Freedom and Authority in Religions and Religious Education

Edited by
Brian Gates

CASSELL

Cassell

Wellington House
125 Strand
London WC2R 0BB

127 West 24th Street
New York
NY 10011

First published 1996

British Library Cataloguing-in-Publication Data
A catalogue record for this book is available from the British Library.

ISBN 0-304-32483-3 (hardback)
     0-304-32419-1 (paperback)

Typeset by Action Typesetting Ltd, Gloucester
Printed and bound in Great Britain by
Redwood Books, Trowbridge, Wiltshire

Contents

Introduction

By What Authority? With What Freedom?

It is commonplace among liberal-minded commentators to make remarks about a world-wide rush to fundamentalisms. Faced with a climate in which uncertainties abound, people are portrayed as looking desperately for secure shelter. It is said they find it by retrenching in traditional religion, or some new age equivalent. The time is ripe for authoritarian rule.

By the same token, from other points of view within the faith communities them-selves, there is evidence of a view that intellectual pundits and politicians have misled their followers. Once on the academic and political escalators, those in authority lose touch with the delights and dangers of ordinary life and death. More generally, it is judged that the modern world as characterized by technology and scientific reasonable-ness has somehow lost its way. Some re-examination of the assumptions taken for granted in Western modernity is urgently called for.

Although it may seem otherwise, if there is a crisis of authority, it was ever thus. So far as we can tell, human beings have always, at least potentially, had the freedom to think and do things differently from what parental society has expected. That question-ing may take the form of thinking which is discontinuous from its conditioning context. Alternatively, it may express itself in terms of outright disobedience. But the scale of all such challenging has become more obviously apparent as we have come to know more about our collective humanity. Our propensity for deviance in thought and action is magnified, not only in documentary television and investigative journalism, but also in personal diaries and artistic explorations in drama, fictional writing and film. Arguably, tensions between freedom and authority, as between chaos and order, are as fundamental to our primal past as they are to our present. In their absence we would cease to be human.

Schools are public market-places which contain all these strains at once. Even before the days of the magnifying glass, to find stress in them should be no surprise. Now, it will be continually apparent, because each school finds itself prey to the variously competing pressures of funding, health, family breakdown, cultural and/or ethnic diver-sity, high and low expectations, changes in official education policy, and prevailing social and national moods.

Tensions also arise directly from whichever model of education is deployed in the school. With the *instructional model*, the authority of teachers resides in the superior knowledge base into which it is their duty to induct the pupils. Such is the enormous wealth of human knowledge, that the individual teacher knows that what is imparted must be highly selective. In that very process of selection, there may be tension between teacher and syllabus or textbook. However, whether teacher or textbook 'says so', the authority with which it is said may be only partially visible, with the consequence that the pupil is encouraged to 'take it on trust'. As a result, although what is taught may be publicly authoritative, the approach employed may still be perceived as authoritarian, because it is lacking in available corroboration by the pupils.

By contrast, in the *discovery model* the emphasis is on enabling children to find out for themselves. They are encouraged to reason their way to a particular conclusion in some maths conundrum or miniature science experiment. Similarly, rather than taking them over second-hand, they are to feel the weight of words and images they use in English or art lessons. The teacher's task is to manage the pupils' learning in such a way that they can subsequently do it of their own accord. On this model, it matters greatly that the teacher understands each pupil and where he or she is at in their thinking, so that what is being taught may be appropriately mediated to the particular pupil. The emphasis on pupils first, and subject knowledge second, leads critics of this approach to judge that teaching authority has been abdicated and discretion wrongly passed to children, which will only serve to reinforce a false sense of freedom and power that they cannot possibly deserve.

National curricula tend to assert the authority of an established order of life, with self-evident standards and norms. Their face value is to give priority to inducting pupils into prespecified concepts, skills and attitudes. As such this is in a clearly instructional mode. However, in so far as there is also an emphasis on outcomes in how well pupils can manipulate concepts, use skills and make effective judgements, aspects characteristic of the discovery mode are also involved. Either way, the teacher is at the same time bound and free in the process of teaching, and pupils are exposed to the attendant tensions. These are the more obvious to the teacher when elements of arbitrariness obtrude in syllabus specifications, where the political establishment pushes one particular view of what counts as correct, for instance in the teaching of history, English or RE.

Religions can be subjected to the same critique as education. Those which defer to the power of external revelation, without any accompanying proof immediately acceptable to common sense, are presented as authoritarian and prone to divisiveness. Their defences in persons (Ayatollah, Mao or Pope X), in places (Ayodhya, Jerusalem or an African Zion) or in parchments (Qur'an, Granth or Book of Mormon) are dismissed as sectional and involving special pleading. Those which rely instead on interior illumination are accused of simply subjective trips. By a short cut, they may even be presented as well on the way to a cult of selfish excess – peaking individualism or total obliteration; either way they are the enemies of social responsibility. Such distortions, along with the criticisms which go with them, are direct counterparts to those which are found in the contrasting instructional and discovery modes of education. Accordingly, in RE which brings together the two fields of religion and education, it is no surprise to find that there too the tension is to be found between instruction and discovery. Accordingly, the challenge for the teacher, as for anyone who would operate responsibly in this territory, is daunting.

In the chapters which follow, there is companionship for meeting that challenge with greater confidence. The book began as an anniversary conference theme of the Shap Working Party on World Religions in Education. It remains largely that. Most of its contributors are Shap members. In common with the Shap aspiration, first expressed in 1969, they believe that every human being would be enriched by a better understanding of religion. For full effect in a plural world this cannot fairly be singularly done. Without any imputation that all religions are equally true (or false), there is conviction that any one faith remains the poorer if it is not held or heard in conversation with others. The position which rejects all religious claims to truth is comparably impoverished unless it in turn has allowed, in an educational setting, entertainment and interrogation from those who believe otherwise.

The book is in two main parts. The first concentrates on the boundaries which define religious experience and tradition. It begins with a dire warning from John Bowker that political neglect of the significance of religion in the fundamental human make-up is as great a threat to human survival as any hole in the ozone. It then focuses in turn on the nature and sources of authority in each of six major religions and on how freedom is perceived and achieved in them. It goes on to examine the religious contexts of two examples of nations divided within themselves: Northern Ireland and Israel.

The second part is concerned more with the process of education, the tensions between freedom and authority within this, and their implications for RE. John Hull explores the social and psychological dimensions of religion and religious development in both negative and positive forms. He presents the challenge to RE as no less than that of overcoming human estrangement. There follow a series of studies of how children from each of the six faith backgrounds are responding to the tensions of living in a society which is secular and multifaith. Finally, there are overviews of the different developments in RE provision as found in Europe and North America. It becomes difficult to escape the conclusion that the absence or presence of effective RE has critical significance for the future of every continent and country.

Contributors to the Book

John Bowker is Gresham Professor of Divinity at Gresham College in London, and is also an Adjunct Professor at the Universities of Pennsylvania and North Carolina State. Among his recent books are *Hallowed Ground: Religions and the Poetry of Place* (SPCK, 1993), *Voices of Islam* (One World, 1995), and *Is God a Virus? Genes, Culture and Religion* (SPCK, 1995). *The Meanings of Death* (Cambridge University Press, 1991) was awarded the biennial HarperCollins prize in 1993. He is at present editing *Annotated Religion* and *The Oxford Companion to World Religions*.

W. Owen Cole is a lecturer, writer and consultant in RE; his doctoral studies were in Sikhism. He is a Research Fellow and continues to teach at the Chichester Institute of Higher Education, where he was Head of Religious Studies until 1989. He is Chairman of the Education Committee of the London Diocese Board of Schools and of the RE panel of the Council of Churches for Britain and Ireland Committee for Relations with People of Other Faiths. His publications include *Religion in the Multifaith School*, *Six Religions in the Twentieth Century*, *Teaching Christianity* and *Teach Yourself Sikhism*.

Riadh El Droubie is currently Arabic Editor of *Computer News Middle East*, and owner-manager of Newlook Translators and DTP, Croydon. Born in Baghdad, he has been based in Britain for over forty years and much engaged in the explication of Islam to non-Muslims. For 18 years he was Publications Manager of the Islamic Cultural Centre and in 1965 he established Minaret House, publishing an educational magazine *The Minaret* and a series of RE booklets for teachers and pupils. He has written and co-authored several school textbooks on Islam, and is responsible for printing the annual *Shap Calendar of Religious Festivals*.

Brian E. Gates is Head of Religious Studies and Social Ethics at the University College of St Martin, Lancaster. His doctoral studies were on children's religious and moral development. He has served on the Religious Education Council of England and Wales since its inception, and as its Chairman or Deputy from 1980 to 1994. His publications are principally in the fields of religious and moral education; they include

Afro-Caribbean Religions and *Time for RE and Teachers to Match*. His current interests are comparative ethics, the interrelationships between religion and health, and the development of electronic databases and network support systems on all aspects of religion, ethics and education.

Richard Gombrich is Boden Professor of Sanskrit at Oxford University and a Fellow of Balliol College. He is President of the Pali Text Society, and a member of Academia Europaea. His main academic interest is in Buddhism, both ancient and modern, and he has published extensively on Buddhism in Sri Lanka, and on the earliest Buddhist texts. His books include *Precept and Practice* (1977), *Theravada Buddhism: A Social History* (1988), and *Indian Ritual and Its Exegesis* (1988). He has established that the Buddha was born early in the fifth century BCE, about eighty years later than stated in most textbooks.

John Greer, in spite of severe ill health, maintains a keen interest in current educational and political developments. He was Reader in Education in the Faculty of Education at the University of Coleraine in Northern Ireland until 1991. His doctoral research focused on classroom pedagogy and the learning and attitudes of children and young people. These are reflected in such publications as *A Questioning Generation: A Report on Sixth Form Religion* (1972) and successive articles in the *British Journal of Religious Education, Character Potential, Educational Research*, and the *Journal of Social Psychology*. In his teaching and writing he has been committed to promoting a deeper understanding for the Churches and society at large.

Hugo Gryn is Senior Rabbi of the West London Synagogue (since 1964), President of the Reform Synagogues of Great Britain, and Vice-President of the Leo Baeck College (where he teaches Practical Rabbinics) and of the World Union for Progressive Judaism. He was educated in his native Czechoslovakia and in Switzerland. After two years in Nazi concentration camps, he studied at universities in England and was ordained rabbi in 1957 at the Hebrew Union College–Institute of Jewish Education, in Cincinnati, USA. From its inception he has been Chairman of the Standing Conference on Inter Faith Dialogue in Education.

Hans-Mikael Holt, lektor, teaches History and Religious Studies at Risskov Amtgymnasium (Sixth Form College), Århus. He is author and co-editor of several textbooks: *Historisk Årstalsliste* (15th edn, 1994), *Tematiske Læsninger i Gammel Testamente* (1976), *USA i Støbeskeen* (2nd edn, 1980) and, with Peter Schreiner, *Who's Who in RE in Europe* (1995). He was Chairman of the Danish Association of Teachers of RE in Upper Secondary Schools 1975–80, co-founder of the European Forum for RE Teachers in 1980, and its secretary from 1980 to 1994. Since 1988, he has been a member of the Board of the InterEuropean Commission of Church and School.

John M. Hull is Professor of Religious Education in the University of Birmingham. He is a graduate of the Universities of Melbourne, Cambridge and Birmingham, and was awarded the DTheol (honoris causa) by the University of Frankfurt in 1995. He has been editor of the *British Journal of Religious Education* since 1971 and is the General Secretary of the International Seminar on Religious Education and Values. His books include *What Prevents Christian Adults from Learning?* (1995) and *The Holy Trinity* and *Christian Education in a Pluralist World* (1995). His autobiographical study *Touching the Rock* (1990) has been translated into many foreign languages.

Robert Jackson is Professor in the Institute of Education at the University of Warwick, where he is Director of the Warwick Religions and Education Research Unit. He is a former of the Conference of University Lecturers in Religious Education and, since 1978, Editor of *Resource*, a thrice-yearly magazine for anyone interested in the teaching of RE. He is author of many articles and several books, including *Approaches to Hinduism* (John Murray, 1988) and *Moral Issues in the Hindu Tradition* (Trentham, 1991), and co-author with Eleanor Nesbitt of *Hindu Children in Britain* (Trentham, 1993).

Kanwaljit Kaur-Singh is a Local Education Authority Inspector with special responsibility for primary school education. She was previously headteacher of a primary school, having taught in that sector for over twenty years. Her doctoral studies focus on the role of Sikh women. Over the last ten years she has served successively on the Schools Examination and Assessment Council, the National Curriculum Council, and the School Curriculum Assessment Authority's Working and Monitoring Groups for National Model Syllabuses. She is currently Chairperson of the British Sikh Education Council, a regular broadcaster, and author of a variety of school textbooks on Sikhism.

Clive Lawton is currently chief executive of a new charitable community development and educational agency called Jewish Continuity, which is London based. Formerly, he was Deputy Director of Liverpool Local Education Authority, before which he was headmaster of King David High School, also in Liverpool. He has written and broadcast extensively on Judaism and on both religious and moral education. He has been the editor and compiler of the *Shap Calendar of Religious Festivals* for more than a decade.

John Levy is Director of two Anglo-Israel educational foundations: The Academic Study Group on Israel and the Middle East, and Friends of Israel Educational Trust. Educated in London, a graduate of Bedford College, he spent nearly a year as a social worker in south London, before joining the Zionist Federation in 1970. Friends of Israel Educational Trust was established in 1976. His twin concerns are the promotion of an informed and analytic understanding of Israel and the Middle East, and the forging of collaborative ties between academics and other experts in the UK and their professional counterparts in Israel.

Peggy Morgan is Senior Lecturer in Theology and Religious Studies at Westminster College, Oxford, a lecturer at Mansfield College and a member of the University of Oxford Faculty of Theology. She is also a consultant for the International Interfaith Centre and is on the advisory board of the World Congress of Faiths journal, *World Faiths Encounter*. Her main publishing has been on Buddhists and Buddhism, but she has also co-authored *Six Religions in the Twentieth Century* (with W. Owen Cole) and *Ethical Issues in Six Religious Traditions* (with Clive Lawton).

Eleanor Nesbitt is the Senior Research Fellow of the Religions and Education Research Unit in the Institute of Education at the University of Warwick. Her doctoral research was on Sikh children in Coventry. She is Reviews Editor of the *International Journal of Punjab Studies* and co-editor of *Sikh Bulletin*. Her publications include 'Sikhism' in R.C. Zaehner (ed.) *Hutchinson Encyclopaedia of Living Faiths* (London, 1988), and 'The transmission of Christian tradition in an ethnically diverse society' in R. Barot (ed.) *Religion and Ethnicity* (Kampen, 1993). With Robert Jackson she has co-authored a curriculum book, *Listening to Hindus* (Unwin Hyman, 1990), and *Hindu Children in Britain* (Trentham, 1993).

Piara Singh Sambhi died in 1992, soon after Chapter 7 had been drafted. He was a past president of the Leeds Gurdwara, a founder member of the Central Committee for British Sikhs, and author of *Understanding Your Sikh Neighbour, Sikhism* and *The Guru Granth Sahib*. He co-authored a number of books with Owen Cole, including *The Sikhs: Their Religious Beliefs and Practices* and *Sikhism and Christianity: A Comparative Study*.

Herbert Schultze is a historian, theologian and educationalist who has taught in schools and universities. He was formerly director of the Comenius-Institut, in Münster, a national centre for research on school education and RE, and president of the Inter-European Commission on Church and School. In each capacity he produced several books and reports. He is presently chairman of the European Association for World Religions in Education. He is involved part-time in teacher education in the University of Essen and in several international research projects, including comparative religious education, schoolbook research and international syllabus comparison, Islam in education and Holocaust education.

Ninian Smart currently teaches at the University of California, Santa Barbara. He was founding professor in the Department of Religious Studies at the University of Lancaster, and has been visiting professor for a term or more in Yale, Harvard, Wisconsin, Princeton, Banaras, Queensland, Otago, Cape Town, Bangalore and Hong Kong. His writings cover areas in the history and philosophy of religion, methods in religious studies, politics, Christian theology, Indian philosophy and current affairs, religious dialogue, and nationalism. Among his books are *Reasons and Faiths, The Religious Experience, The World's Religions*, and *Buddhism and Christianity: Rivals and Allies*.

Wim Westerman was trained as a primary school teacher and holds a degree in pedagogical science. He worked in schools for primary, secondary and special education, and was involved in teacher training in Amsterdam and in a National Educational Advisory Centre. In this centre he provided support for teacher education institutions and the organization of intercultural and religious education. He is secretary of the European Association for World Religions in Education. Since 1991 he has been involved in international educational projects in developing countries and Eastern Europe and the former Societ Union. He has published in several languages, on teacher training, intercultural and religious education, and comparative education.

Frank Whaling was educated at Pontefract, Christ's College Cambridge and later Harvard University. He has doctorates from Cambridge and Harvard. He lived in India for four years in the 1960s and is presently Reader in Religious Studies at Edinburgh University. He has won research awards from Fulbright, Carnegie, Cook, Farmington, the British Academy and the British Council, and taught, written and advised widely on world religions, theology of religion, religious education and interfaith matters. His eleven books and 80 articles cover these areas. He is also an ordained Methodist minister.

Peter Woodward is a former secondary school teacher and college lecturer in the field of RE. For 13 years he was General Inspector of Schools for the City of Birmingham. Since then he has engaged in research with the Department of Education of the University of Cambridge and the Department of Arts Education of the University of Warwick. He is currently Senior Lecturer in Religious Studies at Homerton College, Cambridge. He has acted as adviser and scriptwriter to two nationally networked television series, Central Independent Television's multi-faith educational presentations *Believe It Or Not* and *What's It Like...?*

Part One

Religions

Chapter 1

World Religions: the Boundaries of Belief and Unbelief

John Bowker

In an interview for the programme *Sunday*, shortly after the introduction of the 1988 Education Reform Act for England and Wales, the then Secretary of State for Education defended the absence of Religious Studies from the new National Curriculum on the grounds that the study of religion was not an academic subject.

The defence clearly rests on an error: not only has the study of religion been an academic subject, at all levels of education, for many years, but provision for it as such is made in the Act. The error presumably arose because of the way in which, both in this and in the previous 1944 Education Act, RE was provided in conjunction with acts of worship. By linking the two to each other, and both to the local community, an emphasis has clearly been on respecting the wishes of parents (and of others, such as Church leaders) to initiate children into communities of faith – or not; hence the conscience clauses.

But the price to be paid for denying that the study of religion is an academic subject, in the sense that it should have belonged to the National Curriculum as first conceived, will always be extremely high. The subject was, by definition, marginalized, despite the fact that the legal safeguards were stronger than they had been. Since then, the situation has changed in that a minimum norm of 5 per cent RE curriculum time for all pupils in maintained schools has been approved by central government, and the School Curriculum and Assessment Authority has published national model syllabuses for RE that cover six religions during the course of both primary and secondary years of schooling. However, all this has done little to address the problem of how to guarantee that good-quality RE teaching is actually provided by schools, when specialist teachers are in short supply, and not all head teachers appreciate the significance of the subject.[1]

Why is it then that RE is an academic subject of any importance? One reason undoubtedly stands out. On pragmatic grounds alone, the study of religions is necessary, since without it, it is impossible to understand the nature of so many bitter conflicts in the world today. For years I have been pointing out that religions are likely to destroy human life as we know it now on this planet.

Religions contribute to virtually all the intransigent and seemingly insoluble conflicts in the world. They are rarely the sole cause of those conflicts. There are always other contingent and contributing factors. But equally, it is false to say, as many do, that it is not the religions which cause the conflicts, but rather the misuse of religions for political or ideological ends. The truth is that religions cannot easily be disentangled from the politics and the ideologies in which they are immersed.

So it comes about that it is particularly easy to predict future conflicts of a serious kind: take a map of the world and draw on it the boundaries where religions (or subsystems within a religion) meet; or where they are advancing towards each other, since the religious map is always on the move. There is nothing new in this. What is new is the scale and extent of the weapons with which these conflicts can be conducted. Yet far from realizing, at a moment when this country is a great deal more pluralistic religiously than it has been in the past, that we need to understand the nature and dynamics of religions dispassionately and academically, we have kept the subject tied to the commitments in very subtle ways. Paradoxically, we are often too polite about religions for fear of appearing intolerant. As I put it in 1987:

> Religions are extremely dangerous animals; and one might well put up on their boundary the notice I saw once in a game reserve in Africa, 'Advance and be bitten'. And yet, despite the obvious involvement of religious beliefs and ideology in so many of the dangerous and destructive problems in the world, it is virtually impossible to find any politician or economist (let alone people who make the operative decisions in the worlds of commerce or industry) who has any serious knowledge of what religions are or why. As I put it in an article on this theme: 'One of the most obvious reasons why we seem to drift from one disastrous ineptitude to another is, ironically, that far too few politicians have read Religious Studies in Higher Education. As a result, they literally do not know what they are talking about on almost any of the major international issues. They simply cannot.'[2]

It was no satisfaction – it was a frustrating misery – to see and hear this demonstrated in the Gulf crisis and war and again in the former Yugoslavia.

In the first chapter of the same book, and now in more detail in *Is God a Virus? Genes, Culture and Religion*,[3] I have tried to show why religions are so dangerous, and why we need a more extensive understanding of them. In brief, religions are bad news because they are good news. Religions are extremely long-running and strong systems, which protect information. They are the oldest cultural systems, to which we have access through evidence, for the protection of gene-replication and the nurture of children – hence the preoccupation of religions with food and sex. But manifestly, religions protect the transmission of information (from life to life and from generation to generation) of a far more extensive kind than that. Religions are the resource of virtually every kind of human creativity and achievement, even to the point where they became the context in which humans discovered that they were themselves discovered and created by God.

Fundamentally, therefore, religions are systems in which symbols are generated and sustained through which individuals and groups can maintain their lives coherently (both in terms of meaning and in terms of social reality), and through which also the structured properties of the human brain (the 'preparedness' from the genes of biogenetic structuralism) can be given adequate, and often new, expression.

It is here that we can see why issues of authority can be tense, though they are not always so. Religions must necessarily be conservative as systems: they must conserve the symbol system which has, up to that point, been life-giving. Yet equally, the incorporation of symbols may be powerfully innovative and creative. So a religious system (that is to say, the operators of, and participants in, a religious system) may give conservation such high priority that maintaining the system and the transmission of information becomes an end in itself; or it may be highly innovative, seeing the maintenance of the system as a means to some other end, which may range from personal enlightenment to the coming of *the* End. Systems are by no means identical to each other, simply by virtue of being systems. To understand the conversation of any religion with the world around it, one needs to understand what the priorities are which are set within the system itself. That is an academic subject, which requires great attention to detail, and which has enormous political implications.

This can be seen through the example referred to allusively above, 'the coming of the End'. But what 'end'? Religions differ greatly in their answer to that question. But at the same time, all the major and continuing religions portray, or at least point to, both proximate and ultimate futures which constrain their present behaviours. This is what I have called 'cultural prolepsis' (in contrast to what anthropologists call 'cultural lag'). Religions live towards immediate futures, in which appropriate behaviours are mapped and described; and they live also towards eschatological futures, which can also be mapped and described; and in both cases (immediate and eschatological) the consequences are causative on present behaviour.

This is a dramatic example, therefore, of what is known as 'downward causation'. In biological terms, this means that in an evolutionary advance of exploration into new environments, in which successful mutations are encoded for subsequent generations, the conditions of success are set by the environmental circumstances into which the mutation (and its organism) are projected. In that sense the future causes the present. That is to say (using the language of 'constraint' rather than 'cause', for reasons developed at greater length in *Licensed Insanities* and *Is God a Virus?*), conditions which lie in the future, from the point in time of the organism, are a part of the network of constraint which delimits the range of possibility into its eventuality – into its being that which comes to pass. Thus in hierarchically organized biological systems, the conditions of each of the higher (more complex) orders determine in part the distribution of lower-level events and substances. The organizational levels of molecule, cell, tissue, organ, organism, breeding population, species, ecosystem, social system, are not arbitrary. At each level, the processes at the lower levels are constrained by, and act in conformity with, the requirements and laws of the higher levels.

This means that in the organization of available energy, the higher levels of organization, including the macrosocial phenomena of contemporary human life, are as real and causal as the atoms and molecules on which they depend. While this means that it is not possible to reduce higher-level behaviours to the chemistry and physics on which they nevertheless depend, it also means, the other way around, that the futures which humans construct act as powerful constraints on their present behaviours. We can trivialize this at the level of horoscopes and tea-leaves, or we can ennoble it by the promises we make and try to keep: 'Will you take this woman to be your wedded wife? Will you love her, comfort her, honour and protect her, and, forsaking all others, be faithful to her as long as you both shall live?'

In the case of religions, the future constraint can be even more decisive in the forming of present behaviours, particularly when it relates the believer to eternal reward or punishment. That is why, despite a politician's surprise at the fact, it was possible for *both* sides to win the Gulf war, even though one of them is left in a derelict condition. Religions live towards futures which are encoded in strong symbols. These allow religious believers to decode present circumstances in ways which do not necessarily conform to other kinds of analysis. The complex codes of religious symbol systems need to be learned – and that is a task far beyond the impressive linguistic competence which such institutions as a State Department and Foreign Office already and undoubtedly require if we are to have some chance of understanding the politics of the contemporary world.

The key to such understanding lies in recognizing the dynamics of continuity in the case of religious systems, since clearly the dilemma of any religion is how to sustain the system in the face of threats to it. The threats may be physical and literal, or they may be conceptual. Thus secularization is often described as a competing ideology – as what Don Cupitt calls 'the shift from myths to maths'. But in fact displacement theories of secularization are proving increasingly barren. Nevertheless, in so far as secularization is a word which describes the consequences arising from the proliferation of choices, of which choice among ideas, including religious ideas, is a part, it clearly creates strategic problems for religious systems. Secularization is not a 'thing', prowling about and seeking what religions it may devour. It is a term which summarizes the preferential option for options which characterizes Western styles of democracy. For religions (immersed in such democracies) whose own style, particularly in relation to political decision-making, does not allow for such openness of choice, the problem is extreme. David O'Brien has traced the painful process through which Roman Catholics in the USA had to come to terms with the fact that the separation of Church and state in the Constitution would not allow them to implement a European style of Catholic control, not even indirectly through the 'Catholicization' of US institutions. So he concluded:

> If American Catholicism is to survive, even more if it is to make a substantial contribution to public life, it will have to engage directly the reality of voluntarism, the evangelical imperatives, and the reliance on popular support which are the inevitable by-products of religious pluralism in a democratic society.[4]

But all this can represent a profound threat to those who see it as their responsibility to protect and transmit non-negotiable information (information, of course, means much more than verbal items) to subsequent generations. One predictable response is to mark the boundaries more securely and more defensively – or offensively, if that is regarded as the better form of defence. And where boundaries exist, border incidents will always occur.

Such incidents are not always incidents of conflict. They may be explorations of the conditions of coexistence, for all religions have voices of inclusion as well as exclusion. But this again only emphasizes how important it is to bring the study of religion much more centrally (and academically) into the curriculum. Religions are not going to go away or be eroded by a new world-view (the wrong understanding of secularization). They are long-running systems which have given meaning and value, vision and truth, to virtually the whole human population for millennia – as to most people they still do. It is all the more important, therefore, to reinforce the voices of inclusion and coexistence, so that the incipient schisms in the human communities of knowledge and understanding are not rent open even more widely than they already have been.

The study of religion, then, seeks to understand the kind of stories which people tell through their lives, and how the components of those stories are sustained and made

available in particular societies or families – or schools. It is here that religious authority is located, because it arises from the nature of the resource which supplies a
particular story into life. The various 'Guides, Gurus and Gods' (to quote the title of a
BBC series) may be very different, and what they offer may be extremely different. But
they have authority because they become, at least to some extent, authors or joint
authors of those other lives. In the Latin dictionary of Lewis and Short, *auctor* is
defined as he who brings about the existence of any object, or promotes the increase of
prosperity of it, whether he first originates it, or by his efforts gives greater perma-
nence or continuance to it. It is an excellent definition of religious understandings of
creation; and from it flows the meaning of *auctoritas*: basically, it has to do with bringing something into being, an invention. So it also means an opinion, or advice, or
encouragement. It means weight, or importance, and hence power and our sense of
authority: to have the power to bring something into being, and to do so, is to be the
author of its being.

   In all religions, authorship and authority may be exercised in a dictatorial manner – a
literal 'dictation' of the stories that ought to be told: Vatican Catholicism under the
present Pope is a spectacular, albeit tragic, example of a religious system discerning
threats to its boundaries and reacting defensively. The tragedy arises because it creates
a radical dissonance between the stories that Catholics tell through their lives and the
stories the Vatican is attempting to tell through them. All religions have the means
within themselves to act in a comparable way. But since secularization means the proliferation of choices, there would be a far greater wisdom in religions (at least if they are
looking to their own future) integrating the religious choice as being of paramount
worth within the multiplicity of options, rather than setting it against the world as
though all the world's options are inimical. Thus (to give just one example), the notion
of *taqlid* in Islam could well be seen as a warrant for an aggressive imposition of
authority. In Schacht's succinct definition, *taqlid* means 'clothing with authority' in
matters of religion, the 'adoption of the utterances or the actions of another as authoritative with faith in their correctness without investigating his reasons'. And certainly
the meaning of the verb *qallada* reinforces that impression of blind obedience – 'to put
a rope around the neck of an animal in order to lead it along'. But while *taqlid* undoubtedly means accepting the authority of earlier generations in interpreting *fiqh*, it does not
imply unquestioning conformity to their decisions with no further reflection. If that
appears to be happening in Islam, then there would be a greater wisdom in establishing
dispassionately (and academically) why it is a contradiction of Islam. Blind reliance on
authority is rejected in Islam, whatever the impressions to the contrary; and that is why
at the head of al-Bukhari's collection of *ahādith* stands a tradition which states: 'Surely
actions will be judged *biniyya* [by intention], and a person will have what he intends.'

   The issue of authority in religion, therefore, is always the issue of constraint: how is
the transference to be effected (if it is effected) from external authority to the internalization of the constraints which are the necessary condition of attainment and of
freedom? We are familiar, in biology, with the observation that the greater the network
of constraints, the greater the resulting degrees of freedom for the organism concerned.
We are equally familiar with this in all other aspects of learning, whether of physics,
French or the flute. In the last case, it requires the internalization of the constraints of
notation, fingering and scales, as well as the limitation on options in spare time, before
you are eventually brought into the far greater freedom of playing your own music. The

same applies, *mutatis mutandis*, to religious life. The crisis of religions at the present time is brought about by, on the one side, those outside religions who refuse to acknowledge the profound place that religious symbol systems still play in the construction of human lives (e.g. the nineteenth-century attitudes which seem to prevail amongst civil servants responsible for education), and on the other, those inside religions who refuse to allow the internalization of constraints to lead to imaginative and creative freedom.

Putting the two extremes together, religion is written off by the one extreme as fundamentalist fanaticism, which the other extreme then promptly confirms by its behaviours.

Mediating between the extremes is RE as it has been unfolding in the post-war years, against great odds, but with nevertheless enormous achievements on which to build. Shap initiatives constitute but one voice within this appeal, that to understand the destructive and intransigent problems of the world, we need immensely better (and much more widespread) understanding of religions. Religions are only bad news because they are such good news. We have to appreciate all that religions have meant to people in constructing through their lives virtually all the memorable achievements of what we now call civilization. Because religions matter so much, those who belong to them become 'edgy' (to say the least) when they perceive the necessary boundaries of the system coming under threat. The study of all this, and in particular of the dynamics of religious systems, is manifestly an academic subject. When will this or any other government take it seriously as such?

NOTES

1. See most recently: Chief Inspector of Schools, Office for Standards in Education (1995) *Religious Education: A Review of Inspection Findings 1993–4*. London: HMSO, para. 29.
2. John Bowker (1987) *Licensed Insanities: Religions and Belief in God in the Contemporary World*. London: Darton, Longman and Todd, p. 2.
3. John Bowker (1995) *Is God a Virus? Genes, Culture and Religion*. London: SPCK.
4. David O'Brien (1987) *Public Theology, Civil Religion and American Catholicism*. Philadelphia: University of Pennsylvania, p. 25.

Freedom and Authority in Particular Traditions

Chapter 2

Freedom and Authority in Buddhism

Richard Gombrich

FREEDOM

Among the many hundreds of the Buddha's sermons recorded in the Pali Canon, there is one which modern Buddhists are especially fond of quoting and which may indeed claim to be unique among the scriptural traditions of the world religions. It is the Buddha's sermon to some people called the Kalamas. They have come to him and complained that visiting holy men all preach different doctrines and disparage each other, so that they are confused and wonder who is right. After sympathizing with their confusion, the Buddha says:

> Do not be led by reports, or tradition, or hearsay. Be led neither by the authority of religious texts, nor by mere logic or inference, nor by considering appearances, nor by the delight in speculative opinions, nor by seeming possibilities, nor by the idea: 'This is our teacher.' But, O Kalamas, when you find out for yourselves that certain things are unwholesome and wrong and bad, then give them up. And when you find out for yourselves that certain things are wholesome and good, then accept them and live by them.[1]

This passage contains two exhortations: to think for oneself rather than accepting authority, and to be pragmatic rather than indulging in abstract theorizing. Both themes recur elsewhere in the Canon; it is the former which concerns us here. In the narrative of the Buddha's last days, the Maha Parinibbana Sutta, it is recorded that Ananda, the Buddha's personal attendant, asked the Buddha who would lead the Order of monks and nuns when he was gone. To this the Buddha replied: 'What does the Order expect of me? I have taught the truth without making any distinction between esoteric and exoteric, without keeping anything back in the teacher's fist.'[2] He had, he said, no intention of leading the Order or notion that the Order depended on him; let whoever thought of himself in those terms speak up. 'So, Ananda, make yourselves your islands and your only refuge...'

Other passages in that narrative are in the same spirit. On his very deathbed the Buddha allows the monks to abolish the minor rules of the Order when he is gone.[3] (Tradition has it, however, that since they failed to ask him which rules were to be considered minor they decided not to abolish any.) T. W. Rhys Davids' famous translation of the Buddha's very last words, though extremely free, catches their spirit: 'Decay is inherent in all component things! Work out your salvation with diligence!'[4]

Certainly the Buddha preached that all worldly things, including Buddhism itself as a historical phenomenon, were subject to change, decay, and final dissolution. Certainly, too, he instructed his followers to cultivate their mental powers, notably their intelligence, and had little time for blind faith or unthinking obedience. Whatever may have happened in the course of Buddhist history (thus confirming the Buddha's prediction of decay), the elements of humanism and rationalism are unmistakably strong in the Pali Canon.

The spirit of rational inquiry is opposed to authoritarianism and hierarchy: an idea is to be judged on its own merits, regardless of its source. Throughout human history this attitude has been more commended than practised. But in Buddhism there are telling examples of its being put into practice. There is on the outskirts of Bangkok an extremely popular and prosperous monastery, Wat Dhammakaya, in which most of the permanent monks hold university degrees. I am authoritatively informed[5] that they take instruction in meditation from a semi-literate old lady who works in the kitchen. This is reminiscent of the respect in which his fellows held an illiterate monk who worked as a stoker at a great Ch'an (= Zen) monastery in central China in the 1930s: his moral character was more esteemed than all the learning and piety which the monastery functioned to promote.[6]

It is difficult to exaggerate the awe of the teacher in Indian culture. In Hinduism the teacher is invested with absolute authority – indeed, he is often said to be a form of God – and no pupil may learn anything in the religious sphere without the entitlement (*adhikara*) which only the teacher may bestow, and bestows by initiation (*diksa*). It is to this that the Buddha is referring when he says that he has taught without distinguishing esoteric from exoteric. The terms *adhikara* and *diksa* are alien to Buddhism before (some time round the middle of the first millennium CE) it became overwhelmingly influenced by Hinduism in the movement known as *tantra*. In all the older forms of Buddhism, all fully ordained monks are equal in any matter concerning religion; where there is a practical need for a rank order, it is supplied by seniority, a completely neutral principle. Even more remarkably, the code of monastic rules says[7] that where a pupil notices his teacher going wrong he should say so; I think that this must be unique in Indian tradition.

Nor, apparently, did the Buddha attach importance to whether people proclaimed themselves his converts. After a discussion with another religious wanderer, the Buddha said:

> Well, my friend, though we discuss our views and practices, don't think that I am trying to convert you to my side. I don't want to do so. You may go on your own way, but let us see whether we both practise as we teach.[8]

On another occasion the Buddha had a religious discussion with a lay Jain (Mahavira, the Jain teacher,[9] and the Buddha were contemporaries) and convinced him, but was reluctant to accept his allegiance and told him not to stop supporting Jain monks.[10] The Buddha clearly believed in freedom of affiliation.

There is remarkable evidence that this benign attitude – surpassing mere toleration – towards other religions was not confined to the precepts of the texts but also influenced practice in ancient India. In the middle of the third century BCE the Emperor Asoka, in his twelfth major rock edict, exhorted his subjects not to glorify their own religions and disparage others, but to listen to religious teachers of all persuasions and spread religious information. (He thus anticipated the programme of the Shap Working Party by more than two thousand years.) Turning again to the Maha Parinibbana Sutta, we there[11] find the Buddha telling an ascetic that the only test for the validity of a religious teaching is whether it includes the Noble Eightfold Path (for which see below). Thus the modern Buddhist claim that anyone, be they Christian, Muslim, Jew or atheist, can in principle be a good Buddhist is justified by ancient Buddhist tradition.

AUTHORITY

Nevertheless, the salience often given nowadays to the Buddha's words to the Kalamas seems to me to distort the picture, and when people say (as I have often heard them do) that Buddhism has no beliefs or no dogmas, they are exaggerating. A religion which has only freedom and no authority could hardly survive the death of its founder. This was as evident to the Buddha as it is to us. From the very beginning of his preaching career he set about founding an institution, the Order of monks, and after some years it began to admit nuns as well. The final deathbed scene of the Maha Parinibbana Sutta begins with the Buddha saying:

> You may all think, Ananda, 'The message has lost its teacher; we have no teacher.' But you should not see it like that. After my death your teacher will be the truth I have taught and the rules I have laid down.[12]

We must now explore this statement.

The Buddha preached self-reliance: salvation, the realization of nirvana, is something each individual can only attain by his or her own efforts. That is Buddhism's supreme goal. Most Buddhists believe that they will only be able to attain that goal after many lives. But Buddhism is a world religion with something to offer everyone, however lowly or spiritually undeveloped. Anyone can – and a traditional Buddhist does – recite a formula to 'take refuge' in Three Jewels. The Three Jewels are therefore also known as the Three Refuges. In Pali these are the *Buddha*, the *dhamma* and the *sangha*: the Enlightened Teacher, the Truth he taught, and the Order or Community he founded. Let me consider these in reverse order.

The sangha's authority

Our modern assumption that a religion is the same for everyone and in all circumstances is not valid for ancient India. The Buddha preached a path to salvation and assumed that those who took it seriously would make it their full-time vocation to follow that path. This would mean renouncing the world and becoming full-time monks or nuns. Though there were at that time many other religious teachers and followers who had left their homes and family life (not so unlike Jesus and his Apostles), it was the Buddha who founded monasticism, creating for his followers a kind of home from home, a community outside the normal community of town or village. For this community, the sangha, he laid down a body of disciplinary rules. Some of the rules governed a monk's or nun's personal conduct, and others regulated their community life. In all cases, like our modern laws, they governed externals, not what went on in people's minds.

It is important to emphasize, since the topic is widely misunderstood (even among modern Buddhists), that there has been just one code of monastic rules, with only trivial discrepancies between different versions, and that though monks and nuns have split up into different groupings, this has nothing to do with disagreements over doctrine – as a Christian might naturally assume. We know from the accounts of Chinese pilgrims that in India in the first millennium CE there were monks who followed the Mahayana and monks who adhered to the older forms of Buddhism harmoniously living together in the same monasteries. There is in fact no distinct Mahayana monastic code.[13] In Tibet and China, as well as in ancient India, masses of Mahayana monks have kept to the original monastic rules (with a few local modifications, of course). It is perhaps the fact that Japan received only the Mahayana form of Buddhism and that in Japan the monastic code came to be followed by very few that has given people a wrong idea of Buddhist history.

The sangha can split, and has split, over matters of practice. The splits have tended to be over minor points, even matters so marginal that the rules do not cover them. For instance, there is disagreement in the sangha of Sri Lanka over whether monks have to shave off their eyebrows (like the Thai monks) or not (like the Burmese). There is no conceivable way of guarding for all time against such niggling disputes. But the early Buddhists did their best. Another passage in the Maha Parinibbana Sutta[14] says that from whatever source someone claims to have picked up a doctrine or a monastic rule, what he says is to be compared with the teachings recorded in the canonical texts, and to be rejected if it is not found there. Modern scholars argue about whether the Canon precisely represents 'the Buddha's word', but traditionally that has not been seen as a problem. It is the Buddha's word, and that alone, that is authoritative. And the survival of the sangha shows that this has not worked too badly, for it is one of the world's oldest institutions.

How are the monastic rules enforced? In some Buddhist traditions (notably in the Far East) abbots have a certain amount of power, and in Thailand there is even a national monastic hierarchy with a *sangharaja* ('king of the Order') at its apex. But these monastic officials are ultimately only as powerful as the civil government will allow them to be, and their positions are not recognized by the monastic code itself. The Buddha's plan was for the sangha to be self-governing, much like a modern professional association, and the ancient forms of self-regulation are still widely followed. But what happens if people disobey the rules?

If the infringement is very serious, the individual is considered to have automatically disrobed himself or herself and thereby to have left the sangha. So what happens if they refuse to go quietly? To this the sangha contains no answer within itself. It depends on the co-operation of the civil power. Through Buddhist history, probably since the death of the Buddha, the authority of the code of monastic discipline has ultimately depended for its enforcement on the government (usually a king). For lesser infringements, the code prescribes penalties, which always involve confession of the fault, and may rise to a period of probation, when one is not in full communion with one's fellows. In many periods these penalties and procedures have not been fully enforced, for the sangha has little power against recalcitrants. But the sangha has undergone recurrent 'purifications', as they are known, whenever the civil power has taken an interest in its affairs, for in Buddhist countries a virtuous sangha is considered crucial for public welfare. The authority lies with the rules themselves, and anyone who is demonstrably acting in accordance with those rules is generally held to have the right to enforce them.

The dhamma's authority

The sangha, we have seen, has corporate authority, embodied in its code of rules, to deal with behaviour, to enforce orthopraxy. But is there no orthodoxy in Buddhism? Is there really no prescribed belief?

We have seen that the Buddha preached, and Asoka practised, toleration. But that does not mean that anyone could legitimately claim to be a Buddhist. In fact, this has already been revealed in the very quotations we have used. Not merely a monastic rule but also a doctrine, whatever its source, is to be rejected if it is not recorded as the Buddha's word. A religious teaching is valid if it includes the Noble Eightfold Path. That is distinctively Buddhist, in that it is part of the Buddha's formulation of his essential message, and so recorded in what tradition considers his first sermon. Finally, and most tellingly, my first quotation from the Maha Parinibbana Sutta was incomplete. The full quotation reads: 'So, Ananda, make yourselves your islands and refuges, your only refuges; make the *Dhamma* your island and refuge, your only refuge.' The point is the same as that made in the Buddha's deathbed statement: no further human intermediary is required; from now on the Buddha's followers are to rely on his teachings alone. The term *dhamma* (which is Pali; the Sanskrit equivalent is *dharma*) has many English translations: here 'teaching', 'doctrine' and 'truth' would all be possible. Any of these words would do, because in the context of the Buddha's teaching they are simply synonymous: what he preached *is* the truth.

Even the quotation with which we began, that from the sermon to the Kalamas, has to be understood in that context. The Kalamas are told to think for themselves, but the Buddha is confident – as any religious teacher would be – that their thoughts will lead them to the conclusions to which he has come himself. As Steven Collins has neatly put it,[15] the Buddha is inviting them not to make their own truth, but to make the truth their own.

What, then, are the doctrines which have the stamp of the Buddha's authority? This is not the place for an account of them; for that, I recommend that the reader turn to *What the Buddha Taught*,[16] or some other authoritative exposition – authoritative because demonstrably based on the texts. However, we have cited the Noble Eightfold Path as the Buddha's touchstone for true religion. That path consists of right views, right intention, right speech, right action, right livelihood, right effort, right awareness, right concentration. The first step is right views; what are they?

Steven Collins writes:

> There are three overlapping but distinguishable senses in which Buddhism uses the term right view: firstly, that of a general and pan-Indian pro-attitude to the belief system of *karma* and *samsara*; secondly, that of knowledge of Buddhist doctrine and the motivation to accept and introject it; and thirdly, that of progress towards, and attainment of liberating insight. These three senses correspond to a classification of people into three groups: the 'ordinary man', the 'learner' and the 'adept'.[17]

It is the first that particularly concerns us here.

Buddhism shares with other indigenous Indian religions a belief in the law of *karma*: that the universe is so constructed that good deeds must inevitably bring rewards and bad deeds punishments. If the reward or punishment does not appear in this life – as we often see – it is sure to arrive in a future life, the round of rebirth called *samsara*, unless we manage to bring that process to an end by attaining enlightenment. Buddhists regard what Christians call going to Heaven or Hell as forms of rebirth. For the Buddha, it is the idea that one is sure to benefit by doing good, and the converse, that is absolutely crucial. In the sermon to the Kalamas he says[18] that even if there is no other world – i.e. no rebirth – a person who is kind and compassionate will benefit in this world by leading a happy life. In most texts, however, to deny the existence of another world is condemned as wicked foolishness. In a standard account of six wrong-headed religious teachers, the first four all deny in various ways the distinction between vice and virtue and the validity of moral effort.

As Collins says, believing in the moral law of *karma* does not suffice to make one a Buddhist. But the Buddha presents it as an essential prerequisite: its opposite is definitely 'wrong view' and impermissible for a Buddhist.[19] Not only in the sermon to the Kalamas does the Buddha present prudential reasons for being moral; he frequently uses that line of argument with non-Buddhists. Those who accept it are ready to become 'learners' and to be told some specifically Buddhist doctrines. As the learner progresses, he or she becomes morally good for disinterested reasons; but the initial bait of self-interest is necessary. In sum, though all are free to ruin themselves, someone who is cynical about morality has rejected the Buddha's authority and cannot be accounted a Buddhist.

The Buddha's authority

Was the Buddha's teaching true because it was he who preached it, or was he the Buddha (Enlightened) just because he had discovered the truth? His own position was the latter. But it is easy to lose sight of the distinction, and in fact many Buddhists seem to have lost sight of it.

Trying to dissuade a monk from giving him too much personal veneration, the Buddha said: 'He who sees me sees the *Dhamma* and he who sees the *Dhamma* sees me.'[20] He meant, I think, that he was authoritative only by virtue of the fact that he had understood the truth.

However, the passage came in the Mahayana to be the basis for a complex doctrine of the Buddha's bodies. His metaphor was taken to mean that he has a metaphysical body which is the *dharma*, the way things truly are; thus the Buddha in his 'Dharma body' becomes immanent in the whole universe like a World Spirit. He also acquired, in the Buddhist imagination, divine or supernatural bodies, which appeared to people in dreams and other visions (including visions cultivated by meditative practice)[21] and sometimes enunciated fresh doctrines. Most of the fundamental texts of the Mahayana were composed in India in the first three or four centuries CE, and though they vary greatly in character and content most of them contain new teachings which are ascribed to a Buddha and are hence authoritative.

One of these early Mahayana scriptures was the Lotus Sutra (Saddharmapundarika).

Composed in India in the first or second century CE, it became the most popular of all Buddhist texts in the Far East. It is unusual, though not unique, in being extremely polemical. The Buddha is represented as jeering at those who were foolish enough to take his earlier teachings (those in the Canon) at face value; for example, he did not really die at all, for here he is now, preaching. A great deal of the Lotus Sutra is taken up with its own glorification. A long passage near the end of the third chapter dilates on the horrid rebirths awaiting anyone who presumes to criticize this text. The Buddha goes on:

> For this reason I expressly tell you,
> In the midst of ignorant men Do not preach this scripture.
> If there are those of keen faculties, Of knowledge clear and bright,
> Of much learning and strong memory, Who seek the Buddha Path,
> For men like these, And only for them, may you preach ... .
> If a man is deferential And has no other thoughts,
> Separating himself from common fools And dwelling alone in mountains and marshes,
> For men like him, And only for them, may you preach ... .
> If there is a monk Who for the sake of Omniscience
> Seeks the Dharma in all four directions, With joined palms receiving it on the crown of his head,
> Desiring merely to receive and keep The scriptures of the Mahayana,
> Not accepting so much As a single verse from the other scriptures,
> For men like him, And only for them may you preach ... .
> Such a person shall never again Wish to seek other scriptures,
> Nor has he ever before thought Of the books of the unbelievers.[22]

This is a far cry from the sermon to the Kalamas.

The Three Jewels: a single authority structure

It may already have struck the perceptive reader that from the point of view of the ordinary Buddhist through most of history, the Three Jewels must necessarily have functioned as different facets of a single authority. From that point of view the question whether the Buddha was authoritative contingently, because he happened to have discovered the dhamma, or necessarily, because he somehow embodied the dhamma, never arose; it was simply not posed. But how was the ordinary Buddhist to learn of that dhamma? In an age of books and universal education we easily forget that before printing few laymen were literate (anywhere in the world) and the vast majority of people received their religious knowledge and instruction orally, from religious professionals. The Buddhist Canon was first committed to writing in the first century BCE, and until very recent times, though monks and nuns wrote and sometimes used manuscripts, their training consisted largely of memorizing texts, and their service to the world of preaching from those texts. 'Children of the Buddha', they were the models who aspired to walk in the Buddha's footsteps and at the same time preserved his teaching for the world. All Three Jewels were interdependent. For practical purposes, Buddhist authority was embodied in the sangha.

NOTES

1. Anguttara Nikaya 1, 189, quoted in Walpola Rahula (1959) *What the Buddha Taught*. Bedford: Gordon Fraser, pp. 2–3. I have slightly changed Rahula's translation.
2. Digha Nikaya II, 100.
3. Digha Nikaya II, 154.
4. *Dialogues of the Buddha*, Part II (= *Sacred Books of the Buddhists*, vol. III). London: Pali Text Society, 1910, p. 173.
5. By the Ven. Mettanando, a monk at the monastery, in 1988.
6. Holmes Welch (1967) *The Practice of Chinese Buddhism 1900–1950*. Cambridge, MA: Harvard University Press, p. 34.
7. Vinaya Pitaka I, 46 and 49. For more detail on this and on other matters concerning freedom and authority in the Order, see Richard Gombrich (1988) *Theravada Buddhism: A Social History from Ancient Benares to Modern Colombo*. London and New York: Routledge and Kegan Paul, ch. 4.
8. Ven. B. Ananda Maitreya (1990) *The Buddha and his Way*, ed. Ven. Pesala. New York: Buddhist Literature Society, p. 9.
9   His followers, the Jains, do not consider him the founder of their religion but the reviver of something far more ancient.
10. Ananda Maitreya, *op. cit.*, p. 8; Rahula, *op. cit.*, p. 4.
11. Digha Nikaya II, 151.
12. Digha Nikaya II, 154.
13. This is a slight oversimplification. There is a Chinese text, composed perhaps in the seventh century CE, which contains rules of personal conduct, though none for regulating the community, and which functioned as a kind of monastic code in some Chinese and Japanese sects. It poses as a translation of an Indian text, the Brahmajala Sutra, but in fact has nothing to do with the canonical text of that name. See J.J.M. De Groot (1893) *Le Code du Mahayana en Chine*. Amsterdam: Johannes Muller.
14. Digha Nikaya II, 123–6.
15. In conversation with me.
16. Rahula, *op. cit.*
17. Steven Collins (1982) *Selfless Persons*. Cambridge: Cambridge University Press, p. 92.
18. Anguttara Nikaya I, 192.
19. By 'Buddhist' I here mean a committed follower (*upasaka*). I have argued (Gombrich, *op. cit.*, p. 95) that there was in ancient India no hard and fast line between a Buddhist and a non-Buddhist layman.
20. Samyutta Nikaya III, 120.
21. Paul Williams (1989) *Mahayana Buddhism: The Doctrinal Foundations*. London and New York: Routledge and Kegan Paul, p. 30.
22. I have used (and slightly changed) Leon Hurvitz's translation from the Chinese translation by Kumarajiva, because that is the form in which the text has mostly been used in the Far East: *Scripture of the Lotus Blossom of the Fine Dharma* (1976). New York: Columbia University Press, pp. 80–2.

Chapter 3

Freedom and Authority in Christianity

Brian Gates

I tell thee that man is tormented by no greater anxiety than to find some one quickly to whom he can hand over that gift of freedom with which the ill-fated creature is born ... . But what happened? Instead of taking men's freedom from them, Thou didst make it greater than ever! Didst Thou forget that man prefers peace, and even death, to freedom of choice in the knowledge of good and evil. Nothing is more seductive for man than his freedom of conscience, but nothing is a greater cause of suffering ... . Instead of taking possession of men's freedom, Thou didst increase it, and burdened the spiritual kingdom of mankind with its sufferings for ever ... .

Mankind as a whole has always striven to organise a universal state. There have been many great nations with great histories, but the more highly they were developed the more unhappy they were, for they felt more acutely than other people the craving for world-wide union ... . Hadst Thou taken the world and Caesar's purple, Thou wouldst have founded the universal state and have given universal peace ... .[1]

Even from the earliest extant writings of the faith, there have been many different ways of being Christian. This diversity has been magnified over the centuries, the more so when approximately a third of the world's present population of two thousand million variously calls itself Christian. It is salutary to realize that there are more Christians alive now than there have been cumulatively from the beginning of the tradition up to 1900.[2] This diversity is evident at both an individual and an institutional level. Historically, the major divisions of Christendom are three: Eastern Orthodox, Protestant and Roman Catholic. Their followers, respectively, comprise approximately one-tenth, two-fifths and three-fifths of all Christians, of whom the majority live elsewhere in the world than Europe and North America.

THREE TRADITIONAL SOURCES OF AUTHORITY

Christians commonly acknowledge one or more reference points to order and authenticate their faith. The Scriptures, Church tradition and individual experience are the three most central.

Biblical authority

The charter documents of the faith are found in the Bible. They express a deeply sensed relationship between God and humankind. This is first set out in the form of scriptures centred on law *(torah)*, writings of the prophets *(nebiim)* and other writings *(kethubim)*. This *Tenak*, or Hebrew Bible, is perceived by Christians, as well as Jews, as representing the aboriginal covenant relationship – hence the term Old Covenant/Testament.[3] Alongside this are the complementary writings endorsing and extending that relationship – the New Covenant/Testament – comprising in Greek the four gospels of Jesus as the Christ, and the letters of Paul and other early Christian leaders. Altogether, these make up the canon of scriptures which from at least the fourth century CE has been fixed in form and regarded generally as authoritative for all Christians.

So far there is little of contention. To be sure, there has been debate about which writings were 'in' and which 'out'; hence the respective old and new apocryphas. Notoriously, from Marcion in the second century, there was the attempt to exclude all Jewish ingredients.[4] This eliminated all of the Old Testament (OT) and much of the New Testament (NT) too. Overall, however, the Bible has been the Bible and its books treasured as such.

What is contentious, however, is the way in which the Scriptures are regarded as authoritative. Tradition speaks of them as inspired word of God, but the nature of the inspiration is open to debate. Some insist that, from the moment of revelation, every word has been inerrant. Others argue that, from as early as the Antiochian and Alexandrian schools of the second century, symbolic interpretation and critical exegesis have been regarded as appropriate.[5] How the Bible is authoritative varies accordingly.

In consequence it is useful to distinguish between what Smart characterizes as deductivist and inductivist views.[6] If the Scriptures are inerrant, God's teachings for human behaviour and belief can be deduced from them in a quite straightforward way. This deductivist view is endorsed by the NT itself: 'all scripture is inspired' (1 Timothy 3:16). Unfortunately, other scriptures (e.g. Qur'an, Gita, Granth) can equally be judged the word of God and validated as such by appeal to internal theologic.

By contrast the inductivist takes the view that the text is to be respected, but goes on to use critical reasoning and scholarship better to understand it. Unfortunately, critical scholarship is in the process of continuous refinement and change. The deductivist provides much surer ground. Significant numbers of Christians take this position, preferring as it were to live with the apparent arbitrariness of accepting one set of scriptures whilst rejecting others, rather than what they regard as the greater arbitrariness of scholarly judgement.

The inductivist is not convinced. The Bible is about revelation; the word of God is that revelation, not the words of the Bible. They themselves are fallible. They express God's truth, but refracted through the lens of human minds and hearts. On this view scripture is authoritative, but not finally so without reference also to other considerations.[7]

Ecclesiastical authority

Such another consideration is our second major reference point, ecclesiastical authority. Historically, without the Church, there would be no Bible. In that sense, as in other traditions, the community of faith is prior to the Scriptures. Subsequently, the words of the Bible have both attracted new members to the Church and provided regular sustenance for the faithful. But the Church has been the guardian of the Scriptures, determining which writings are canonical and providing interpretation.

That role of interpreter and guide has been, in other respects as well, an explicit function of the Church for Christians generally. This is true as much of the Protestant and Independent Churches as of the Catholic and Orthodox Churches. A certain order and discipline has emerged from the fellowship of faith and found expression in prescribed rhythms for liturgy and life. Whether such developments have been communicated through informal osmosis or more codified decree, their influence on Christian self-understanding has been weighty.

As with the Bible, however, the nature of the Churches' authority is contentious. There are instances from the life of the early Church that can be invoked to support any one of several modes of authority: *congregational* (Romans 12 – division of labour in the body of Christ), *conciliar* (Acts 15 – leaders' consultation in Jerusalem) or *apostolic* (Matthew 16:8 – keys of authority given to Peter).

Apostolic authority is understood as deriving directly from God through the person of Jesus. In commissioning Apostles to serve throughout the world, Jesus endowed them to wield the power of God on his behalf, teaching, preaching and dispensing judgement or mercy. Here is the basis of episcopal succession and the rule of bishops, in turn ordaining priests/vicars, to stand 'vicariously' with them, in the place of Christ.

In the Roman Catholic tradition, this authority resides peculiarly in the Pope as Bishop of Rome and successor to Peter, the presiding Apostle. Following a conceptual distinction made in Roman law, he holds it in his official capacity and not in his own person. Thus, he presides over the *magisterium*, the teaching authority, of the Church. The Orthodox and Anglican traditions of patriarchs and archbishops share in this high sense of succession, but without the predominant focus on Rome.[8]

By contrast, *congregational authority* is seated within the local church. Typically, from a shared experience of prayer and fellowship, leaders (often elders) are appointed and judgements made on the basis of the evidence to hand. Aspects of this may be familiar from the 'Free Church', Protestant traditions of Baptists, Congregationalists, Methodists, and Presbyterians.[9] But it is perhaps best illustrated by reference to the weekly gatherings of Quakers, renowned for 'taking the sense of the meeting'.[10] Less obviously, there are parallels also in such disparate locations as the monastic tradition of the Dominicans, the 'base communities' of the Catholic Church in Latin America, and the pressure for participatory democracy from Presbyterian Church leaders in Malawi.[11]

The congregational and apostolic modes of authority may seem totally separate from each other. However, there are elements in each which they share with the *conciliar authority*. For instance, in the interests of providing co-ordination between the many different local churches, concessions were made from congregational authority to some form of centralized committee or council. Similarly, apostolic authority has been seen as having a collegial aspect, not least in the case of the election of the Bishop of Rome. In both instances, some conciliar dimension is involved.[12]

From very early in the history of the Church, councils of its leaders have been held, as, archetypally, in Jerusalem in 49 CE between Peter, Paul, James and others. The range of territory covered by a council might be a diocese, a province, or, if it was an 'ecumenical' council, the Church throughout the known world. Thus, the famous RC Councils, Vatican I (1870) and II (1959–64), include in their lineage those earlier ones associated with the ratification of creeds, Nicaea in 325, and Chalcedon in 451. Synodical councils, as currently implemented within the Anglican communion, bringing together clergy and laity in the government of the Church, were also held earlier in the Catholic tradition, as at Whitby in 664. Of comparable significance within the Protestant Churches was the development first of national and international councils of particular denominations, and then of inter-denominational councils at local, regional and world levels, culminating in the formation of the World Council of Churches in 1948.[13]

Conciliar authority is a mixture of the apostolic and the congregational. It therefore ranges from that which is formally promulgated, as with canon law in some sense binding on all members of a particular Church, to what is simply of an advisory nature.[14] Taken altogether, ecclesiastical authority, like that of the Bible, is capable of quite different interpretations.

It is worth noting that, in some theological reckonings, the conciliar church is the arena for continuing revelation. At the same time, any tendency, in the name of that more extensive interpretation of revelation, to cut too far adrift from earlier tradition has often been rebuked in the name of biblical authenticity. In this connection the renewed emphasis on biblical scholarship, in its own right, within the Roman Catholic Church is especially significant.[15]

Individual authority

Just as references to Bible and to the Church often interact one with the other, they also interact with our third reference point: the experience of the individual. The foundations of individual authority are also more varied than a first glance would suggest. They include those of inwardness or mysticism, of rationality and enlightenment, and of moral compulsion or conscience.

Mysticism is here taken to encompass all those experiences reported by Christians as breaking in from beyond themselves. Thus, there is the experience of speaking with tongues, or glossolalia, first mentioned in connection with the birth of the Church in Jerusalem, shortly thereafter in Corinth and again amongst followers of Montanus in the second century, or of Joachim of Fiore in the twelfth, but now widespread in the Pentecostal Churches of Southern Africa, Western Europe and North America.[16] There are also the visionary experiences of the desert fathers, of a Teresa of Avila, or a Bernadette. And to these must be added the unpublicized experiences of countless men and women, who, to this day, attest to a dawning sense of divine spirit within them, associated perhaps with extremes of desolation or happiness, or, simply, everyday routine.[17] There is an authority in such experience, which is self-authenticating. Given such, it can confidently challenge other authorities and frequently be an embarrassment to positions established on other grounds.[18]

Rationality is closer to mysticism than is widely recognized.[19] The image of light is associated with each of them. They are both inward and subjective in orientation, and, in the history of Christian thought, emphasis on the one has usually been followed by attention to the other. With public credibility in view, however, rationality endeavours to be objective in the arguments advanced from its inner reasoning. Thus its theological language is intended both to arise from personal experience and to correspond with common and natural sense.

Within common human experience it finds signals of transcendence, in other words, theistic evidences.[20] They may begin with reference to the universal occurrence of mystical experience, widespread beyond the bounds of institutional religious belonging. They include:

- bemusement over the contingency that there is a universe, as well as you and I within it, when there might be none at all;
- wondering at the order and pattern in the natural world, as also in human relationships and civilization;
- recognition of living towards some meaningful end, with life having some overall point and purpose to it.

This is the stuff of natural, rational theology. Here are the makings of traditional pointers to the reality of God. Their appeal is to individual rational experience.

Examples of such argument abound throughout the history of Christianity. It is the language of such as Thomas Aquinas, Friedrich Schleiermacher, Hans Küng, and Kyung Chung.[21] Significantly, it provides a bridge for relating both to secular culture and also to other religious traditions. Such potential for universal correspondence makes much of the language of reason. Like John's Gospel, it speaks of it as an inner source of light illuminating every human being. Indeed, this is a major clue to understanding the significance of Jesus, for it is that light of reason, in all its creative power and wisdom, which Christians recognize him as bringing to fullest human expression.

Both rationality and mystical sense are rooted in individual experience, and prominently alongside them is a sense of moral obligation and oughtness. It may be variably present or absent in particular individuals, and anthropologists can speculate about societies in which it is hard to find. Even so, there is evidence of it transculturally, almost as a universal. In Christian tradition this is named as conscience, and already by Paul identified as more fundamental to humans generally than any law of state or religion.[22] The incidence of individual Christians 'taking a moral stance' is therefore very common.

On the authority of individual moral experience unjust laws have been protested, charity given, taxes withheld, chastity celebrated or eschewed, and wars conscientiously objected to. In all conscience, Martin Luther 'could not do other' than challenge the established ways of the Church, Thomas More resists to the death the self-seeking ways of his king, and Oliver Cromwell, after 'waiting on the Lord' in moral agony, resolves to kill a different king. In each case the force of conscience is powerfully felt. In certain circumstances it even suffices to counter the authority of Scripture or Church tradition.

Authority then, for Christians, has several aspects to it. Any one of them can be magnified in a way that conceals the others. This is the case, quite commonly, when, singly, Bible, Church or conscience is 'infallibilized' and made absolute, to become in itself the voice of God. That any such tendency is intellectually dubious is hard to deny in the face of literary criticism, historical scholarship, or Freudian insights into the superego.[23] The evidence from these sources only serves to confirm the Pauline judgement that transcendent power is God's alone: apostolic witness and the other reference points are but 'pots of earthenware to contain this treasure' (2 Corinthians 4:7).

Yet they remain authorities, and compelling ones. The compulsion can be felt heteronomously, imposed as some alien law from the outside, and reinforced with all the weight of tradition. It is difficult, however, to find such an authoritarian frame of mind in the New Testament (NT). There, the compelling claim may be experienced in the spirit of what Jesus says or does, or equally in that same spirit in the fellowship of Christians and life of the world. But, in addition, it also 'rings true', entails 'dawning personal recognition', and makes intrinsic sense for the individual respondent. In Weberian terms, there is both charisma *and* rationality.[24] By holding together all three reference points, Bible, Church and conscience, Christians may legitimately assert that human autonomy is not demolished, but transmuted from within.

THE SCOPE FOR FREEDOM

The image of liberation from bondage is recurrent in the experience of the early Christians. They are heirs to the tradition of a people freed from slavery in Egypt. From their association with Jesus, whom with God they called the giver of life, they laid claim to a new sense of vitality and freedom in their own lives.

Theologically, the contrast is drawn between that version of the Jewish tradition which appeared to emphasize the formality of rule-following, and that which, in the words of the prophet Jeremiah, has the law known from within, because written on human hearts. Psychologically, this roots human actions in the intentions and motivations that give rise to them, rather than the requirements of some externally imposed conformity. Either way, liberation has an inward source.

Freedom of this kind is contrasted sharply with legalism. Equally, however, it is distinguished from licence, into which, so we are told by Paul from the experience of his journeys round the Roman Empire, the overenthusiastic may be carried away by disregard for the letter of the law. The check against both is the double-sided principle of loving God and neighbour, as fully fleshed out in the Gospels. Thus, true freedom is bound on the inside by the law of love, and that binding itself is described as 'perfect freedom'. Knowledge of that truth is itself the force of liberation (John 8:32). By contrast, carelessness, or disaffection from any other as neighbour, is a sign of ignorance and a fall back from the potential for freedom.

Over the centuries of the Christian tradition, the scope for freedom provided by the Churches has varied. On the one hand, it has been extended to the point of anarchy. On the other, it has been reduced to the point of elimination by total control.

Anarchical expressions are easily caricatured. Thus, for instance, in a notorious spoof, Terry Southern portrayed his heroine, one Candy Christian, as a devotee of free love. So freely was her loving available and applied that, sexually, she was everyone's mate, however incongruously. Or, again, in the Peter Sellars film *Heavens Above*, the new vicar is so freely committed to the plight of the poor that he scarcely notices the inconvenience of the vicarage being taken over by a large gipsy family or the lead disappearing from the roof of the church.

There is historical precedent for such actions as these. Invoking the spirit of freedom in Christ, normal routines and legal proprieties have been deliberately ignored. In place of monogamy, there has been polygamy or experiments with the sharing of husbands and wives. Similarly, in place of property ownership, there has been the pooling of all goods and belongings. Extremes of licence are reported from amongst gnostic Christians in the early Church, amongst Cathars in medieval Christendom, and perhaps most elaborately in the period following the Reformation. In Germany, it is associated with Johannes Agricola or Thomas Münzer; in Holland, with Jan of Leyden; and in England, with such strange-sounding sects as My One Flesh or the Diggers.[25]

Whilst never accepted in the mainstream of Church life, such instances as these can only have been generated in the name of Christ because the emphasis on freedom is so fundamental a feature of the tradition. However, they have generally been viewed by the Churches with as much embarrassment as was the vicar in *Heavens Above*: he was put in a rocket and sent into outer space, where he could safely be ignored.

Such banishment is an example of the other tendency in the Church, to restrict the scope of freedom by total control. This tendency is at its strongest whensoever Christians have been tempted to 'infallibilize' their authority. If one or other of the Bible, the Church or conscience is perceived as absolute truth, there is a logical transition from that to a desire to control the lives and thoughts of individuals, who come or ought to come within its sway.

Without benefit of such control, it might well be feared that they could err, or persist in error. That, in turn, would entail the risk of terrible consequences, not only during their lifetimes, but beyond death as well. Moreover, it would be possible, or even very likely, that others might be similarly led astray. On this basis, it is in everyone's best interests that all deviance is controlled.

There is a parallel to this in the totalitarian stance of Marxist-Leninism, where freedom is described as 'the recognition of necessity', and, in turn, what is necessary is subject to the judgement of the official interpretation of history by the Communist Party. Purges, expulsions, even pogroms are a well-documented feature of communist regimes in Eastern Europe,[26] as also in South East Asia. They have featured also in the history of the Churches.

The most notorious examples of the Church engaging in acts of total control are perhaps those relating to the activities of the Inquisition and to treatment of Jews. Thomas of Torquemada, in his zeal for the faith of Christ, combined the Deuteronomic injunction to exterminate apostates with the Pauline encouragement to avoid and expel heretics.[27] In Spain, from the 1490s onwards, Jews, Muslims and Protestants all suffered mightily in consequence. More generally, throughout Europe, whether in the East on Orthodox territory or in the West in deference to the Roman Church, the cycle of obligatory yellow star, forced conversion and intermittent burnings was in operation.[28] The scale of comparable Protestant activities may have been smaller, but Luther's verbal indictment of the Jews was ferocious and Calvin's involvement with the execution of Servetus for heresy indisputable.[29]

New attention has been given in recent years to another example of Christian intolerance: that of male Church leaders against female healers, labelled as witches. This was not confined to the old world of Europe, but extended to the new world of North America. The scale of actual killings is contentious, but probably extends to thousands, even tens of thousands, rather than just a few hundreds. In this respect, as in the others too, it is salutary for male Christians to realize that the policy of total control has been largely a male preserve.[30]

The biblical enthusiasm for freedom, with which we began, is better displayed in the twentieth century by formal declarations from the Churches on the principles of religious freedom and of social justice. The two are even combined in the movement known as liberation theology.

In principle, from a Christian point of view, religious freedom is grounded theologically in the affirmation that all human beings derive from God, irrespective of whether they are born underneath or outside the ecclesiastical umbrella. This was earlier made plain in the writings of Nicholas of Cusa, John Milton, and John Locke, but has been powerfully reiterated from Geneva and Rome.

It is an open secret that the World Council of Churches (WCC) had a major part in promoting the need for the Declaration of Human Rights which was finally agreed by the United Nations. Indeed, the final and fuller form of words contained therein on freedom of conscience directly reflects WCC handiwork. Similarly, the Declaration on Religious Liberty from Vatican II was a watershed in the public appreciation of human diversity by the Roman Catholic Church.[31] It is no coincidence that both the WCC and the Vatican have subsequently given high priority to encouraging dialogue, both formal and informal, between Christians and folk of other faiths.

Social justice has loomed comparably large. Papal encyclicals, not least the successive anniversary publications in the *Rerum Novarum* tradition, have trumpeted this cause, drawing on the best of secular intelligence as well as that of insiders to the faith.[32] And the same has been true in the WCC-sponsored programmes to combat racism or for an attainable and sustainable condition of justice, peace and the integrity of creation.[33]

Illustrating many of these same concerns is the movement which has come to be known as liberation theology. Best known from Latin America, but with manifestations elsewhere, including Southern Africa, this has harnessed the cause of the poor to that of the kingdom of God. 'Base communities' have addressed the question of how the gospel's message of freedom can be translated into economic and political terms, and this has been seen to have powerful implications for established institutional self-interest of all kinds.[34]

The parallel between base communities and the significance of monastic foundations in the history of the Church is worth remarking. They too are radical experiments in freedom. Except in well-advertised periods of corruption, their lifestyle is not one of licence, but of equality in poverty, chaste love and common obedience. In both, freedom brings with it its own internal discipline and order. At least potentially, their impact on the social environment within which they are set is massive.

In sum, freedom is a crucial belief and value for Christians. Its pursuit has evidently not been wholehearted by all who have called themselves such. However, none from any world-view has been more resolute in its advocacy and practice than the Christians who have actually been true to their faith. On good authority they believe that this is their calling.

NOTES

1. Fyodor Dostoyevsky (1880) *The Brothers Karamazov*. ET Constance Garnett, New York: Random House, pp. 302–6.
2. These and the other demographic data which follow are extrapolated from David B. Barrett (1982) *World Christian Encyclopaedia*. Oxford: Oxford University Press.
3. The term 'old' can sometimes be used pejoratively, as compared with the new, and the

Jewish community is understandably sensitive at any Christian usage which appears to render Torah as *démodé*. However, just as the terms 'older' and 'younger' generation need not build barriers to mutual respect, so in continuing to use the term Old Testament no doctrine of supersedence, of a kind which vaunts Christian supremacy, is necessarily implied.

4. According to Marcion the Christian gospel of love, represented by ten of Paul's Epistles and an edited version of Luke's Gospel, was diametrically opposed to the Jewish God of law, revealed by the Old Testament as fickle and cruel.

5. In its first centuries the Christian Church had substantial centres in each of the many cities of the Roman Empire, often with a distinct theological bent of their own. That in Antioch was strong in historical, even critical, interpretation of scripture, whereas that in Alexandria inclined to allegorize and to look for mystical meaning.

6. Ninian Smart (1964) *The Teacher and Christian Belief*. London: James Clarke.

7. James Barr (1983) *Holy Scripture: Canon, Authority and Criticism*. Oxford: Clarendon Press; Richard P. C. and Anthony T. Hanson (1989) *The Bible Without Illusions*. London: SCM Press.

8. 'The hierarchical constitution of the Church'. In *Catechism of the Catholic Church* (1994). London: Geoffrey Chapman, pp. 203–8. For Orthodox and Anglican views, see, respectively: G. Florovsky (1972) *Bible, Church, Tradition: An Eastern Orthodox View*. Belmont: Nordland; and Robert Wright (1987) 'An Anglican comment on papal authority in the light of recent developments'. In Stephen W. Sykes (ed.) *Authority in the Anglican Communion*. Toronto: Anglican Book Centre.

9. The distinctive sociological features are characterized ideal-typically in David Martin (1964) *Pacifism*. London: Routledge and Kegan Paul, pp. 208–24. For sweep of historical presence and impact, see Sydney Ahlstrom (1972) *A Religious History of the American People*. New Haven: Yale University Press.

10. John Punshon (1987) *Encounter with Silence*. Richmond, IN: Friends United Press.

11. See successively: Ernest Barker (1913) *Dominican Order and Convocation: A Study of the Growth of Representation in the Church during the Thirteenth Century*. Oxford: Oxford University Press; Christian Smith (1991) *Emergence of Liberation Theology*. Chicago: Chicago University Press; and Kenneth Ross (1993) *Presbyterian Theology and Participatory Democracy*. Edinburgh: St Andrew's Press.

12. Paul M. Harrison (1959) *Authority and Power in the Free Church Tradition: A Sociological Study of the American Baptist Convention*. Carbondale, IL: Southern Illinois University Press; Bill McSweeney (1980) *Roman Catholicism: The Search for Relevance*. Oxford: Blackwell.

13. *WCC Year Book 1995* (1994). Geneva: World Council of Churches, gives details of member Churches, plus a comprehensive list of regional ecumenical conferences and national councils by continent and country.

14. Canon Law Society of Great Britain and Ireland (1995) *The Canon Law: Letter and Spirit*. London: Geoffrey Chapman/Dublin: Veritas.

15. The importance, for example for doing ethics, is discussed in James M. Gustafson (1978) *Protestant and Roman Catholic Ethics*. London: SCM Press, pp. 21–9.

16. For a general overview see Walter J. Hollenweger (1972) *The Pentecostals*. London: SCM Press; and more particularly David Martin (1990) *Tongues of Fire: The Explosion of Protestantism in Latin America*. Oxford; Blackwell.

17. Cheslyn Jones (ed.) (1976) *Study of Spirituality*. London: SPCK.

18. Gilbert Markus (ed.) (1992) *The Radical Tradition: Revolutionary Saints in the Battle for Justice and Human Rights*. London: Darton, Longman and Todd.

19. See Paul Tillich (1976) *Perspectives on Nineteenth and Twentieth Century Protestant Theology*. London: SCM Press, pp. 19–23.

20. The term canvassed by James Richmond as an alternative to 'proofs' for the existence of God: James Richmond (1970) *Theology and Metaphysics*. London: SCM Press.

21. Timothy McDermott (ed.) (1989) *St Thomas Aquinas' Summa Theologiae (1275): A Concise Translation*. London: Methuen; Friedrich Scheiermacher *On Religion: Addresses in Response to Its Cultured Critics*. ET (1893) London: Routledge; Hans Küng (1977) *On*

Being a Christian. London: Collins; and Kyung Chung (1990) *Struggle to Be the Sun Again*. New York: Orbis.

22. Romans 2:12-18.
23. See in turn: James Barr (1984) *Escaping from Fundamentalism*. London: SCM Press; John Kent (1987) *The Unacceptable Face: The Modern Church in the Eyes of the Historian*. London: SCM Press; Sigmund Freud, variously, e.g. (1938) *New Introductory Lectures on Psychoanalysis*. New York: W. W. Norton & Co., p. 88.
24. Max Weber (1920) *The Theory of Social and Economic Organisations*. ET (1947) Oxford: Oxford University Press, Section IV. The 'charismatic' as well as the 'legal-rational' is vital if the latter is not to be reduced to the iron cage described in Weber (1930) *Protestant Ethic and the Spirit of Capitalism* (1904). ET (1930): London: Allen & Unwin, pp. 180–3. Such a fate may have been reached in the undiscerning extension of mechanical accountancy models to professional life, including teaching, in the course of the last decade.
25. Norman Cohn (1961) *The Pursuit of the Millenium*. 2nd edn. New York: Harper.
26. Dimitry V. Pospielovsky (1988) *A History of Soviet Atheism in Theory and Practice*, Vol. 2: *Soviet Anti-religious Campaigns and Persecutions*. London: Macmillan; Theodore Freedman (ed.) (1984) *Anti-Semitism in the Soviet Union: Its Roots and Consequences*. New York: Freedom Library Press.
27. Deuteronomy 13:12–16 and 1 Corinthians 5:13 and 16:22.
28. Friedrich Heer (1967) *God's First Love*. London: Weidenfeld & Nicolson.
29. Roland H. Bainton (1951) *The Travail of Religious Liberty*. Philadelphia: Westminster, ch. 3.
30. Compactly represented in Barbara G. Walker (1983) *The Woman's Encyclopedia of Myths and Secrets*. New York: HarperCollins, entries 'Torture', 'Witch', 'Witchcraft'.
31. Pope Paul VI, 'Declaration on Religious Freedom'. In A. Flannery (ed.) (1981) *Vatican II: Conciliar and Post-Conciliar Documents*. Leominster: Fowler Wright.
32. The 1991 papal encyclical *Centesimus Annus* is one of a succession of such encyclicals published to mark each decade's anniversary of *Rerum Novarum*, itself perceived as a striking expression of concern for social justice. Cf. the special issue of *Ecumenical Review* **43**, 4, October 1991.
33. E.g. D. Preman Niles (1992) *Between the Flood and the Rainbow*. Geneva: World Council of Churches.
34. Alfred T. Hennelly (ed.) (1990) *Liberation Theology: A Documentary History*. New York: Orbis.

Chapter 4

Authority and Freedom in Hinduism

Frank Whaling

AN INTRODUCTORY CAVEAT: THE COMPLEXITY OF THE HINDU TRADITION

Beware the complexity of the Hindu tradition! The caveat, although trite, is very necessary. The careful and detailed work of Wilfred Cantwell Smith has highlighted the inappropriateness of the term 'Hinduism' with its connotations of a monolithic and static entity.[1] However, even when we move in our thinking to the use of the phrase 'the Hindu tradition' in place of 'Hinduism', the problem of complexity is only somewhat resolved, for within the history of the Hindu tradition there has been tremendous change and development. Indeed, it may legitimately be questioned whether there is such a thing as the Hindu tradition, for it appears to be a congeries of traditions developing and interacting side by side.[2] Moreover, when we isolate any one of the particular Hindu groups or symbols for particular enquiry we find within it different layers of meaning and levels of interpretation. Now we see this so-called Hindu tradition and now we don't! In relation to our topic the question is raised in regard to *what* Hindu tradition and at *what* time and at *what* level are we investigating the issue of authority and freedom?

There are many manifestations of complexity. In the first place *change* has been endemic within the Hindu tradition. For example, when we look at the basic corpus of Hindu sacred texts, the Veda, we see tremendous developments within them from the original Rg Veda to the major Upanisads. Although nestling within the same canon, the same *sruti*, the same set of heard and revealed texts, the insights of the Rg Veda and the Upanisads point to dramatic changes within what we now call the Hindu tradition. These changes are, of course, reconcilable to Hindus, many of whom do not understand the stress that is placed upon historical development by sympathetic outsiders.[3] Nevertheless, to the historian of religion those changes are real. The emphasis upon the gods of the Rg Veda, such as Indra, Varuna and Agni, is transferred, in the Upanisads, to the Absolute Reality behind everything, namely Brahman. The stress upon sacrifice to the gods in the Rg Veda is transferred, in the Upanisads, to the search for inner realization of the relationship between one's own inner self, the Atman, and the Ultimate

Reality Brahman. Whereas the Rg Veda had recognized the importance of the priests who had officiated at the Vedic sacrifices, the Upanisads turn the spotlight upon the seers and sages who intuit the knowledge necessary for inward realization. Whereas the Rg Veda had envisaged a life after death in heaven following a one-life sojourn on earth, the Upanisads accept the notion of many rebirths according to the working out of *karma* and *samsara*. Arising out of this switch in world-view, the Upanisads insist that there is a fourth aim of life, namely *moksa*, or release from the round of rebirths that is added to and is more important than the first three aims set out in the Rg Veda, namely *kama* or pleasure and leisure, *artha* or making a living, and *dharma* or ethics and appropriate living. Likewise, the Upanisads add a fourth stage of life to the Rg Vedic stages of being a student, a householder with family, and a semi-retired contemplative, namely *sannyasa* or renunciation of the world in the final search for *moksa*. In line with this development, yoga became a heightened interest in the Upanisads and at the same time the caste system became more systematized and crystallized.[4] Our Hindu friends are right to point out the continuities within the Hindu process from its rise in the mists of history to the maturing of the Hindu tradition as a world religion in our own time. However, it is undeniable that there have been extraordinary developments within that history, and these complicate our search for a settled notion of authority and freedom within the Hindu tradition. The Lord Jagannatha of Puri 'majestically stands there on His throne graciously smiling to his devotees: stands as a unique symbol of the great flexibility and dynamics of Hinduism, of its capacity to absorb, integrate and remodel'.[5] In so far as the continuity of the Hindu tradition lies in its flexibility and dynamics, where does this leave the notion of authority and freedom within that tradition?

In the second place, there is *infinite variety* within the Hindu tradition. It contains 14 different language groups lying behind which are ethnic differences – in marked contrast, for example, with China, where 93 per cent of the population are of Han extraction. It has no historical founder, no hierarchy of religious authority, and no validated body of doctrine. Many gods, great and small, are contained within its fold. One is reminded of the seeker who approaches Yajnavalkya in the Brhadaranyaka Upanisad with the query 'how many gods are there?'[6] The first answer is 3306, but in response to further queries it declines to 33, six, three, two, one and a half, and one. The Brahman underlying the gods may be one, but they themselves are legion. A bewildering variety of religious organizations, *sampradayas*, have grown up around the main deities. Countless individual gurus have attracted followers, and organizations have sometimes grown up in connection with them. However, although an occasional charismatic spiritual leader may attract attention, and although in an undefined sense the Sankaracaryas of the four great monastic institutions reputedly established by Sankara at Badrinath, Puri, Dvaraka and Srngeri in the four corners of India have some wider standing in the Hindu community, there is no one who can speak for the Hindu tradition as such.

Consequently, attempts to define what constitutes the Hindu tradition have never been wholly successful. For Dandekar, 'a Hindu is one who is born of Hindu parents and who has not *openly* abjured Hinduism';[7] for others caste is the key; for others the Hindu sects and schools are crucial; yet others would view the Veda as the scriptural crux to what is a Hindu; yet again implicit beliefs in certain key doctrines such as Brahman as Absolute Reality, the Atman as the real self of human beings, and life being centred upon rebirth (*samsara*) according to deeds (*karma*) requiring *moksa* (release) would gain the definitional vote of others.[8] In fact none of the definitional approaches is wholly convincing or satisfactory. As Dandekar puts it, 'the true glory of Hinduism consists in presenting all these polarities and paradoxes as also the various levels of doctrine and practice as constituting a single well-conditioned religious system'.[9] The problem remains of how we locate authority and freedom in this 'well-conditioned religious system'.

In the third place there are *various layers and levels of meaning* within virtually every aspect of the Hindu tradition. If we go back to the Rg Veda itself we find that Agni can function at three levels of religious nuance. At the mundane level Agni is fire, the everyday fire whereby we cook and keep ourselves warm. At another level Agni emits smoke which reaches up to heaven and Agni is therefore an intermediary between the mundane world and the heavenly world. At yet another level Agni is a fully fledged Vedic god amenable to worship, respect and honour.

In the modern context a simple Siva Nataraja (Siva as Lord of the Dance) sitting in a temple, in a museum, in our home or in the mind of the believer evinces different layers of interpretation. In this icon of the four-armed Siva dancing in a ring of fire we see Siva as creating the world and destroying the world, we see Siva trampling a demon underfoot and at the same time extending his mercy by means of a hand gesture, we see Siva's wild dance and frenzied hair combined with a seraphic facial expression, we see Siva holding the drum of creation and the fire of destruction, and we see the flaming circle in which Siva dances as real and illusory (*maya*), as positive and negative. If we are empathetic to the Hindu Siva our mind flicks over to other Siva images – to the Siva *linga* with its erotic as well as its pure undertones, to Siva as the meditating ascetic (*daksinamurti*), to Siva the consort of the goddess Parvati, to Siva the destroyer of demons (*tripurantaka*), to Siva half-male and half-female, and so on.[10] If we think we have fathomed the depths of the Hindu tradition or any aspect of it this is a fairly sure sign that we have not understood it.

It may be felt that this comprehensive and detailed caveat has hindered our ability to arrive at any real understanding of the Hindu view of authority and freedom. Yet this is not really so. It depends upon the perspective we bring to the problem. If our gaze is upon the minutiae of the Hindu tradition we will rightly be sceptical of sweeping generalizations. But if our gaze is global, and it is only in this decade that we can take a global sweep of religious history and earthly destiny, then we can see the many-crannied details of the Hindu structure in the light of the whole edifice and we can see that edifice in the light of the cosmos as a whole.

THREE PERSPECTIVES ON AUTHORITY AND FREEDOM IN THE HINDU TRADITION

In this chapter, therefore, taking seriously the points that have been raised so far, we will look at authority and freedom in the Hindu tradition in the light of the political history of India, in the light of the social, cultural and ritual background to that history, above all as seen in the caste system as interpreted by Louis Dumont, and finally in the light of the religious and spiritual dimension within which Hindus have lived their lives, and in the light of which they have lived, and moved and had their being.

Political history

The term 'authority' usually conjures up the notion of a political or military authority over against which we exercise or do not exercise some sort of freedom. It conjures up the notion of the background of Christendom, of the close inter-relationship within Islam of religious and political oversight, of the intertwining within Theravada Buddhism between the pious ruler, the sangha and the laity, of the Confucian political hegemony in China, and of the poignant oscillation within Judaism between the Davidic type of kingdom and the state of Israel over against exile and persecution.

It is a striking and little-rehearsed fact of Indian history that of the five great uniting rulers within the history of the subcontinent only one was obviously Hindu, namely Candra Gupta. Of the others, Asoka was a Buddhist, Akbar was a Muslim, the British Raj was reputedly Christian, and the Nehru dynasty in modern India is secularly Hindu. Let us pause for a moment to examine this singular phenomenon: it implies that Hindu authority has not been primarily located in the political arena, or linked to military prowess. Such an examination may also offer us clues as to the actual sources of authority and freedom within the Hindu tradition.

Asoka, who died around 232 BCE, was a Buddhist monarch, albeit in the state-dominating mode of Constantine rather than the more piously dominant mode of the Mughal Aurangzeb. There is reasonable evidence to show that during his reign Buddhism transcended the role of an Indian religious group and began its career as a missionary religion. In his famous rock and pillar inscriptions Asoka becomes alive. He states

> the Beloved of the Gods desires safety, self-control, justice and happiness for all beings. The Beloved of the Gods considers that the greatest of all victories is the victory of Righteousness, and that the Beloved of the Gods has already won, here and on all his borders.[11]

It is not unjust that the insignia of the modern Indian state incorporates an Asokan column into its design. Yet it was during the years surrounding the rule of this Buddhist monarch that some of the basic features of Hindu authority became established. Although Asoka's inscriptions were in Magadhan Prakrit, which together with Pali was the language favoured by the Buddhists and Jains, it was around this period that the great triumvirate of Sanskrit grammarians, Panini, Katyayana and Patanjali, were evolving the glories of classical Sanskrit, which combined a strict grammar and syntax with infinite opportunity for the expansion of vocabulary and situational language. Such was their success that Asvaghosa and his later Mahayana Buddhist successors were to switch to Sanskrit as their medium of expression. The process of Sanskritization was in being. Whatever the political situation, therefore, the religious and cultural agenda was being set by Hindu thought-forms set out in Sanskrit sacred texts, the Epics and later the Puranas. The sacred geography of India was delimited by Hindu sacred places in the four corners of the land: Badrinath in the north, Puri in the east, Ramesvaram in the south, and Dvaraka in the west. The Ganges river and the Himalaya mountains were the best-known of a myriad of holy places that became assimilated into and interpreted by Hindu mythology.[12]

Equally important, it was during this period that the Code of Manu originated, which was to become the key to Hindu social organization and ethics, which was to become the archstone of *dharma*. Alongside this systematization of *dharma*, there also emerged the *grhya sutras*, the rituals of the householders. These established the norms for the observance of the great rites of passage of birth, marriage, initiation and death. They formed the basis for Hindu civilization. To use the language of the anthropologists, a great tradition was emerging at the ritual, social, cultural and linguistic level that was able to assimilate into itself numerous little traditions throughout the length and breadth of India which, without losing their variety, were able to see themselves as part of a greater whole whether they themselves attracted glory as in the case of Krsna or whether they remained small and unknown.[13]

The political culmination of the process described above came in the reigns of the great Gupta kings, *Candra Gupta I* (320–335 CE), *Samudra Gupta* (335–376 CE), and *Candra Gupta II* (376-415 CE). They united the greater part of India prior to the Hun invasions; the prosperity and well-being they engendered is described by the Chinese Buddhist visitor Fa-hsien; and they represented not only the zenith of ancient Indian culture but also the high watermark of world civilization in their day.[14] However, the fact that the Guptas were Hindu monarchs is neither unimportant nor vital. The process of Hinduization we have outlined would have continued anyway because it was not directly dependent upon the politics of the day. The social agents lying behind it were not the political rulers, the *ksatriyas*, but the dominant minority of priests, the *brahmins*.

A number of reasons are given for the demise of Buddhism in India after this period. They include internal weaknesses within the Buddhist tradition, the philosophical work of Sankara in absorbing Mahayana Buddhist notions into Vedanta, the growth of *bhakti* Hinduism which incorporated the Buddha into the Hindu pantheon as the ninth *avatara* of Visnu, the work of Kumarila and the general assimilatory effect of Hinduism, the supposed corroding effects of Tantrism, and finally the catastrophe for Buddhism of the Muslim invasions. It seems to me that a more basic reason for the decline of Buddhism was the slow disappearance of Buddhist monks from a number of Indian villages. The Buddhist sangha set up an extraordinary norm beyond the caste system and the Vedic texts, and Buddhist monks lived peacefully in Indian villages side-by-side with their Hindu neighbours. But theirs was an exemplary role and if they disappeared for any reason (for example to study at the great monastic university at Nalanda) their loss was crucial, whereas, whether or not there was a Hindu monk or saint in the village, the traditional social and religious organization of the village continued together with the norms of Hindu authority and freedom associated with it.[15]

The next great unifying ruler in India history, *Akbar*, was a Muslim. He was a genius intoxicated by the audacity of his own originality. The first of the great Mughal emperors, ruling from 1555 to 1606, he was tolerant in religion, humane in rule, supportive of inter-communal marriages, innovative in inter-religious dialogue, and prominent in the arts.[16] Not all of his fellow Muslim rulers were as ecumenical or enlightened as he was. Indian political historians have highlighted the importance of Hindu rulers who resisted the Mughal Empire, such as the Ranas of Mewar and the southern kings of Vijayanagar. As we have indicated earlier, the key to Hindu life and authority lay not in the political realm but in the areas of social, ritual and cultural organization. The Muslims represented a monotheistic world-view that was alien to Indian thought-forms.[17] But beneath the umbrella of Muslim rule the Hindus maintained their social organization over against the Muslims, and in religious matters they both reacted against the Muslims and were influenced by them. The sixteenth century was in fact one of the great ages of Hindu *bhakti*, featuring the rise of the great vernacular devotional movements associated with the names of Guru Nanak and the rise of the Sikhs, Tulsi

Das and the glory of Rama, Caitanya and the ecstasy associated with Krsna, Sur Das and the emergence of Radha alongside Krsna, and so on.[18]

The next great unifying force in Indian history was the *British Raj*. Again, the ruling political force was clearly not Hindu, it was implicitly Christian. Nevertheless, the Hindu tradition, although admittedly not strong at the beginning of the nineteenth century, survived sociologically and revived intellectually. The neo-Hindus were at the forefront of the Hindu renaissance, which took seriously the Christian and Western world-view as a force for renewal, with its stress upon mission, scripture and God, and its stress upon education, democracy, social reform and science. The Hindu stress upon tolerance and upon assimilation enabled this adjustment to take place in different stages. Ram Mohun Roy (1772–1833) admitted his debt to Western models in his work for social reform, in his founding of the Brahmo Samaj, and in his support for Western education; Ramakrishna, through his deep spiritual experience, felt that Hinduism had much to give the West; later reformers such as Vivekananda, Gandhi, Radhakrishnan and Aurobindo implied that the richness of the Hindu tradition's spiritual heritage outweighed the material splendour of Western science and technology – that the Hindus had more to give than to receive.[19] Some Hindu commentators, and eminent Western scholars such as Paul Hacker, have suggested that too much has been made of neo-Hinduism, because it has been relayed in the English language. The key to Hinduism remained, for them, the caste system and social and cultural organization of India as seen in the *varnasrama* structure centred upon the castes, rituals and life-stages of the Hindus.[20] There would appear to be truth in both these viewpoints.

Finally, in our own day India has become an *independent secular state*, tolerating all religious positions. The Nehru dynasty, which has superintended the affairs of India for most of the contemporary period, has included Indira Gandhi, whose husband was a Parsi, and Rajiv Gandhi, who married an Italian Catholic. By contrast with Pakistan, which opted to go in a Muslim direction, India turned its face away from the option of a Hindu state. This has not been without its problems, insofar as liberal Hindus such as Gandhi, while supporting the idea of a secular state, retain, as their ideal of what the state should be like, Hindu ideal images such as Ramarajya, the kingdom of Rama.[21] Nevertheless, present-day Hindu nationalist groups such as the Hindu Mahasabha, the Rashtriya Swayamsevak Sangh (founded in 1925) and the Bharatiya Jana Sangh (founded in 1951) have only recently found strong support. Their stress upon Hindutva, 'Hinduness', as a political principle, their stress upon Sanskrit and Hindi as 'Hindu languages', their stress upon the need for a Hindu state, their veneration for the caste system and the cow, and their emphasis upon Hindu communalism partly inspired by Dayananda Saraswati, the founder of the Arya Samaj (1824–83), and B. G. Tilak (1856–1920), have been slow to find favour for the reasons underlined throughout this chapter, namely that authority and freedom within the Hindu tradition are not to be sought or found within the political sphere.[22]

Where then are they to be found? We have seen also that credal and doctrinal ortho-doxy are not prized within the Hindu tradition as they were until recently within the Christian tradition, for which theology is a central category. Hindus have stressed the notion of the *istadevata*, one's own chosen deity. That deity may be Visnu, Siva, the Goddess, Rama, Krsna, or a number of other focuses of divinity. For oneself, one's own deity may be all in all. It may be the functional equivalent for the Hindu believer of the whole Christian trinity. Yet at the same time, the Hindu is willing to admit that for someone else a different deity may have the same force.[23] Allied to this inbuilt internal tolerance is the intuition that different religious traditions are equal paths to the same goal, and that there is transcendental unity of all religions.[24] In addition to the lack of theological exclusivism among most Hindus, there is the institutional reality that there is no organizational focus of orthodoxy, and there are few formal religious structures within the Hindu framework whereby beliefs can be designated as systematically true or false.

Social, cultural and ritual background

We have already hinted throughout this presentation that an important inherent source of authority and freedom within the Hindu tradition has been the *varnasrama* system, with its stress upon caste, ritual, the stages of life, and Hindu social organization. This is vividly conveyed by the epoch-making work of Louis Dumont, as outlined in his celebrated *Homo Hierarchicus* and other studies.[25] Dumont insisted that Hindu social organization should be seen in its own right. We cannot understand it in terms of Western class or racism; it is not to be compared with Western notions of equality or individualism. It is a total system within which there are three essential elements: hierarchy, separation and interdependence based upon the opposition between pure and impure.

Although the caste system is, strictly speaking, based upon thousands of subcastes, *jatis*, Dumont felt that the original Vedic ranking of the four *varnas*, the four estates, was important. At the top were the *brahmins* or priests, second came the *ksatriyas* or warriors, third came the *vaisyas* or merchants, and finally came the *sudras* or servants. Within these groupings there was a hierarchy ranging from the brahmin, who was superior, to the sudra, who was inferior. Nevertheless they were interdependent: each depended upon the other, each played a role in relation to everybody else. The hierarchy was holistic. Each person lived proportionate to his or her status, and each was part of the whole. Hierarchy was therefore in a sense unequal, but it was also interdependent. Authority was conveyed by one's position in the hierarchy, but so was freedom. Freedom and justice in a hierarchically ordered society are equated with interdependence, with exercising your *dharma* or role in accordance with your position in society.[26]

Marriage and eating are important factors in Hindu social organization – the notion of marrying within and eating within your own subcaste according to the principle of separation which is encompassed within hierarchy.[27] This is not just a matter of difference of class, for written into the whole system is a view of purity and impurity. This distinction between pure and impure lies behind the rankings within the caste hierarchy, and it also operates within the family, especially at times of birth or death, in regard to objects of everyday use, for example food and cooking implements, and in regard to the body.[28]

Therefore authority and freedom are provided by the caste system seen as a whole. Some castes are higher than others within the total hierarchy; men have a superior and different role to that of women; persons at a later stage of life within the same caste have precedence over persons at an earlier stage of life within the same caste. The whole system of authority and freedom is validated by religious theories of purity and impurity and also by notions of *karma* and *samsara*. We are born into our present position in life because of what we have done and the way we have lived in past lives. The authority that is given to us is therefore a reasonable one, and to live in accordance with our place in the scheme of things is perfect freedom.

Dumont's gloss upon the *varnasrama* system takes us nearer to a clearer view of authority and freedom within the Hindu tradition. Hindu authority has not taken a political or 'ecclesiastical' form. It has not been exercised with a view to commanding belief in certain prescribed doctrines. Whether we agree with Dumont's formulation of the theory of Hindu social organization or not, it is clear that the caste system and the concepts underlying it are very relevant in regard to authority and freedom. The Hindu may have enviable freedom in regard to belief; the Hindu's social freedom, while it may be genuinely seen as freedom, is severely circumscribed within rigid limits. It may provide an inbuilt apparatus of social security and care in old age but it would appear, at first sight, that this social freedom is exercised at the expense of individual initiative. Nevertheless it represents an interesting alternative to the extremes of political or ecclesiastical autocracy on the one hand and unbridled individualism on the other hand. It is Hindu and it is different.

What then are the possible defects in Dumont's thesis? It is relevant to mention two at this point. It is too abstruse, simplistic and structurally pure; and it contains a whiff of reductionism. In regard to the first point, we saw earlier how it is unwise to lose sight of the complexity of the Hindu tradition. In practice it is more disparate than Dumont's holistically watertight categories cater for. Eminent Indian sociologists of religion such as G. S. Ghurye have shown how it was possible to move up the caste ladder by dint of changing economic circumstances.[29] The focus of caste lies within the subcastes, the *jatis*, rather than within the *varnas*, the estates as such. In practice by no means all brahmins are priests. When I lived in India, we had a brahmin who was a *chaukidar*, a night-watchman, which is a menial job. His chanting of sacred texts kept us awake at night until we stopped him! His authority in the community was contingent upon his job as well as upon his status as a brahmin. The caste situation has varied in different parts of India. It has never been as monolithic as Dumont suggests. His clear-cut categories of pure and impure, borrowed partly from Lévi-Strauss,[30] and of separate estates, borrowed partly from Dumézil[31] (both French scholars) – indeed, the structural purity of his whole conceptual model – are not amenable to exact application to the grass-roots realities of the Hindu tradition. This is especially true of the present era, when the caste system is changing in India. The Hindu Marriage Act of 1955 allowed divorce and, when supplemented by the Hindu Adoptions and Maintenance Act and the Hindu Succession Act, effectively abolished caste as far as the civil law was concerned as a necessary requirement for a valid marriage.[32] Some Hindu secularists such as K. M. Panikkar have denied that there is any real connection between caste and religious Hinduism, so that from their perspective one can be a Hindu while repudiating caste.[33] The neo-Hindus take a mid-way position between the Hindu secularists such as Panikkar and the communalist Hindu parties and traditional Hindu orthodoxy, which would seek to bolster the traditional caste system as an integral part of the Hindu tradition. While affirming the general relevance of the four *varnas*, the neo-Hindus seek to reform the caste system, they attack untouchability as a blot on Hinduism, they aim to purify the attitudes of higher-caste Hindus, they stress the centrality of spiritual experience and Vedanta philosophy, and they accept that Hindu social organization is bound to change in line with the exigencies of the modern world.[34] While it is clear that living in cities, studying at universities, industrialization and secularization do have some effect upon caste practice (although unambiguous research evidence for this is more difficult to find than might be expected) it is also clear that the traditional view of *dharma* as relating to caste and the four stages of life (*varnasramadharma*) remains strong in the villages where 80 per cent of Hindus still live.[35] Thus while it is easy to puncture the monolithic nature of Dumont's thesis, it has more validity as a basis for the sociological grounding of authority and freedom within the Hindu tradition than many liberal Western scholars care to admit.

As far as reductionism is concerned, Dumont states straightforwardly that 'the Hindu belief in gods is secondary and derived in relation to the fundamental religious values of caste'.[36] This is a beguiling half-truth which begs a number of questions and which ultimately subordinates religion, however defined, to caste, however defined. It is difficult to deal with, as relatively little research has been done upon the inter-relationship between religion and caste. We will conclude by looking briefly at four ways of resolving the problem: the way of the Hindu renouncer who renounces the caste system and the everyday world for the sake of a higher authority and freedom; the way of renouncing the caste system on grounds of principle within or without the Hindu tradition; the way of accepting the caste system at the social level but transcending it at the religious level; and the way of seeing the caste system as an integral but not superior part of the totality of the Hindu tradition.

The Hindu renouncer of caste is one who rejects the everyday world, the wheel of rebirth, and conventional ties in order to seek *moksa* directly. He, and it is usually a man, can do this at the end of his life as the final stage of his pilgrimage, or it is possible to miss out some of the middle stages of the classical Hindu progression and proceed immediately from the student stage to renunciation. Through yoga and other spiritual means the *sannyasin* or renouncer seeks to become *jivanmukta*, liberated in life. Within the Hindu tradition there have been and are millions of sannyasis, many of whom belong to one of many ascetic orders which have their own history, institutions, codes of discipline and spiritual ways. The renouncer has obtained freedom from the world and its bondage, and by the same token he is often a figure of authority for people in the world. Insofar as he has transcended worldly concerns, he is in a position to advise about both worldly and spiritual matters from a detached viewpoint.[37] A number of the famous gurus of India from some of the sages or *rsis* of ancient times to men such as Sathya Sai Baba in our own day would fit into this category.[38] Having renounced worldly authority and achieved freedom from that authority, spiritual authority is bestowed upon them by those 'remaining in the world'. Although the renouncers can be seen as complementary to the caste system, and indeed reliant on it for sustenance, there is a sense in which the relationships that individual gurus set up with their followers, and the relationships that families and groups of families often set up with ascetic orders, transcend the caste system. The renouncers, either individually or corporately, often represent an independent system of spiritual authority over and above the caste system and a means of spiritual freedom for householders over and above the bounds of social organization.[39]

A second way of resolving the dilemma concerning caste and religion is to contract out of the caste side of the equation. The Buddhists and the Jains and later the Sikhs, as well as the Christians and the Muslims, took this option. So also did other groups which remained in the Hindu fold, ranging from the Sants, Lingayats and Kabir Panthis to the secular Hindus of our own day.[40] This has not been a popular option for many Hindus, and even when it has occurred within and without the Hindu tradition there has usually been some accommodation with the system that was being rejected. Nevertheless, caste has not been a consistent feature of being Hindu to all Hindus either in time or in space. Therefore, we must beware of emphasizing caste authority unreservedly in any discussion of authority and freedom within the Hindu tradition.

In the third place, the Hindu tradition has been skilful in balancing the needs of social and religious activity. Especially among the *bhakti* groups it has been common to observe caste restrictions at the social level but to waive them within religious gatherings. Thus religious leadership and authority might take different directions from caste leadership and authority. The way was opened up for people of lower caste and also women to exercise authority in the religious sphere which they could not have expected to purvey in the social sphere. Nor was it necessarily the case that religious leaders should be renouncers. They could be part of the caste system at the social level but because of the religious qualities they exhibited or were held to reside within them they were given esteem and honour in the religious realm. The different schools within the Sri Vaisnava tradition have debated in theory and in practice this point of the relationship between social and spiritual authority, and it has been a lively issue for discussion among the *bhakti* schools in general. Hindu tradition has it that in early Vedic times there were a number of women saints. As Ghanananda puts it, 'in the Rg-Veda we find names of so many women who realised the highest spiritual truths'.[41] However, it was in the *bhakti* tradition that women such as the South Indian Alvar Andal, and the North Indian poetess Mira Bai, were able to exercise spiritual authority with an authenticity that would not have been open to them at the social level. It is of course true to say that women in general superintend the home and a fair part of the living practice of Hinduism, even though they are subordinate castewise to men. Spiritual charisma and authority, guruhood, and saintliness know no caste boundaries. Although brahmins have been charismatic spiritual leaders, gurus and saints, this has not always been the case. Insofar as this is so, authority and freedom in matters of the spirit have developed a spiritual sovereignty of their own that is exercised along personal, not along, caste lines.[42]

This brings us to our final point. In our zeal to show that authority and freedom in the Hindu tradition are not in thrall to political and military authority, nor to institutional or doctrinal authority, we have laid some emphasis upon the evolving social and religious authority inherent in the developing caste system. Within the *varnasrama-dharma* centred upon caste hierarchy, the stages and aims of life, the householder rituals, and the *dharma* inherent in Manu and the Sanskrit texts, there developed a matrix of authority sufficient for life in the world. However, we have also shown that lines of Hindu spiritual authority, although to some extent interwoven with caste authority, are not reducible to them. In conclusion we will develop the theme that the caste system is only a part, albeit an important part, of the Hindu tradition. It is part of a wider whole and by no means the sole reference point of authority for Hindus.

The religious and spiritual dimension

In order to elucidate this point about the integral nature of the Hindu tradition I will refer briefly to my own model, which I have written about elsewhere.[43] Lying behind the Hindu tradition is *a transcendent reference*, namely Brahman. Every Hindu – indeed, Hindus would argue every person – has access to Brahman. Brahman is irreducible to anything or anyone else. Persons may be inhibited from realizing Brahman in this life by their inherited *karma*, by their desire to pursue the path of rebirth rather than that of *moksa*, and so on. But their very human nature, and the Atman hidden within their heart, bears witness to the transcendent reality under which they are set and by which they are potentially apprehended. Through a mediating focus, usually a personal God or a growing awareness of their real self, their Atman, and its relationship to Brahman, they are brought within range of *moksa*, release from the round of rebirths.

In practical terms eight elements conspire together to help them in their quest. The amalgam of these eight elements constitutes the Hindu tradition available to particular persons at particular times. They may avail themselves of some or all of these elements. Together they form a nexus that we inelegantly call the Hindu tradition. First, there is a set of religious communities, or *sampradayas*, usually centred upon a personal deity such as Siva, Visnu, the Goddess, Rama, Krsna, etc. Second, there are various rituals clustered under three headings: householder rituals to do with the sacramental rites of passage such as birth, initiation, marriage and death; temple rituals to do with temple worship; and festival rituals to do with great festivals that punctuate the Hindu year. Third, there is the element of ethics subsumed under the aegis of the blessed word *dharma*, and this spills over into the fourth element of social involvement which is centred upon the caste system. Fifth, there are the Hindu sacred texts deriving from the Veda but spilling over into numerous *smrti*, remembered texts, that are precious to particular groups, including the epic *Mahabharata* and *Ramayana*, the Puranas, the Tantras, the Bhagavata Purana for devotees of Krsna, and Tulsi Das's Ramacaritamanas for devotees of Rama. Sixth, there are a cluster of basic beliefs, such as the notions of Brahman, Atman, *karma* and *samsara* and *moksa*, that are taken for granted by most Hindus, together with philosophical insights into the nature of the relationship between Brahman and ourselves and the world. These usually derive from one of the Vedanta schools: Sankara's Advaita non-dualism between Brahman, ourselves and the world; Ramanuja's qualified non-dualism between Brahman, ourselves and the world; and Madhva's dualism between Brahman, ourselves and the world. These spill over into the seventh element of spirituality, the kind of yoga and devotional attitudes that we adopt, depending upon whether we are aiming at absorption into Brahman by realization, or a continuing personal relationship with Brahman, with whom we will have communion rather than union. And finally there is the element of aesthetics: the use of images, temple buildings, dance, music, painting, sculpture and iconography, whereby we can have *darsana* of our heart's desire, whereby we can see and be seen by the reality that transcends yet enfolds us.[44]

It will be seen from the above rapid survey that the Hindu tradition itself, and authority and freedom within the Hindu tradition, are not exhausted by the rituals, *dharma* and social hierarchy of the caste system. In one sense the other elements in the model point to a *moksa* situation rather than a this-worldly *dharma* situation, with their focus upon religious community, scripture, beliefs, spirituality and aesthetics. They point to a religious and spiritual view of authority, whether found in the person of renouncers or not. In another sense it is not quite so simple. *Moksa* and *dharma* are separate yet they belong together; they divide and yet they criss-cross. In so far as all Hindus are willy-nilly involved in worldly affairs by the very fact of birth, it is natural that matters of social organization to do with caste and *varnasramadharma* should preoccupy most Hindus. Yet their ultimate aim is fixed on *moksa*. Even if only a minority feel called to focus upon *moksa* in this life, their turn for concentration upon *moksa* will come later and therefore those religious leaders, those saints, those gurus who are wise in *moksa* are revered for their knowledge, their spirituality, and their exemplary function. They point us beyond the worldly dharmic concerns that motivate our life to the Brahman who draws us, to the reality that enfolds us, to the *moksa* that is our birthright even if we choose to forgo it now.

In short there is a yin–yang, a both-together side, to the Hindu tradition. *Dharma* and *moksa* both matter. The outrageous Krsna who defies convention in the soaring ecstacy of his blissful play (*kanu bina gita nahin* – without Krsna there is no song) is comple-mented by the conventional Rama, who is an example of *dharma* and human relationships.[45] We return again to the ineffable complexity of the Hindu tradition, which encapsulates within itself different models of authority and freedom that enrich one another. Although the authority engendered by Hindu arrangements for social orga-nization has commended itself most to social scientists such as Dumont, a more subtle sort of authority and freedom linked to religious and spiritual reality centred upon *moksa* and those who manifest its possibilities stands alongside sociological authority. They illuminate one another, they complement one another, and to give priority to the one or the other may be apposite in particular contexts but to do so absolutely is to offend against the Hindu genius for integration and assimilation that has delivered Hindus from political, military, doctrinal and institutional authoritarianism into a post-independence situation fraught with problems that can yet triumphantly be solved. It is perhaps no accident that India is now the world's largest democracy, for the Hindu tradition which has now advanced into many other parts of the world retains its capacity to absorb, integrate and remodel. It will exercise these virtues in relation to the models of authority and freedom that it has inherited and in so doing will be of help to others in the global world that is now being shaped.[46]

NOTES

1. See W. Cantwell Smith (1964) *The Meaning and End of Religion*. New York: New Ameri-can Library (Mentor), p. 61.
2. George Huntston Williams pioneered the phrase 'Christianity is a congeries of religions' in Frank Whaling (ed.) (1984) *The World's Religious Traditions: Current Perspectives in Reli-gious Studies*. Edinburgh: T. & T. Clark, p. 92. The Hindu situation points even more to a 'congeries of traditions'.
3. An insightful essay by J. L. Mehta, on the Hindu approach to the notion of history, is to be found in Whaling (ed.), *op. cit.*, pp. 33–54.
4. A helpful survey along these lines is to be found in D. S. Sarma (1978) *Hinduism Through the Ages*. Bombay: Bharatiya Vidya Bhavan (1st edn 1956).
5. G. C. Tripathi (1978) 'Jagannatha: the ageless deity of the Hindus'. In A. Eschmann, H. Kulke and G. C. Ripathi, *The Cult of Jagannatha and the Regional Tradition of Orissa*. New Delhi: Manohar, p. 490.
6. Brhadaranyak Upanisad III.ix.1. See, for example, *Brhadaranyaka Upanisad with the Commentary of Sankaracarya* (1965) trans. Swami Madhavananda. Calcutta: Advaita Ashrama, p. 531.
7. R. N. Dandekar (1979) *Insights into Hinduism*. Delhi: Ajanta Publications, p. 4.

8. See Frank Whaling (1987) 'The Hindu tradition in today's world'. In F. Whaling (ed.) (1987) *Religion in Today's World*. Edinburgh: T. & T. Clark, pp. 130–2.
9. Dandekar, *op. cit.*, p. 8.
10. For a helpful brief insight into Siva images and other images, see Diana L. Eck (1981) *Darsan: Seeing the Divine Image in India*. Chambersburg, PA: Anima.
11. Quoted in A. L. Basham (1959) *The Wonder That Was India*. New York: Grove Press, p. 54.
12. See Frank Whaling, 'The Hindu tradition in today's world', *op. cit.*, pp. 164–7.
13. The classical exposition of the 'great tradition' notion is in Robert Redfield (1953) *The Primitive World and Its Transformations*. Ithaca, NY: Cornell University Press.
14. A famous interpretation of the Gupta and other periods in Indian history is to be found in K. M. Panikkar (1962) *The Determining Periods of Indian History*. Bombay: Bharatiya Vidya Bhava.
15. For an analysis of the decline of Buddhism in India, see F. Whaling (1979) Sankara and Buddhism. *Indian Journal of Philosophy* **7**, 1–42.
16. For Akbar's religious outlook, see Theodore de Bary (ed.) (1967) *Sources of Indian Tradition*, vol. I. New York: Columbia University Press, pp. 430–7.
17. R. C. Zaehner brought this difference out radically in his comparison between the poles of Israel and India, of which Islam and Hinduism were archetypal examples.
18. It was also one of the great ages of world *bhakti* when we take into account the Protestant Reformation, the Shi'ite revival in Persia, and developments within Pure Land Buddhism elsewhere.
19. On the neo-Hindu reformers see V. S. Naravane (1964) *Modern Indian Thought: A Philosophical Survey*. Bombay: Asia Publishing House; Sarma, *op. cit.*, pp. 60–278; Whaling, 'The Hindu tradition in today's world', *op. cit.*, pp. 136–51.
20. See Paul Hacker (1978) 'Aspects of neo-Hinduism as contrasted with surviving traditional Hinduism'. In Paul Hacker, *Kleine Schriften*. Wiesbaden: Franz Steiner Verlag, pp. 580–608.
21. See F. Whaling (1980) *The Rise of the Religious Significance of Rama*. Delhi, Varanasi, Patna: Motilal Banarsidass, pp. 69–75.
22. See P. H. Ashby (1974) *Modern Trends in Hinduism*. New York and London: Columbia University Press.
23. An earlier alternative to this had been categorized by Max Müller as kathenotheism, the sequential yet devout worship of particular gods.
24. The notion of religions as being different paths to the same ultimate goal, a kind of teleological relativism, has grown in importance from the time of Ramakrishna through the work of the neo-Hindu reformers; the notion of the transcendental unity of all religions is also a fundamental insight of the *philosophia perennis* school of thought.
25. Louis Dumont (1970) *Homo Hierarchicus*. Chicago: Chicago University Press.
26. This insight is basic to Dumont's approach, which was epoch-making in its day.
27. The same insights are found elsewhere in Dumont's writings, e.g. Louis Dumont (1970) *Religion, Politics and History in India*. Paris, The Hague: Mouton.
28. Anthropologists who have studied this same phenomenon in wider terms include Mary Douglas (1966) *Purity and Danger*. London: Routledge and Kegan Paul; and (1973) *Rules and Meaning*. Harmondsworth: Penguin; and Claude Lévi-Strauss (1963) *Structural Anthropology*. New York: Basic Books; and (1969) *The Raw and the Cooked*. New York: Harper.
29. G. S. Ghurye (1962) *Gods and Men*. Bombay: Popular Book Depot; and (1953) *Indian Sadhus*. Bombay: Popular Book Depot.
30. See also C. Lévi-Strauss (1966) *The Savage Mind*. London: Weidenfeld and Nicolson.
31. G. Dumézil (1968–73) *Mythe et Épopée*, vols 1–3. Paris: Gallimard.
32. Although in civil law caste became irrelevant to marriage as far as the courts were concerned, social custom does not necessarily (at any rate immediately) follow legal precepts.
33. The same position is implied by Nehru, albeit more cautiously stated, in *The Discovery of India* (1961). Bombay: Asia Publishing House.
34. Vivekananda and Radhakrishnan would be exemplars of this line of thought.
35. See Frank Whaling, 'The Hindu tradition in today's world', *op. cit.*, pp. 140–4.

36. Dumont, *Religion, Politics and History in India*, *op. cit.*, p. 16.
37. For studies of contemporary renouncers, see P. Brent (1972) *Godmen of India*. London: Penguin; Khushwant Singh (1975) *Gurus, Godmen and Good People*. Bombay: Orient Longman.
38. Charles S. White (1988) 'Indian developments: Sainthood in Hinduism'. In R. Kieckhefer and G. D. Bond (eds) *Sainthood: Its Manifestations in World Religions*. Berkeley: University of California Press, pp. 98–139.
39. See Gurye, *Indian Sadhus*, *op. cit.*
40. The level, vociferousness, and completeness of retreat from caste of course differ from group to group.
41. Swami Ghanananda (ed.) (1955) *Women Saints of East and West*. London: Ramakrishna Vedanta Centre, p. 3.
42. The same point would apply in a different way to figures such as Gandhi, who were not renouncers in the orthodox sense but who developed a personal spiritual authority akin to that of some of the great renouncers.
43. See, for example, F. Whaling (1986) *Christian Theology and World Religions: A Global Approach*. Basingstoke: Marshall Pickering, pp. 37–47.
44. Diana L. Eck (1983) *Banaras City of Light*. London: Routledge and Kegan Paul, brings out this aspect of the life of a famous Hindu holy city.
45. See David R. Kinsley (1979) *The Divine Player*. Delhi: Motilal Banarsidass.
46. The Gandhian model of creative non-violence and the plural-religious model have global implications as well as more inwardly religious Hindu models of freedom and authority.

Chapter 5

Authority and Freedom in Islam

Riadh El-Droubie

In dealing with the subject of authority and freedom in Islam, it is important to recognize that Islam is *ᶜAqida*, belief or faith, as well as a comprehensive code of law, or *Shariᶜa*. The belief aspect of Islam is that theoretical part of it which defines the terms of faith required of Muslim believers, as expounded and taught by the Prophet Muhammad, may God's peace and blessings be upon him. The Shariᶜa defines the legal and practical framework of rules and regulations that govern a Muslim's relationship with the Creator, with his fellow Muslims, with other human beings and with the rest of creation as a whole.

According to Islam, faith is the basis upon which the whole body of the law is founded, while the Shariᶜa itself is the system that regulates Muslim life. The Shariᶜa cannot be seen to exist without the faith. This gives the Shariᶜa a very special, and revered, place in the Muslim mind. To follow the Shariᶜa's rules and regulations willingly and freely ('Let there be no compulsion in religion'[1]) is a central part of the faith and a fulfilment of religious obligations. To accept one without the other, or to negate either of these two aspects of Islam, would impair one's belief in and identification with the religion of Islam.

Giving evidence at the trial arising from the assassination of the Egyptian writer Farag Foudah in Cairo, the prominent moderate Muslim scholar, Sheikh Muhammed al-Gazali, said that whoever denied the Islamic Shariᶜa would be considered an apostate and the penalty would be capital punishment.[2] According to a former Sheikh of al-Azhar, Mahmud Shaltut:

> Apostasy is a denial of the established principles of Islam and comes as a result of any act to ridicule or negate them. On this matter, the Qur'an says: '... and if any of you turn back from their faith and die in unbelief their works will bear no fruit in this life and in the Hereafter; they will be companion of the Fire and will abide therein.'[3] This is a clear condemnation of apostasy, punishment for which will be hell-fire, in the hereafter. The temporal punishment for apostasy is set out by *ᶜulama* [Muslim religious scholars], on the basis of *one* Hadith (saying) of Prophet Muhammad's that 'whoever changes his faith should be killed'.[4] This saying has been a matter of debate among scholars who enquired and tried to establish whether it applied to Muslims only, or to Jews who had become Christian, for example, and whether it applied to women as well as men.[5]

Shaltut goes on to say that many scholars oppose the idea that punishment in Islam could be based on a *single* saying by the Prophet and thus they do not consider rejection of the faith of Islam, on its own, as sufficient justification for capital punishment. What they take as a good reason for that is active hostile opposition to Muslims and the effort to promote sedition or create strife and turmoil amongst them. The Qur'an says: 'Let there be no compulsion in religion'[6] and 'If it had been thy Lord's Will, They would all have believed, all who are on earth! Will you then compel mankind against their will, to believe!'[7]

The Shari^ca embodies all the laws and regulations laid down by God and which Muslims are required to obey and follow in all their dealings with their Lord and their fellow humans. This is referred to in the Qur'an thus:

> The same religion has He established for you as that which He enjoined on Noah, and that which We have sent by inspiration to you, and that which We enjoined on Abraham, Moses, and Jesus: Namely, that you should remain steadfast in Religion, and make no division therein ...'.[8]

Despite its complexity and diversity, the Islamic Shari^ca is basically divided into two main sections. One section relates to those actions required of a Muslim as part of his obligations towards God, and is known as *^cibadat*, personal 'religious' matters or worship. The other section is known as *mu^camalat* and deals with all aspects of the collective relationships with the Muslim society and the actions of its members to preserve and protect their common interest of safety, prosperity, freedom and justice. It also covers the wider arena of relationships between Muslim and non-Muslim societies. Some of the topics that come under mu^camalat include family affairs, inheritance, finance, commerce, penal laws and international relations.

The Islamic Shari^ca warns very strongly against disobedience of divine teachings in general and emphasizes the severe punishment awaiting those who persist in it. The underlying reason for this is the need to deter individuals and protect society against the harm that could be inflicted upon it. It has stipulated fines and punishments that can be meted out by the relevant competent authorities here in this life and punishments that could be received in the Hereafter. Thus divine and temporal authorities combine to deter individuals from pursuing harmful activities and maintain the stability and cohesion of society as a whole.

The worldly penalties are defined in the Islamic Shari^ca by two methods. One is through the specific text of the Qur'an or the Prophet's *sunna*, sayings or actions, referring to specific crimes, and the other is the interpreting, implementing and opinion on applicability to a particular issue or, in the absence of an applicable text, giving individual opinions of *^cUlama*, people of knowledge and competent scholars or experts. To every Muslim, such authority is dependent on its compliance with the Qur'anic and prophetic text and on the fulfilment of their objectives.[9]

SOURCES OF ISLAMIC SHARI^CA

The sources for any legislation, in any society, emerge as a result of the realization by its members of their collective need for a comprehensive set of legal codes to regulate their lives. This is followed by their agreement on a mechanism for representation that would lead to the selection of an effective authority capable of devising laws and regulations and implementing them. Religious systems, however, differ from this quite radically. They are divine, God-ordained and are set out, on the whole, outside the sphere of human choice or influence. God's will, inasmuch as it is contained in the religion, is thereby handed over to society, whose religious authorities interpret the religious law and convert and develop it into applicable and meaningful systems which the people will willingly obey.[10]

Yet, Islam differs from this slightly. Muslims firmly believe that Islam is a divinely inspired God-ordained system, taught and expounded by the Prophet Muhammad, may God's peace and blessings be upon him. They believe that Islam is the final, and therefore the most complete, divine revelation sent to man and that Muhammad is the last and final Messenger. Nevertheless, Islam cannot be considered a theocracy even though the Qur'an says authority rests with God alone: 'the Command is for none but Allah: He has commanded that ye worship none but Him.'[11] The Qur'an also identifies man as God's representative on earth, and not a particular class or caste of men. It says: 'Behold! your Lord said to the angels; I will create a vicegerent on earth.'[12] This implies that man's task on earth is to implement God's authority as expounded in the Qur'an.

The Islamic Shari^{c}a has two kinds of sources, primary sources and secondary sources.

Primary sources

The Qur'an

This consists of text and the possible interpretation of the text. It is necessary to point out here that the most important factor is that God, and God alone, is the author of and the reference for all the laws of the Shari^{c}a. Human beings have no authority to promulgate fundamental laws other than those laid down by God. However, in matters where no such divine pronouncements are found in the Qur'an, the Shari^{c}a requires knowledgeable and qualified people of authority in society to lay down rules and regulations in accordance with well-defined methods and parameters.[13]

This is made clear in the Qur'an when it says 'the Command is for none but Allah' and 'We have sent down to you the Book in truth, that you mightest judge between people by that which Allah has shown you'.[14] It also totally rejects acting outside the texts of the Shari^{c}a and describes such action as a denial of God's will, a transgression against Him and a corruption: 'If any do fail to judge by what Allah hath revealed, they are unbelievers.'[15]

The Sunnah

This refers to Prophet Muhammad's sayings, actions and assent over all matters of law, provided their authenticity and accuracy is established in accordance with the science of *hadith* by the ^{c}Ulama. This is supported by Qur'anic texts such as 'But no, by your

Lord, they can have no (real) faith until they make you judge in all disputes between them'[16] and

> It is not fitting for a believer, man or woman, when a matter has been decided by Allah and His messenger, to have any option about their decision. If any one disobeys Allah and His messenger, he is indeed on a clearly wrong path.[17]

Consensus of opinion, or ijmaᶜa

This is also established by the Qur'anic verse which says 'O ye who believe! Obey Allah, and obey the Messenger, and those charged with authority among you. If ye differ in anything among yourself, refer it to Allah and His Messenger.'[18] Yusuf Ali, in his commentary on this *Aya*, says that *Ulu-l-amr* are those charged with authority or responsibility or decision, or the settlement of affairs. All ultimate authority rests in Allah. Prophets of Allah derive their authority from Him. As Islam makes no sharp division between sacred and secular affairs, it expects the governing Muslim authorities to be imbued with righteousness. Likewise, Islam expects Muslims to respect the authority of such government, for otherwise there can be no order or discipline.

Also 'those in authority' here are known in the Islamic term as *ahl al-hall wa al-'aqd*. They are the ultimate temporal authority to whom ordinary people would refer, and whose collective opinion would reflect the consensus of the community as a whole.[19] *Ijmaᶜa*, or consensus, on the interpretation of the Shariᶜa derives its efficacy and legality as a source of law from Qur'anic text and from the Prophet's saying: 'My people would never have a collective agreement on something wrong.'[20] *Ijmaᶜa* is very closely related to another Islamic term, *ijtihad*, which refers to the diligence and effort exerted by scholars and rulers to deduce or arrive at the correct and equitable ruling with respect to any particular matter that is raised or occurs in society. *Ijtihad* is an individual vocation and does not assume legal status until it is adopted collectively by the community's scholars and rulers through *ijmaᶜa* of *ahl al-hall wa al-'aqd*. For these scholars to qualify for contribution to *ijmaᶜa*, they must meet certain standards of knowledge and intellectual calibre. They have to have full understanding of the Qur'an and the Prophet's sunnah, the works, opinions and intellectual and juristic legacy of scholars and jurists of earlier generations, especially that of the Prophet's own contemporaries and their contemporaries, mastery of the Arabic language and the science of logic and deduction.[21]

According to this process, if a ruling is found in the Qur'an, no reference need be made to any other source. If this is not the case, then reference must be made to the established sunnah of the Prophet, and if a ruling is found there, no reference should have to be made to any other source. If no satisfactory ruling is found in either the Qur'an or the sunnah, the issue then becomes a matter for debate and interpretation among the qualified scholars who are eligible to exercise *ijtihad*, according to the criteria and requirements given earlier.

Since *ijmaᶜa* comes about as a result of a consideration and an assessment of public interest, which in turn differs according to places, times and circumstances, those who exercise *ijtihad*, or those who succeed them, have the right and the prerogative to revise or alter their ruling in the light of new evidence or conditions, as long as the new opinion serves the common good and leads to better results. Once it gains the *ijmaᶜa* of the qualified scholars, the new *ijtihad* then assumes the status of law or official ruling, binding on the whole community.

Individual *ijtihad* can only be binding on the person who expounded or arrived at it, and it is the prerogative of anyone, man or woman, ruler or citizen, who possesses the required qualifications of knowledge and piety. The ruler, or caliph, is not to be seen as infallible, and nor has he the right to impose his own opinions on the community, unless those opinions are supported by irrefutable and unambiguous statements from the Qur'an and the sunnah.

Ijmaᶜa is a source of legislation and collective religious opinion in matters where no textual support from either the Qur'an or the sunnah, or both, is available. It comes about as a result of the consensus among those individuals in the community who have knowledge, expertise and intellectual prowess to be able to pronounce judgements and opinions to deal with various conditions, issues and situations that arise in society. This must not be the same as the consensus that might be found at a public level over various issues. It is not to be confused with the concept of 'public opinion' or 'consensus of the majority'.

Analogy, or Qiyas

This is the application of deductive reasoning to the Qur'an and the sunnah in order to extract precedents and common grounds that would allow the formulation of a new ruling that would provide a solution for a new issue or situation. It also involves the use of certain established formulae and criteria such as 'the presumption of permissibility' and 'the preservation of public interest' and 'necessities overrule prohibitions' and 'mitigation of damage takes precedence over the pursuit of benefit'.

Secondary sources: procedural methods of reaching judgements

1. *Discretion or istihsan*: giving preference to one rule over another, although the latter would be more appropriate.
2. *Istislah*: giving prime consideration to the public good in a matter on which neither the Qur'an nor the sunnah has a definite ruling.
3. *Al-ᶜUrf*: tradition, convention and general custom which do not contradict or clash with the latter or the spirit of Islam and the Qur'an and sunnah.

These secondary procedures for applying the Shariᶜa are not binding on scholars and it is a matter of discretion on their part whether to make use of them or not. The reason for this is that they were not known to have been in existence during the time of the Prophet Muhammad, when only the Qur'an and the Prophet were the sources of legislation and religious guidance. Indeed, the Prophet's own example and sayings were ruled by the Qur'an, the ultimate reference. Nevertheless, this did not completely eliminate individual opinion and personal judgement. The following might illustrate this better.

The Prophet had appointed one of his companions, Mu'adh ibn Jabal, as ruler of Yemen. As he was seeing him off, the Prophet asked him:

'On what basis shall you judge when you are confronted with a problem of the people?' to which Mu'adh had replied: 'According to the God's Book', meaning the Qur'an. 'But', the prophet asked, 'what if you do not find the answer there, what will you do?' Mu'adh replied, 'I shall adopt the rule of the sunnah of the Messenger of God'. The Prophet continued, 'What if you do not find an answer there?' and Mu'adh said, 'I shall then exert myself [make *ijtihad*] and exercise my own judgement', whereupon the Prophet said, 'Praise be to God who has guided the messenger of His Messenger to what pleases God and His Messenger'.

There can be no 'exertion' to arrive at one's 'own judgement' without a given space of free thought and individual opinion, and this freedom of thought does not in any way infringe on or contravene the teachings of the Qur'an or the sunnah.[22]

In all matters of forming one's own opinion, for his own personal usage, he may be able, through his knowledge and experience, to do so, and he will be responsible in front of God on the Day of Judgement for that. But if he cannot do so, he is permitted to follow the advice and judgement of those who have the knowledge; however, the responsibility is still his for making such a choice.

As for the learned people who shoulder the responsibility of their own opinion and the responsibility of those who follow them, in the sight of God and in front of the law, the responsibility is much greater.

This ability to form an opinion and make judgement (*fatwa*) on a certain matter for the people to follow, or to formulate a law and regulation, requires a complete liberty and freedom with knowledge and piety.

When talking about liberty, we have to remember that everyone in society has rights and obligations. These are based on two main principles: equality and freedom. *Equality* has many aspects, including equality in front of God, as defined in the Qur'an:

People, We (God) have created you from a male and a female and made you into nations and tribes in order for you to know one another. The most honourable of you in the sight of God are the God-fearing.[23]

There is also equality before the law, as defined by the Prophet, peace and blessing of God be upon him, when he said:

Those before you had been destroyed because if a nobleman among them committed larceny they let him go unpunished, but if a helpless one did the same they punished him. By God, if Fatima, the daughter of Muhammad, committed larceny I would cut off her wrist.[24]

According to Islam, official authorities should not infringe or interfere in the *personal freedom* of the individual members of society. Whatever a person does that is of benefit to him, but does not infringe on the liberties or interests of other members of society, cannot be restricted. At this point, it has to be acknowledged that although governments in Muslim countries today may claim to be Islamic, they are in fact not quite so if they have adopted only certain Islamic laws and principles and have deeply violated the personal and public rights of their people.

Every citizen has the right to choose his or her occupation and place of living without the government having any authority to interfere or force them. Every individual is free and has the right to own things within the general law of the land without causing harm to himself or to someone else. Parents have unchallenged authority over their children, within the ethical and disciplinary rules of Islam, as long as they do not corrupt or neglect them. If they are not capable of looking after their children, the authorities have the power to provide welfare for them.

Islam also guarantees freedom of thought within the overall framework of Islam as defined by the Qur'an and the practice of the prophet Muhammad, or defined by the prevailing contemporary needs and requirements of life.

In this connection, the Islamic Shari^ca has laid down general principles and rules for public freedom, including the freedom of religion, as affirmed in the Qur'an and the practice of the Prophet. Religious differences are no justification for hostility or hatred, as expressed clearly in the following verse: 'Let there be no compulsion in religion: Truth stands out clear from error.'

Islam permits its followers to conclude agreements and sign treaties with people from other faiths, as long as these do not infringe upon any of Islam's principles or undermine the interests of the Muslim community.

Islam has gone a long way to protect the rights of the adherents of other religions. In Imam Shafi'i's view, when a spouse converts to Islam, he or she does not even have the right to ask the other spouse to convert too, and it is considered a form of coercion, if tried.[25]

Freedom of speech is a basic right in the Muslim society, which the individual cannot relinquish and the official authority cannot prohibit. One of the most basic duties of Muslims in society is to promote good behaviour and oppose or prevent harmful activities, both of which can never be carried out without freedom of action and freedom of speech. This is one of the principles of Islamic freedom: 'Let there arise out of you a band of people inviting to all that is good, enjoining what is right and forbidding what is wrong.'[26] The same applies for the development and practice of jurisprudence in Muslim law, which require such practice as *ijtihad* and *qiyas* which cannot be achieved in the absence of intellectual and political freedom.

It is not enough to recognize freedom of speech and thought only in principle. People themselves are required to have the necessary courage and resolve to demand and protect those freedoms; otherwise society as a whole will suffer. The Prophet was reported as saying: 'If my nation begins to fear calling an oppressor an oppressor, all hope would be lost.' A believing Muslim knows that only God can harm or benefit him and would therefore have no reason to fear anyone else.

Freedom of speech would of course cover all means of propagation, such as publishing and the media. But these have to operate within the framework of Islamic ethics and principles of justice and respect for other people. The media must not be used as an instrument for spreading false rumours, degrading or corrupting ideas and material, or anything that threatens or undermines the health and welfare of society as a whole.

Accordingly, in Muslim society, freedom of speech more generally is not absolute or totally unrestricted, but must be exercised within the overall religious and moral framework of Islam, and should be used to establish the truth and reinforce justice and honesty. Citizens are entitled to oppose the ruling authority but have no right to corrupt society or eliminate their opponents or in any way take the law into their own hands. Caliph Ali said to his opponents: 'We shall never take up arms against you unless you corrupt the people.' Corruption here, of course, includes moral, political and religious, as well as intellectual.

Just as the ruler is expected to respect his subjects' basic freedom, the public are also expected to guard their freedom and defend it. Imam Ghazali warned very strongly against the infringement of freedom by the ruling authorities. He thought that political power poses a much bigger threat to public freedom than slavery, because it leads to humbling and subjugation, and it is a form of administrative oppression against free thinking by free minds. In other words, it is slavery of the mind.[27] It was said that Caliph al-Ma'moun once asked the accomplished man of politics, Abdullah ibn Taher, 'Which do you prefer, your house or the palace of the Caliph?' Ibn Taher replied: 'I prefer my own house where I would be the master, rather than the Caliph's palace where I have no freedom.'

NOTES

1. The Holy Qur'an 2:256. All Qur'anic verse translations are quoted from Yusuf Ali (1968) *The Holy Qur'an, English Translation of the Meaning and Commentary*. Beirut: Dar Al Arabia.
2. *Al-Arab Daily*, issue no. 4128, London, 6 August 1993.
3. The Holy Qur'an 2:217.
4. Hadith, saying of the Prophet Muhammad, report by Bukhari and Muslim.
5. Mahmud Shaltut (1952) *Al-Islam Aqidah wa Shari^cah*. Al-Azhar: Public Department for Islamic Education.
6. The Holy Qur'an 2:256.
7. The Holy Qur'an 10:99.
8. The Holy Qur'an 42:13.
9. Said Ramadan (1961) *Islamic Law, Its Scope and Equity*. London: Macmillan.
10. *Ibid.*
11. The Holy Qur'an 12:40.
12. The Holy Qur'an 2:30.
13. Afif Tabbarah (1978) *The Spirit of Islam, Doctrine and Teaching*. Beirut: Librairie du Liban.
14. The Holy Qur'an 4:105.
15. The Holy Qur'an 5:44.
16. The Holy Qur'an 4:65.
17. The Holy Qur'an 33:36.
18. The Holy Qur'an 4:59.
19. Muhammad Abdu, *Al Manar*, **5**, p. 181.
20. Ahamad Atiya (1963) *Al-Qamus Al Islami*. Cairo: Al-Nahda Al Misriya Library.
21. Mahmud Shaltut, *Al-Islam Aqidah wa Shari^cah*.
22. Said Ramadan, *Islamic Law, Its Scope and Equity*.
23. The Holy Qur'an 4:1–2.
24. Hadith 4188.
25. A. Zaidan (1987) *Individual and State in the Islamic Shari^cah*. Cairo: Dar al-Ulum.
26. The Holy Qur'an 3:104.
27. al-Ghazali, *Ihya' Ulum al-Din*, Vol. 3, p. 241.

FURTHER READING

Akhtar, Shabbir (1990) *A Faith for All Seasons: Islam and Western Modernity*. London: Bellew Publishing.
Arin, Elizabeth M. (1991) *Islam and Human Rights*. London: Pinter.
Hourani, George F. (1985) *Reason and Tradition in Islamic Ethics*. Cambridge: Cambridge University Press.
Hovanissian, R. G. (ed.) (1985) *Ethics in Islam*. Malibu: Undena Press.
Khadduri, Majid (ed.) (1984) *The Islamic Concept of Justice*. Baltimore: Johns Hopkins University Press.

Rahman, Fazlur (1982) *Islam and Modernity*. Chicago: Chicago University Press.
Rippon, Andrew and Knappert, Jan (eds) (1986) *Textual Sources for the Study of Islam*. Manchester: Manchester University Press.
Sardar, Ziauddin (ed.) (1989) *An Early Crescent: The Future of Knowledge and the Environment in Islam*. London: Mansell.

Chapter 6

Freedom and Authority in Judaism

Hugo Gryn

It is helpful to consider the theme of freedom and authority in the Jewish tradition under the twin subtitles of the authority of God and the authority of human agencies, notably and chiefly the role of the rabbis, both in the formative Pharisaic period, and through some of the ways in which this authority devolved on successive generations and schools of thought.

The authority of the word of God is a very sophisticated concept. God speaks to men and women and the people can hear. Indeed, there are occasions when they have no alternative but to listen. Of the many well-known instances in the Torah where this happens, it is possible to see a progression in the effect that divine communication has on subsequent events. Adam is addressed by God, he hears the voice of God, but he hides. Abraham also hears the voice of God and he responds. Indeed, he, in turn, pleads with God. God also speaks to Sarah, she hears – and she laughs. Likewise, Moses hears and eventually he acts. The episode at the Burning Bush is well documented as an instance where Moses, the individual, receives communication and responds; and because of this encounter his entire life undergoes a radical transformation. Equally well documented is the encounter between God and the entire collective of Israel at Sinai. There everyone listened and heard something. The response of the people prior to the revelation has become a paradigmatic feature of the Jewish attitude to the word of God. The people, when asked by Moses whether they are prepared to be addressed by God, respond: *na'ase v'nishma* – 'We will do and we will hear'. It is instructive to note that in Hebrew *shema* connotes both hearing and understanding. It is also interesting that it is 'do' then 'hear' – an apparent inversion of accepted logic. Action results in understanding. The pattern of revelation is the presence of a potential conflict which then reaches a proportion of crisis in which a choice becomes readily apparent. In the act of revelation there is a sudden illumination followed by certainty and the vanishing of all doubt.

The classic example is the account of the Theophany in Exodus 33 and 34. All the foregoing elements are present. However, it is interesting here to note the comments of the great medieval philosopher Moses Maimonides. Moses makes a radical request: 'Show me, I pray Thee, Thy glory' (33:18). It is the ultimate request in revelation and one that God resists. Instead God suggests a compromise: 'I will make all My goodness

pass before thee ... (but) thou canst not see My face; for no man shall see Me and live ... thou shalt see My back; but My face shall not be seen' (33:19–23).

Most biblical scholars and commentaries agree that this episode indicates the opportunity for men and women to make certain discoveries about the nature of God through God's effects on creation and the experience of God's creatures and their understanding of the physical and spiritual phenomena around them. Maimonides does not share this accepted wisdom. He offers the analogy of a man walking some distance behind another man. From the way the one in front moves his body and holds his head the one behind believes this has to be his friend so-and-so. But the fact is that unless the two can look at each other, face to face, there has to be an element of doubt. So, Maimonides concludes, it is with God. It is simply not possible for human beings to have that absolute certainty. There must always be an element of doubt in asserting this or that quality or action in God: 'And that is how it is.' Reflecting on this medieval insight at the end of the twentieth century, we may add that this is a 'saving doubt' and perhaps the surest way to avoid falling into the many and attractive traps of religious fanaticism.

The biblical account of the prophets reveals experiences very similar to those of Moses. Issues of personal morality or social concern reach towards a climax whose resolution comes about in an act of revelation. Amos is overwhelmingly concerned with social justice. For Hosea, God's love is interpreted through a traumatic personal experience. Isaiah and Ezekiel have mystic visions. The general reaction of the prophets is that there is an initial reluctance to accept the mandate which flows from an act of revelation. But once this is overcome there is no going back. In time there emerged prophetic guilds, professionals who claimed ability to contact and discern the will of God, as it were, at will, but these guilds soon fell into disrepute. The amateurs ultimately won immortality.

Throughout the Bible authority is derived from God. There is generally a two-way system of communication and a discernible pattern in which this takes place. When the Bible is 'edited', it also becomes 'authorized' and something of its authority becomes an essential and indeed decisive element in all subsequent developments in Jewish law and morality. As the biblical period gives way to the rabbinic one, *Halacha* – literally 'the way' and a generic term for Jewish law – evolves and becomes the most decisive influence in the course of the subsequent centuries.

The problem for the leaders of the Pharisees who emerge as the religious authority in the first century BCE and in the course of the next six centuries before the Mishnah and the Gemarah,[1] the twin elements that comprise the Talmud, is to determine how laws change.

The most obvious and 'authoritative' way is through revelation – but no one makes such claims after the prophets. Legislation was a very reliable instrument for change as well. The Sanhedrin, a supreme religious court, whose seat was in Jerusalem and which had a membership of 71, did legislate and its decisions were universally accepted. However, the Sanhedrin and its power to implement and enforce its rulings came to an end with the fall of Jerusalem in 70 CE. For the subsequent generations there remained two other and more problematic instruments. One was interpretation. The rabbis devised agreed hermeneutic rules of exegesis. Norms as well as changes derived their authority from biblical texts and their acceptance was a matter of consensus wherever possible. Where this was not possible, the authority of a given scholar was generally the deciding factor. The other instrumentality of change derived from the *minhag* or custom. It was regional rather than universal. Where a community or group of communities had evolved certain religious practices, in the fullness of time they had assumed the force of law. It was a flexible but also limited mode of change.

In this period, too, there emerged the rabbinic notion or doctrine of the two-fold Torah. There was the *Torah Shebichtav*, 'the written Torah', revealed by God at Sinai and committed to writing by Moses in the form of the text of the Pentateuch. There was another revelation at Sinai as well in the form of the *Torah sheb'al pe*, 'the oral Torah', which was preserved in its totality, handed down by means of oral tradition and considered as authoritative as the written text. These 'oral' laws amended and supplemented the biblical legislation. In time, and because of the ever-widening dispersion of the Jewish people, the 'oral Torah' was also cast into written form. Academies in Judea and in the numerically larger community of Babylonia had produced two parallel versions of the Talmud which remain the basic and authoritative literature to this day.

A justification for this authority is succinctly expressed in the Talmudic tractate of *Baba Batra* (12a): 'Prophecy was taken from the prophets and given to the sages.' In a general way it is possible to state that the function of the biblical prophets was to show the ways of God to humanity. The emphasis of the rabbis on the Talmud is more of a search for ways in which men and women can imitate God. Unlike the prophets, the rabbis were prepared to compromise and were satisfied with approaching the ideal even if not fully realizing it. A paradigmatic principle in tractate *Pesachim* (50b) asserts: 'Man should always be occupied with Torah and the commandments even if not *lishma* (for the sake of heaven – meaning, purely for its own sake) because from what may not be initially *lishma* he will come to *lishma*.' In another passage the rabbis went so far as to state: 'A sage teacher is better than a prophetic dreamer' (*Baba Batra* 12a).

For the rabbis there were no theological problems. The Torah was of divine origin but it was given 'in human language' and the fact that the rabbis located and classified 613 laws was a sign of divine favour. It should be noted that one of the favourite rabbinic terms for God is *Rachamana* – 'the compassionate one'.

There are certain caveats. There is a strong feeling throughout rabbinic literature that the sages must somehow be right. This is sometimes carried to an extreme but inevitable conclusion: 'Even if they (the Rabbis) tell you that left is right and right is left, hearken unto their words until they tell you that right is right and left is left' (Jerusalem Talmud *Horayot* 1:145d). The freedom to interpret and expound texts is a constant concern. In the Midrash, which is a homiletical collection that parallels the Talmud, the question is asked whether it was possible for Moses to learn the entire Torah in the course of the 40 days he spent on Mount Sinai. They concluded that 'God taught Moses the principles' (Exodus *Raba* 41:6). The medieval philosopher Joseph Albo interpreted this to mean that

> the Law of God cannot be (given) in a complete form so as to be adequate for all times ...
> and therefore at Sinai Moses was given general principles ... by means of which the sages
> in every generation may formulate the details as they present themselves.
>
> (*Ikkarim* 3:23)

There was already in the Talmudic period a problem about coping with the 'weight of the past'. The possibility is recognized that future scholars might not be as learned or as wise as their predecessors. Nevertheless, there is an unexpected mandate that contemporary scholars and judges be regarded with the same esteem as those of past generations.

'Whoever is appointed leader of the Community, even if he be the least worthy, is to be regarded with the same esteem as the mightiest of earlier generations.' There is a healthy corrective in the statement that follows it: 'Say not "How was it that the former days were better than these?" for it is not out of wisdom that you inquire concerning this' (*Rosh Hashanah* 25b).

There were two tendencies which became clearly discernible and remain a feature to the present on the part of religious authorities. There is the *machmir*, literally 'the heavy one', and there is the *meikil* – 'the light one'. It reflects an understanding that there are those who are instinctively severe, inclined to say 'no', and there are those who are temperamentally inclined to be liberal and look for ways in which they can say 'yes'.

Time and again the rabbis find ways to express the prophetic thought that the ways of God and the ways of men and women are not at all the same. In a classic collection of homilies known as the *Midrash Tanchuma*, we find the following: 'What difference does it make to God how we slaughter an animal and what foods we eat? Except that He desires by such laws to benefit His creatures by ennobling their characters.' Indeed, the laws were almost invariably considered as a means to an end: moral perfection.

Something of this radicalism is also reflected in the Talmudic maxim 'Not all the ritual laws of the Torah can equal a single moral principle of the Torah' (Jerusalem *Peah* 16d), and the injunction that goes to the heart of spiritual understanding: 'To preserve the spirit of the Torah you can abrogate the letter of the Torah' (*Menachot* 99a/b). The first of the true underlying principles appears to be that 'The Law' is to further the course of humanity and that every human being has some capacity to contribute to the cause of humanity and in that way help in the realization of God's plan for His creation. The law shifted from the purely divine to the realm of human consensus. Indeed, the very imagery of *halacha*, namely of walking in godly ways, implies a fluidity.

There is a dual image of *halacha* which finds expression in two fundamental and apparently contradictory dicta. On the one hand, there is a basic tenet that the Torah is from Heaven, and, on the other, the principle that the Torah is not in Heaven. A classic story in the Talmud (*Baba Mezia* 59b) describes a fierce dispute over an apparently very trivial matter. It concerns the oven of a man called Aknai. Instead of being made of one piece, it had a series of separate sections with a layer of sand between each section. The head of the academy, Rabbi Eliezer, insisted that the oven is not a single utensil and therefore not liable to ritual uncleanness. His colleagues insisted with equal certainty that the outer coating of the mortar acts as a unifying force and therefore if any part of it becomes unclean the whole is affected. Perhaps the very triviality of this issue only highlights the extraordinary debate that ensued in the passage which I would like to quote in full:

> It has been taught: On that day R. Eliezer brought forward every imaginary argument but they did not accept them. Said he to them: 'If the *halacha* agrees with me, let this carob-tree prove it!' Thereupon the carob-tree was torn a hundred cubits out of its place; others affirm, four hundred cubits. 'No proof can be brought from a carob-tree', they retorted. Again he said to them: 'If the *halacha* agrees with me, let the stream of water prove it!' Whereupon the stream of water flowed backwards. 'No proof can be brought from a stream of water', they rejoined. Again he urged: 'If the *halacha* agrees with me, let the walls of the schoolhouse prove it', whereupon the walls inclined to fall. But R. Joshua rebuked them, saying: 'When scholars are engaged in a halachic dispute, what have you to inter-

fere?' Hence they did not fall, in honour of R. Joshua, nor did they resume the upright, in honour of R. Eliezer; and they are still standing thus inclined. Again he said to them: 'If the *halacha* agrees with me, let it be proved from Heaven!' Whereupon a Heavenly Voice cried out: 'Why do ye dispute with R. Eliezer, seeing that in all matters the *halacha* agrees with him!' But R. Joshua arose and exclaimed: 'It is not in heaven!' [Deuteronomy 30:12]. What did he mean by this? – Said R. Jeremiah: 'That the Torah had already been given at Mount Sinai; we pay no attention to a Heavenly Voice, because Thou hast long since written in the Torah at Mount Sinai.' 'After the majority one inclines' [Exodus 23:2].

(*Baba Mezia* 59b)

The outcome of this debate was not only a victory for that majority of the sages who disagreed with the ruling of Rabbi Eliezer, but the deposing of Eliezer from his position of authority. All accounts of this event consider this action to have been both necessary and tragic. But the story has an even more unexpected postscript. A certain Rabbi Nathan, who was present at the debate, met the prophet Elijah not long after. By then Elijah had become a legendary figure capable of moving between the heavenly and the earthly worlds. Nathan asked Elijah: 'What did the Holy One, blessed be He, do in that hour?' Elijah replied: 'God laughed with joy, saying, "My children have defeated Me, My children have defeated Me!"' They were not swayed by miracles. They had, as it were, come of age and were capable of making their own decisions.

This principle that 'the Torah is not in Heaven' implies that while the source of the *halacha* is divine, its place and life, as well as its development and formulation, rests with humanity and in the life of society. The scholars and sages of Judaism saw no inconsistency in these two principles. They believed that in their exegesis, enactments, innovations and creativity they were merely giving practical expression to the continuous unfolding of the revelation at Sinai.

The medieval scholars of Judaism continued to insist on this freedom to interpret and develop religious authority. The eleventh-century moralist and philosopher, Bahya Ibn Paquda, states explicitly that

On the question whether we are under the obligation to investigate the doctrine of God's unity or not, I assert that anyone capable of investigating this and similar philosophical themes by rational methods is bound to do so according to his powers and capacity. Anyone who neglects to institute such a inquiry is blameworthy and is accounted as belonging to the class of those who fall short in wisdom and conduct.

(*Chovot Ha-Levavot*, 'Duties of the Heart', chapter 3)

Maimonides echoes this view in much of his work and so do many other major Jewish thinkers. The last of the great philosophers of the Middle Ages, Joseph Albo, sums up this tradition of freedom of thought: 'It is clear now that every intelligent person is permitted to investigate the fundamental principles of religion and to interpret the Biblical texts in accordance with the truth as it seems to him' (*Sefer Ha-Ikarim*, 'Book of Principles', Part I, chapter 2).

This freedom is evident in the lack of any official Jewish creed. There are, of course, many proposed creeds which are developed in the course of the centuries and generations. They vary in content, principles and number. Any survey will reveal that from antiquity to the present time Judaism has found room for almost every conception of God known to civilized men and women so long as it is consistent with the one overriding principle: the affirmation of the unity of God.

Most of the development in Jewish law since the end of the Talmudic period took place in the context of what is known as the Responsa method. Individuals or communities would pose in writing questions or problems to recognized and authoritative scholars – but of their own choice. Their answers and reactions were generally accepted and – when appropriate – implemented.

Another method through which religious authority continued to evolve was by means of varying the arrangement and classification of laws and customs. From time to time great scholars would compile and publish their own arrangements, and the very shifts and prioritizing in these codes proved to constitute a very helpful instrument for keeping legal developments in harmony with the social, political and economic conditions of their respective times. The difficulties that these codifiers faced were formidable. They had to know the entire body of the law. They required great breadth of mind and self-confidence. It was in fact much easier to make one's point by way of a commentary on already existing and authoritative texts, especially texts of the Bible and the Talmud. Generally, the codifiers did not engage in Responsa writing and vice versa. The reason is a psychological rather than a philosophical one. After all, when a scholar had done his research, and prepared a Responsum that shed new light or provided fresh insight, he almost inevitably amplified the law. The aim of those who produced codes was generally to simplify the law.

It is, I think, fair to say that the Responsa writers remained authorities par excellence im Jewish experience. A count made in 1930 found over 15,000 volumes of Responsa literature! They originated in Spain, France and Germany as well as North Africa, Turkey, Poland, Russia and Hungary. Their subjects were equally wide-ranging: marriage, divorce, the ordination of rabbis, dietary laws, and laws of inheritance, the ransoming of captives, reactions to persecution and apostasy, laws relating to business, agriculture and industry as well as insurance and banking. Virtually no aspect of individual and communal life goes untreated.

Of the many codes which were also produced in fairly regular and rapid succession, one needs to be singled out because of its great influence and, indeed, authority, which continues to the present time. The *Shulchan Aruch* ('The Prepared Table') was destined to become the last great code in traditional Jewish life. Its author, Joseph Caro, was born in 1488 in Spain and died in 1575 in Safed, the Galilean home of Jewish mysticism. It has four sections: *Orach Chayim* deals with everyday commandments, sabbath and festival observance; *Yoreh De'ah* is concerned with a variety of subjects including dietary laws, interest charges, laws of purity and mourning; *Eveh Ha-Ezer* focuses on marriage and divorce laws; and *Choshen Mishpat* is a 'user-friendly' section of civil and criminal law. The book was first printed in Venice in 1565 and achieved great popularity, paradoxically in consequence of the swift and many attacks on it. The Polish authority, Moses Isserles, though a great admirer of Caro and his work, objected to the absence of the *minhagim* or customs of Central and East European Jewry and he added a series of explanations and supplements to Caro's work under the title of *Mappah* – literally 'the Tablecloth'. The combination of the two texts made it a halachic best-seller without precedent. It should be pointed out that there was great opposition to codes which, as it were, 'laid down' the law. The impression is that while both Caro and Isseles considered their work to be at the most 'a last word' on the question of religious authority for their own age and society, in fact, it became 'the final word', and to this day Orthodox Jews and communities consider it as the definitive statement on Jewish law.

Reform or Progressive Jews do not give the *Shulchan Aruch* and its predecessors the same degree of authority. In a recent 'Collective Theological Essay' published in *MANNA* magazine by the Reform movement in Britain, it is stated:

> Whilst respecting the *halachic* system as a dominating aspect of our inheritance, we do not believe that a system of law is adequate to enable all contemporary Jews to express their relationship with God and other human beings. This is firstly a reflection of the shift from a society which addressed groups and classes to a society which addresses individuals. Secondly, it stems from a process whereby the Jewish Community has handed over responsibility for such areas as criminal and civil law to the State, leaving only the deeply personal area of ritual and subtle issues on ethics to the domain of *halachah*.... We recognize the primacy of individual judgement and conscience, but individuals have to recognize that they exist also as part of a community and a tradition.... Progressive Judaism embraces that process of creative change and development which brings with it new patterns of Jewish practice.[2]

There is a growing body of literature pioneered by the late Solomon Freehof, an outstanding leader of the Reform movement in the USA, which uses the Responsa method in shaping contemporary attitudes and practices but there is great reluctance to produce a comprehensive code. Anyone tempted to do so must be sobered by the realization that there would be no chance of having such a code accepted as binding on all communities and individuals.

My personal conclusion is that the revelation at Sinai continues to reverberate. There is a Rabbinic notion of the *Bat Kol*, literally 'the daughter of the Voice', which is a way of saying that the will and ways of God resonate and echo throughout God's Creation and in all times and places. The task remains to be open and receptive. Is there only one Voice or are there many Voices? At the end of some great controversies between equally learned and sincere teachers and authorities, when a conclusion one way or another was simply not possible the rabbis of old found it both liberating and spiritually realistic to leave such unresolved issues with the humble maxim *elu v'elu divrei elohim chayim hem*, 'These (words) *and* these are both words of the Living God'. Perhaps the most spiritually sensitive and ambitious mandate for the present was given by Rabbi Abraham Isaac Kook (1865-1935), the first Ashkenazi Chief Rabbi of Israel. The task for contemporary Jewry, he insisted, is 'to renew the old and to sanctify the new'.

NOTES

1. The Mishnah in its present form was edited by Rabbi Judah Hannasi ('Judah, the Prince') around 200 CE. It is based on earlier codes of law. Its six volumes or tractates are systematically arranged under the headings of *Zeraim* (Seeds), which deals with laws of agriculture, *Moed* (Set Feasts), laws relating to the observance of the sabbath and festivals, *Nashim* (Women), which deals with marriage and divorce laws, *Nezikim* (Damage) – a collection of tort laws which also includes the well-known collection of ethical aphorisms of *Avot* (the Fathers) – *Kodashim* (Hallowed Things), which deals with the sacrificial cult as practised in the Temple in Jerusalem, and *Tohorot* (Cleannesses), which deals with a wide range of laws of purity and issues of personal and public health.

    The Gemara is a record of the wide-ranging discussions of the rabbis and their decisions based on the rules promulgated in the rather sparse text of the Mishna. The combination of the texts of the Mishna and Gemara is the Talmud, of which there are two versions.

    The Palestinian or Jerusalem Talmud was developed mainly in the academies at Tiberias, Caesarea and Sepphoris. It consists of 39 tractates and was redacted around 450 CE.

    The more authoritative work is the Babylonian Talmud, which was developed in acade-

mies at Nehardea, Pumberdita, Machuza and Sura and was finally redacted around 500 CE.
2.   'Progressive Judaism: a collective theological essay and discussion paper' (1991) *MANNA Theology Supplement*, Section C.2.

FURTHER READING

Alexander, Philip S. (ed.) (1984) *Textual Sources for Study of Judaism*. Manchester: Manchester University Press.
Bermant, Chaim (1977) *The Jews*. London: Weidenfeld and Nicolson.
Goldberg, David J. and Rayner, John D. (1987) *The Jewish People: Their History and Their Religion*. Harmondsworth: Penguin.
Magonet, Jonathan (1991) *A Rabbi's Bible*. London: SCM Press.
Neusner, Jacob (1990) *Torah Through the Ages*. London: SCM Press.
Spero, Shubert (1983) *Morality, Halakha and the Jewish Tradition*. New York: Ktav Publishing House and Yeshiva University Press.

Chapter 7

Freedom and Authority in Sikhism

Piara Singh Sambhi and W. Owen Cole

The Sikh religion originated in the Punjab region of India only 500 years ago.[1] Although it has undergone institutional developments in that time and has had to consider the place of authority within the community, it has never done so with any eagerness. As we shall see, the issue of authority in a practical sense remains unresolved.

A distinctive feature of Sikhism is that although it began with the preachings of a Guru (followed in fact by nine successors), the emphasis has always been on the teaching or *sampradaya*, rather than the teacher. The Gurus are to be respected and Sikhs affirm that they entered the world of time as already enlightened beings, their birth was non-karmic, but no claim has ever been made that they are *avatars*. One of the bards at the court of the fifth Guru Arjan did say:

> O Nanak, the Guru, blessed are thou who lovingly relished the Lord's Name, in the *sat yug* too, you enjoyed the state of *rajyoga*, when you deceived Bali, becoming a dwarf whose form pleased you.
> In the *treta yug* too, when you were called Rama of the Raghu clan.
> In the *duarpa* age too as Krishna, when you emancipated Kansa....
> In the *kali* age you were called Nanak, Angad and Amar Das.
>
> (AG 1389)[2]

These words are merely dismissed as ecstatic praise of a devotee and have never been used as the basis for a Sikh doctrine of *avatar*. Where they have been pressed into service it has been to support the Sikh belief in continuing revelation, that is the view that God's self-revealing activity began at creation and has never ceased, and nor has it ever been confined to any single person or religion. We cannot be certain that some often-quoted words of Guru Arjan were made in response to the bardic enthusiasm of Kal, but it is they which sum up Sikh beliefs about the human Gurus: 'May the mouth burn by which it is said that the Lord becomes incarnate. The Lord neither comes to nor departs from this earth. The God of Nanak is all-absorbing and ever-present' (AG 1136). At the outset of his ministry Guru Nanak stressed his subordination to God. When he was about thirty years old he disappeared while taking his normal daily bath in the nearby River Bein. The Janam Sakhis[3] provide various accounts of what happened, but of far greater importance is Guru Nanak's explanation of the event:

> I was once a worthless bard, then the Divine One gave me work....
> The Mighty One instructed me; 'Night and day sing my praise'.
> The Lord summoned the minstrel to the Divine Court and bestowed on me the robe of honouring and praising God.
>
> (AG 150)

Here Guru Nanak clearly defines his position. His words are those of God, not his own. His actions and the whole of his life are in obedience to the divine will (*Hukam*). At some later point in his ministry he repeated the statement that his message was not his own:

> As the Word of the Master comes to me, so I make it known.
>
> (AG 722)

> I have said what you, my Lord, inspired me to say, Your Name is sweet *amrit* and I am in love with it. Your Name seems sweet to my mind so the abode of pain is destroyed and gladness comes in to my mind at your will. My task is to pray, yours is to bless. You are the self-existent, I have said what you, my Lord, have inspired me to say.
>
> (AG 566)

After the Mughal Emperor Babur's siege of Saidpur, Guru Nanak and his musician-companion, Mardana, were tramping along with the rest of the prisoners when the Guru became conscious of imminent inspiration. He turned to Mardana, who had been given charge of an officer's horse, and told him to be ready to play his rebeck. When Mardana remonstrated with him, saying that he could not play and hold the horse, Guru Nanak replied 'Let the horse go, I feel the Word [*bani*] descending'.[4]

Doubtless there were those who came to Guru Nanak for the kind of general counselling about family matters and social relationships that Gurus are expected to provide in addition to spiritual guidance. Evidence can be found to support this in some of the Guru's hymns.[5] This must be one of the reasons why he decided to appoint a successor shortly before he died. The young community needed someone to provide guidance. In India the Guru–disciple relationship is one which quickly generates dependence and belief in the Guru's divinity, for Hinduism teaches that all human beings are divine. Guru Nanak shared that view: 'The One God is all-pervading and alone dwells in every soul' (AG 433). However, from what has been written so far, we can see that we are dealing with a man who always wished to deflect attention from himself to the Word. Guru Nanak had no authority of his own.

The inclination of the Gurus is always to point beyond themselves to the Guru of gurus. Guru Nanak said:

> The Transcendent is the Guru, whom Nanak has met.
>
> (AG 599)

> My Guru is eternal; neither taking birth nor dying.
>
> (AG 759)

The term 'Guru' in Sikh thought can be confusing. This is not the place to explain it in detail but an understanding of it does impinge upon our discussion of authority. God, *Akal Purukh*, the Timeless One or the Being Beyond Time, is indiscernible. Human beings can only know God if and when God decides to become self-manifest. This God does as Word (*Shabad*). Gurus in the Indian tradition may communicate their sampradaya in many ways, but a common method is by verbal teaching. Taking up this idea, Sikhs speak of the manifest deity as *Sat Guru*, the True Guru, and the divine word as *gurshabad.* The human Gurus were among the many people chosen by God to transmit the divine Word; thus when the phrase *gurprasadi*, 'by the Guru's grace', occurs in the Mul Mantra, it is to be understood as 'by God's grace', not by the grace of the human Gurus. They had no grace of their own: 'I have no virtues, all the virtues are yours' (Guru Arjan, AG 577). A hymn in the Guru Granth Sahib (AG 937–943) describes an encounter between Guru Nanak and the Nath yogis, followers of the teachings of their Guru, Gorakhnath. They ask him such questions as: 'What is your Name?' (i.e. name of your path); 'What path do you follow?'; 'Where is your *asana?*' To these the Guru replies that he abides constantly in the God who lives in all hearts: that the Lord's love is his sect; that his *asana* is meditation on the imperishable One. He continues: 'I have come from God and shall go wherever the divine command directs me. Through the Guru I have come to know myself and have merged in the truest of the true' (AG 938). To the question 'Who is your guru?' he replies: 'The *shabad* is my Guru, upon which I, the disciple [*chela*], greatly love to meditate' (AG 943).

This belief was seen very clearly in practice in Guru Arjan's action when he installed the first copy of the Sikh scriptures in the Harmandir Sahib, now better known as the Golden Temple. He realized that a compilation of the authentic hymns of the Gurus was needed for several reasons: rival Gurus were composing spurious verses which backed their teachings, and the Panth was so large and widespread that it was beyond the physical reach of the human Guru. The status of the collection (*granth* in Punjabi) must have perplexed the Sikhs; after all, this was not a commonplace move on the part of Gurus during their lifetime. To clarify the situation, Guru Arjan prostrated himself before the book, indicating that it was the gurshabad, the Word, which mattered ultimately, not the person.[6] This was in 1604. The line of Gurus continued until 1708 when the tenth, Guru Gobind Singh, just before his death, placed five coins and a coconut in front of a copy of the scripture and declared that it would be the manifest form of the Guru. From this time, the Adi Granth, as the original compilation had been called, is also known as the Guru Granth Sahib. The precedence which Guru Arjan gave to the scripture has become an essential part of Sikh practice. Every Sikh who comes into the presence of the Guru Granth Sahib, at home or in the gurdwara, prostrates himself or herself or bows towards it. Sikhs should never offer obeisance to a picture of one of the human Gurus, and should make sure that such portraits are not placed near the Guru Granth Sahib in such a way that they might seem to vie with it for respect.

Another, less noticed but equally significant development had been taking place during the period from about 1500 to 1708. Sikhism has always been a religion which attached great importance to the community of believers, the *sangat*.[7] In Siddha Gosht, Guru Nanak indicates its high status and worth in this passage:

I salute the One who is the truth, who is infinite and without limit.
I would lay my severed head at that one's feet and give myself body and soul. Truth is also to be found in the fellowship of the saints [*sangat*], through them the soul is led to bliss [*sahaj*].

(AG 938)

The Truth which is God is to be found within oneself and therefore within the community which is committed to truthful living.

This is a logical development or extension of the belief which Guru Nanak held that it was God, not he, who was the Word. The revelation could just as powerfully exist in the sangat as in the Guru. This idea is expressed explicitly in some words of Guru Nanak:

I always associate with saintly people [*sangat*]. The saints have instructed me. That country is blessed where a saint lives. Where God's devotees do not live, that place is a wilderness. By the Guru's grace be aware of God in all hearts. . . .

My attention is fixed on the lotus feet of God who, in mercy, has blessed me. O God, I crave the dust of your saints' feet. Abiding always in God's presence, Nanak meditates on the Lord.

(AG 1183)

In 1699 Guru Gobind Singh instituted the new Sikh family of the *Khalsa*; the word 'brotherhood' has often been used to describe it, but in these non-sexist times it is important to remind ourselves that it, like all aspects of Sikh life and practice, is open to male and female alike on terms of complete equality. Explanations of the Guru's purpose in forming the Khalsa emphasize his wish to remove power from the masands, regional leaders appointed to meet the needs of a widely dispersed Panth over a hundred years earlier, and focus it back on the Guru. He was also affirming the importance of the community. He demonstrated this by himself receiving initiation from the five men he had made the first Khalsa members, just as the family and gender-inclusive aspect was shown by the participation of his wife in the preparation of *amrit*.[8]

In *Guru Sobha* (Radiance of the Guru), a poem written between 1711 and 1745, the Guru's concern for the future of the Panth after his death is described in these words:

On an earlier occasion the Guru had been approached by his Sikhs and had been asked what form the (eternal) Guru would assume (after he had departed this earthly life). He replied that it would be the *Khalsa*, 'The *Khalsa* is the focus of my hopes and desires', he had declared. Upon the *Khalsa* which I have created I will bestow the succession. The *Khalsa* is my physical form and I am one with the *Khalsa*. To all eternity, I shall be manifest in the *Khalsa*. They whose hearts are purged of falsehood will be known as the true *Khalsa*; and the *Khalsa*, freed from error and illusion, will be my Guru.

And my true Guru, boundless and infinite, is the eternal Word, the Word of wisdom which the devout contemplate in their hearts, the Word which brings ineffable peace to all who utter it, the Word which is wisdom immeasurably unfolded, the Word which none may ever describe. This is the light which is given to you, the refuge of all who inhabit the world, and the abode of all who renounce it.[9]

These words present the Sikh ideal of the Guru Panth and bring together the two strands of authority which had hitherto existed somewhat separately, the scripture and the community. The term *Guru Panth* affirms the belief that authority lies in the community assembled in the presence of the Guru Granth Sahib as it had earlier existed in the word of the human Guru and the sangat.

During the eighteenth century, the tradition grew up of meetings known as a Sarbat Khalsa (literally 'all the Khalsa'), held at Diwali and Baisakhi. The Gurus, from the time of Guru Amar Das, had convened assemblies on these occasions. They usually took place at the Akal Takht in Amritsar. The Sarbat Khalsa began with the Sikh prayer Ardas, the business agenda followed, and decisions were reached and accepted by the gathering shouting 'Sat sri akal', and ratified with another Ardas. The election of military leaders, meetings with foreign emissaries, and the formulation and approval of policy took place at the Sarbat Khalsa. Of course, most of the business was conducted by the leading sardars, military commanders, who attempted to woo the assembly to the acceptance of their views, but, in theory at least, all members of the Khalsa had their say. Resolutions passed by the Sarbat Khalsa were known as *gurmatta*. They enjoyed identical authority with the edicts of the human Gurus.

Sir John Malcolm, one of the first Europeans to study the Sikhs, gave this account of a Sarbat Khalsa. He did not attend it himself but it is based on enquiries made in 1805, the year when it was held. He made the mistake of confusing the assembly with the decision. There is no doubt, however, that his description is of a Sarbat Khalsa, and perhaps of the last one for over a century and three quarters, for Maharaja Ranjit Singh abolished it in 1805.

> When a *Guru-mata*, or great national council, is called, as it always is, or ought to be, when any imminent danger threatens the country, or any large expedition is to be undertaken, all the Sikh chiefs assemble at Amritsar. The assembly, which is called the *Guru-mata*, is convened by the *Acalis*; and when the chiefs meet upon this solemn occasion, it is concluded that all private animosities cease and that every man sacrifices his personal feelings at the shrine of the general good; and, actuated by principles of pure patriotism, thinks of nothing but the interests of the religion and commonwealth to which he belongs.
>
> When the chiefs and principal leaders are seated, the *Adi-Grant'h* and *Dasama Padshah ka Grant'h* are placed before them. They all bend their heads before these scriptures, and exclaim, *Wa! Guruji ka Khalsa! Wa! Guruji ki Fateh!* A great quantity of cakes made of wheat, butter, and sugar, are then placed before the volumes of the sacred writings, and covered with a cloth. These holy cakes, which are in commemoration of the injunction of Nanac, to eat and to give to others to eat, next receive the salutations of the assembly, who then rise and the Acalis pray aloud, while the musicians play. The Acalis, when the prayers are finished, desire the council to be seated. They sit down, and the cakes being uncovered, are eaten of by all classes of Sikhs: those distinctions of original tribes, which are, on other occasions kept up, being on this occasion laid aside, in token of their general and complete union in one cause. The *Acalis* then exclaim: '*Sirdars*! (chiefs) this is a *Guru-mata!*' on which prayers are again said aloud. The chiefs, after this, sit closer and say to each other: '*The Sacred Grant'h* is betwixt us, let us swear by our scripture to forget all internal disputes and to be united.' This moment of religious fervour and ardent patriotism is taken to reconcile all animosities. They then proceed to consider the danger with which they are threatened, to settle the best plans for averting it, and to choose the generals who are to lead their armies against the common enemy. The first *Guru-mata* was assembled by Guru Govind; and the latest was called in 1805, when the British army pursued Holkar into the Penjab.[10]

On the death of Guru Gobind Singh, political leadership of the Panth passed to Banda (meaning 'slave') Bahadur Singh, one of his followers.[11] He assumed royal authority, struck coins in the name of the Guru and issued *hukam namas*, letters of royal command. His seal bore the inscription:

> *deg o teg o fateh o nusrat-i-bedrang*
> *yaft az Nanak Guru Gobind Singh*
>
> Through hospitality and the sword unending victory
> granted by Nanak and Guru Gobind Singh.

These words suggest that he attributed his status to the Gurus and accepted their authority. Writers who were not Sikhs, however, sometimes described him as 'guru' and some Sikh historians accept that he may have attempted to claim that status for himself, using the title *Banda Guru* to mean 'Banda the Guru', not 'the slave of the Guru'. Certainly the Panth did not allow him to usurp it, had that been his wish, and a schism occurred, with Mata Sundri, widow of the tenth Guru, repudiating his leadership.[12] Whatever intentions Banda had, the line of Gurus which Guru Gobind Singh had ended was not revived and never has been.

During the eighteenth-century struggle for survival and then for political freedom, the

Sikh resistance to Mughals and Afghans took the form of highly mobile voluntary bands called *jathas*, led by *jathedars*. These groups tended to constitute the Sarbat Khalsa. From time to time a leader arose who could unify this army so that it was a Dal Khalsa, 'Khalsa army', in practice rather than mere theory. The most famous and influential of these was Ranjit Singh. By the age of 20 he was ruler of an independent Punjab which existed until 1849 when it was annexed by the British.

Ranjit Singh was a secular ruler in the Indian and modern Western sense of the word. He anticipated Nehru's concept of 'secular' by ruling his empire in such a way that all religions were respected, and the Sikhs seem to have enjoyed no particular privileges. He drank and enjoyed the company of dancing girls in flagrant violation of the Khalsa code of discipline. It was for his marriage to a Muslim without requiring her to convert to the Sikh faith that he was called to account by the Sarbat Khalsa and condemned to suffer 21 lashes. He was also punished for associating with dancing girls and, on another occasion, criticized for making the gift of an ornamental canopy which he had first enjoyed the use of himself, to the Akal Takht. There can be little wonder that he abolished the Sarbat Khalsa in 1805! He could argue that its role had been superseded now that a Sikh kingdom had been established and it had no need to appoint military commanders and negotiate treaties, but there is no doubt that he was eager to remove the threat of an assembly which could issue gurmatta which might conflict with his political authority and might provide a focus for opposition.

The late nineteenth century saw the Panth under attack again, but this time the assault was ideological. The assailants were members of the Hindu Arya Samaj movement and Christian missionaries. The Sikh response took the form of a renaissance through the establishment of educational institutions and distancing itself from Hinduism by the reforms of Sikh practices. A major obstacle to this was the fact that many gurdwaras had passed into the control of Hindu families during the period of conflict with the Mughals and Afghans. The struggle to recover them ended with the Gurdwaras Act of 1925. In anticipation of this the Shromani Gurdwara Parbandhak Committee (SGPC) had been set up in 1920. It assumed responsibility for the administration of historical gurdwaras in the Punjab under the Act. These are places associated with the Gurus, sometimes being set up by them, or at later times on sites where they preached or some important incident in their lives took place. For the purpose of the Act, 'Punjab' includes the modern states of Hariyana and Himachal Pradesh, and the city of Chandigarh, as well as Punjab itself. Over the intervening eighty years, its role has developed and its importance increased. The SGPC has 175 members. These are elected by Sikhs at elections conducted by the central government. It now regards itself as the voice of Sikhism and claims to be the body that the Indian government should deal with in its attempts to resolve the crisis which led to, and has continued after, Operation Blue Star.[13]

The SGPC appoints the jathedars of the Akal Takht, Amritsar, gurdwaras Keshgarh Sahib, Anandpur, and Damdama Sahib at Talwandi Sabo, Batinda, the three Takhts or seats of authority which are situated in the Punjab. The other two Gurdwara Takhts are Patna Sahib in Bihar, and Nanded in Hyderabad. All are sites of considerable significance in Sikh history. The first of these Takhts was the Akal Takht, which has enjoyed its authority from at least the mid-eighteenth century, being the venue of gatherings of the Sarbat Khalsa. It was to this place that Maharaja Ranjit Singh was summoned to answer the charges mentioned above and receive the punishment which they incurred.

The purpose of the Takhts was originally to ensure orthopraxis. For this reason the jathedars appointed to them were to be men of standing within the Panth, respected for their learning and piety. They were appointed by the Sarbat Khalsa and could also be removed from office at its pleasure. Something of the democracy which was involved in the appointment of jathedars in earlier times survives. Although they are chosen and appointed by the SGPC, the names of persons being considered for the office when a vacancy exists are known publicly and widely discussed in gurdwaras and by the media, so that the SGPC is well aware of popular feelings when it makes appointments.

Here it is probably wise to interject a word of warning about the usage of the phrase 'Sikh High Priests' in the Western media, and in such Indian papers as the *Spokesman Weekly*, a well-known Sikh journal. They do not exist! One can never be certain who is meant when the words are used. It could be one of the jathedars. It could be all five. It might be a *granthi*, the person responsible for worship at a gurdwara. There is also the possibility that the reference is to the Panj Piare of one of the Takhts. These are five persons, almost invariably men, who would be appointed by the Takht to undertake initiation ceremonies or represent it at gatherings. They really have no more status than the Panj Piare that a gurdwara would commission to conduct an Amrit Pahul initiation ceremony, or delegate to speak to a Sikh accused of infringing the rules of the sangat. They have no permanency or authority other than that invested in them for specific purposes.

A major achievement of the SGPC was the Rahit Maryada, the Sikh Code of Discipline. This document was finally published in 1950 after a long period of discussion and argument. The real origins of the Code go back to the times of the Gurus. They issued commands known as *hukam namas* on particular matters and more general *rahit namas*, written codes of discipline.[14] These met the needs of the time satisfactorily but in the context of the reform movement of the last century and the anticipated control of gurdwaras, something else was required. An attempt had been made in 1915 when a book of order for Khalsa rituals was issued, *Gurmat Prakas Bhag Sanskar*, but it never enjoyed wide support, perhaps because of its tendency to equate Sikh with Khalsa, something which has never been totally accepted by the whole Panth, though the Khalsa ideal is one which most Sikhs will affirm and declare to be their aspiration. It may be said that generally the Rahit Maryada is accepted as authoritative, especially in the areas relating to the conduct of worship and other ceremonies.

The Rahit Maryada has a number of sections. They cover: the details of daily personal devotion; the conduct of worship; naming, marriage, and funeral ceremonies; *amrit* initiation; reading the Guru Granth Sahib; the preparation of Karah Parshad; Langar; and the conduct of Khalsa members, including such prohibitions as smoking, drinking alcohol, receiving dowries on the marriage of daughters, and eating halal meat (that which Sikhs eat should be 'jatka', killed by one sword-blow while the words 'Sat sri akal' are said over the animal).

The Code has been widely accepted in matters of worship and the conduct of ceremonies. Some un-Sikh practices may occasionally be detected, especially the Hindu custom of placing a bowl of water near the Guru Granth Sahib.[15] The full participation of women in leadership roles in these activities, for example, reading the Guru Granth Sahib, and giving addresses (*katha*) based on it, is far less than one would expect in a religion which gives theoretical equality to everyone irrespective of gender, caste, or colour. One only occasionally hears of a woman taking part in an Amrit Pahul initiation ceremony as one of the Panj Piare. Personal piety also focuses strongly upon the prescription of the Rahit Maryada, perhaps because it was endorsing what many devout Sikhs already did.

A considerable influence upon corporate and individual conduct, both of ceremonies and personal life, can be exerted by sants, whose pictures are to be found in homes and occasionally in gurdwaras. These are men who have become well known for their piety and understanding of Gurus' teachings. This results in them attracting a following of devotees who turn to them for spiritual and personal guidance. Many of them affirm fully and without alteration the principles and practices found in the Rahit Maryada. Some provide an interpretation which is at variance with it in some respects. They may, for example, exclude women from reading the scriptures at an *Akhand Path*, the continuous reading of the Guru Granth Sahib which is a feature of all important celebrations. They may encourage a personal regime of vegetarianism. It may not be surprising to find this kind of allegiance in a culture which is still very close to that of Hinduism with its many gurus and stress on hierarchy within the family and society. Perhaps it is more remarkable that there are many Sikhs who do not turn to sants to provide authority over their lives.

There are areas where the Rahit Maryada has been less effective. The tradition of giving dowries has not been ended, though the Gurus opposed the custom centuries ago, long before the Indian government made it illegal. There are many Sikhs, outraged at the practice, who have simple weddings at which no lavish presents are given to the groom or his family or to the bride, but there seem to be more Sikh families who participate in the dowry system. The prohibition against smoking seems to be complied with; only rarely does one hear of Sikhs who take tobacco in any form. The same cannot be said for abstinence from alcohol. The non-Khalsa Sikh has not accepted this part of the Rahit, though public opinion favours it. (Sikhs who drink often tend to excuse themselves in a way which suggests that they know that they should be teetotallers.) The prohibition against eating any meat which is not jatka seems to be ignored, certainly in Britain, but it could be argued that this is a recommendation, not a requirement.[16] Halal meat is definitely avoided, but the debate among Sikhs has more to do with vegetarianism than the method of animal slaughter. There is no prohibition against meat-eating in the Rahit Maryada, but many Sikhs are vegetarian, and one can hear its virtues and necessity being preached in gurdwaras, especially by visiting sants. Though meat may be eaten, it is rare to find Sikhs who eat beef.

The cultural influence of Hinduism survives at the level of eating and caste-based marriages. The rule that only vegetarian food should be served in gurdwaras, however, is universally observed and has to do with respect for the consciences of those who are vegetarian, not Hindu concepts of purity and pollution. Panthic concerns outside India have to do with persuading young Sikhs to accept arranged marriages, encouraging them to learn Punjabi, and keeping the *keshas*, the uncut hair. Although one might argue that the Rahit Maryada presupposes that Sikh marriages will be arranged, there is no explicit statement to this effect and one could equally say that the Code gave no consideration to what was the common custom of the day. There is no mention of Punjabi either.

Forty years ago Sikhs were[17] not living in situations which challenged the value of Punjabi, as does British or American society now, by implication if not explicitly. The uncut hair is something which the Khalsa tradition has always considered vital, even of supreme importance. The prohibition against cutting the hair, plucking the beard and dyeing hair is emphatically stated in the Rahit Maryada, but the clean-shaven Sikh who covers his head with a handkerchief is a fairly common sight in most gurdwaras outside India. (In India the identification is less clear, because Hindus often worship in gurd-waras, and usually cover their heads with a handkerchief or scarf.) It is not rare, however, to meet Sikhs who do not keep the *keshas* and who are ready to assert that they are faithful to the teachings of Guru Nanak. They claim that the hair, together with the rest of the five Ks, was introduced by Guru Gobind Singh and may be obligatory on the Khalsa but not on the rest of the Panth, for whom the Rahit Maryada is, at best, only a guide book.

The authority of the Rahit Maryada rests upon the willingness of the Panth as a whole to accept it, as does the authority of the SGPC. In the introduction to the Rahit Maryada,[18] the SGPC is described as 'the Supreme Religious Parliament of the Sikhs'. This it is not. Its writ runs only in the parts of India already mentioned. Delhi has its own SGPC which does not acknowledge that the Amritsar body has authority over its gurdwaras. There is not necessarily an SGPC for every state of the Indian Republic, so many gurdwaras are autonomous sangats. A bill is at present with the Indian Parliament which provides for a Shromani Gurdwara Parbandhak Committee for the whole of India based on the Punjab model, but how authoritative the body will actually be once it comes into existence has yet to be seen.

Meanwhile the movement for the SGPC to be recognized as the religious parliament of the Sikhs presses forward. In the emergency of 1975–77 it spoke as the voice of Sikhism, denouncing, for example, the enforced use of vasectomy as part of the government's policy of birth control. Currently, it seeks to take a lead in ending the Punjab crisis resulting from Operation Blue Star. In doing so it moves into the field of temporal politics and itself can become the victim of politicians who seek to manipulate and control it.

One of the questions which immediately presents itself when a 'religious parliament' is suggested is that of the franchise. Who should be allowed to vote? The answer is obvious: Sikhs. But who is a Sikh? Most recently, in the Delhi Gurdwara Act, 1971, the qualification of electors stipulates residence in the ward for 180 days, and a minimum age of 21. It continues: 'no person shall be registered as an elector who: trims or shaves his beard or keshas; smokes; takes alcohol drink'.

The fact that it would be very difficult to verify these conditions is the least important matter. What we have is an attempt to define a Sikh which, it could be argued, conforms neither to the teachings of Guru Nanak nor to the Khalsa ideal of Guru Gobind Singh. The description of a Sikh is a not very satisfactory compromise.

The terms of the 1925 Gurdwaras Act were slightly less prescriptive. Smoking and taking alcohol were causes of disenfranchisement, but the other restriction was that no one who 'trims or shaves his beard or *keshas*, except the case of *sahajdhari* Sikhs', shall be a voter.

The word *sahajdhari* is claimed to mean 'one who proceeds by easy stages'. The Sikh Gurdwara Act 1925, as amended in 1959, defines one as a person who:

professes the Sikh religion, can recite the *Mul Mantra* [i.e. in good faith], performs all ceremonies according to Sikh rites; does not smoke, use tobacco, *kutha* [halal meat], in any form; does not take alcohol drinks who is not *patit*.

It does not, however, require belief in the Guru Granth Sahib and the Ten Gurus and the declaration that one has no other religion.

A *patit* is 'a person, who having been a *keshadhari* Sikh, trims or shaves his beard or *keshas*, or who, after taking *amrit*, commits any one of the four *kurahits*' (prohibited acts).[19] The inclusion of *sahajdhari* meant that the word 'Sikh' could be interpreted quite broadly. The Delhi Gurdwara Act, 1971, indicates a movement towards a more restrictive definition of Sikhism. It actually defines a Sikh as 'A person who believes in only one God, follows the teachings of the Guru Granth Sahib, Ten Gurus, the *bani* of Guru Gobind Singh and takes *Amrit*, and has faith in no other religion whatsoever'. It goes on to say that should a dispute arise as to whether someone is or is not a Sikh, that person should be required to declare the following: 'I solemnly affirm that I am a *Keshadhari* Sikh, and I believe in and follow the teachings of Shri Guru Granth Sahib and the Ten Gurus only and that I have no other religion.'[20] This reinforces the emphasis on uncut hair and wearing the turban. It is not uncommon today to hear Sikhs echoing this by asserting that only men who keep the uncut hair or have been initiated into the Panth, that is *keshadharis* and *amritdharis*, are Sikhs.

Rules governing those who stand as candidates for the Punjab and Delhi SGPCs are stricter than those for electors. The 1925 Act laid down that they must at least be *keshadhari*. The 1971 Act requires those nominated to be *amritdhari*, and not one of those who trims the beard, as some do.

From the foregoing paragraphs, and the differences to which we have drawn attention between the Gurdwaras Act of 1925 and the 1971 Delhi Gurdwaras Act, it is clear that there is no agreement on the definition of a Sikh and, consequently, whether authority lies with the broad Guru Panth or the narrower and more precise Khalsa Panth.

The SGPC's decisions have no legal authority outside the Punjab as defined above, though their moral influence might be considerable. In the UK, Kenya, the USA, New Zealand, Norway, and anywhere else where Sikhs might live, there is no body which may exercise spiritual or any other kind of jurisdiction over them apart from the law of the land. Authority for a Sikh family in somewhere like Rome, where there is no sangat, takes the form of living according to the Gurus' teachings. What these are understood to be will depend on upbringing, practices learned from parents, and knowledge of the Guru Granth Sahib. Where advice is needed on a particular issue, recourse is likely to be made to the Guru Granth Sahib, if the family possesses one, or a *gutka*, a book containing its main hymns (*shabads*). This will be opened prayerfully, at random, and the first complete verse on the left-hand page will be regarded as the voice of the Guru. By meditating on it the Sikh should be able to discover God's command or will (*Hukam*). The practice is known as *Vak laina*, taking advice.

The local sangat in Crawley, Chicago or anywhere else operates in much the same way. Its general affairs are in the hands of an elected body of men and women. Decisions will be taken by the sangat as a whole. These will be reached through discussion, consulting the Rahit Maryada and the opinions of great Sikh scholars, and, if needs be, the taking of a *Vak*. (The person who may be introduced to visitors as a 'priest' is actually someone appointed to conduct worship and other ceremonies, a granthi. He may possess an authority based on his learning, but he is only one voice and has no *ex officio* status. He is merely a minister responsible to the sangat.) Should a gurdwara be known to be in breach of the tenets of Sikh faith, a *hukam nama*, or decree, could be issued by the jathedar of the Akal Takht or SGPC, denouncing it and instructing Sikhs to have nothing to do with it. However, the jathedar has no power to enforce the decision. It is up to the individual concerned, or the management committee of the local sangat, to abide by it or ignore it.

Cases do arise from time to time. For example, on Baisakhi Day 1981, the management of Richmond Hill Gurdwara, New York, declared itself to be the sixth takht and appointed a jathedar. The same Baisakhi edition of the *Spokesman Weekly* also drew attention to alleged non-Sikh practices at one of the Sikh Takhts, Hazur Sahib, Nanded.[21] It took the form of a special Havan, a Hindu puja focused on the sacred fire, not the Guru Granth Sahib. This was conducted by the 'head pujari' despite the objections of the management committee. It seems to have been only the most flagrant of many breaches of the Rahit Maryada, for the article also mentions bells being rung when the devotee enters the shrine, the blood of a he-goat being used to anoint weapons of Guru Gobind Singh which are preserved there, and the requirement of the 'head pujari' that worshippers should make obeisance to him. Such examples, many Sikhs would say, point to the need for some kind of central authority.

The use of the phrase 'head pujari' throughout the article cited above is interesting and indicates a confusion which still exists within the Panth. *Pujari* is a Hindu term. The appropriate Sikh word is *granthi*, one who reads scripture. He or she does not offer worship, as a pujari does. Worship is offered by the sangat or the individual Sikh; there is no need for priestly meditation. Similarly, a gurdwara is not a 'temple', as we, and other writers, have often described it. Such casual use of language may not seem very important, but it may also indicate something of the lack of distinctiveness between Hinduism and Sikhism which persists in the attitude of many Sikhs and restricts the effective authority of the Rahit Maryada at a practical level.

THE FUTURE

So far Sikhs in India have shown little concern for the consequences of being a religion which exists worldwide or at least in English-speaking countries. Yet already in 1925 there were Sikhs who regretted that the Sikh Gurdwaras Act did not cover the whole of India and give representation to Sikhs living elsewhere in the world.[22] The majority, however, view the needs of the Panth from their own Punjabi standpoint. (This is not surprising and the comment is in no way made as a criticism. One remembers the major impact which the Lambeth Conference of 1988, with its preponderance of black bishops, made upon the Church of England, a denomination which has long been proud to speak of itself as a world church!) However, Sikhs are to be found in every inhabited continent and those who live outside the Punjab are gradually discovering that their interests are not those of that part of the world. Acknowledgement of this is slow because most Sikhs, wherever they are domiciled, still have close links with the Punjab. The ties are not merely emotional. It is the place where their grandparents or even their parents, aunts and uncles live. Worship in all gurdwaras is conducted in Punjabi, which continues to be the language spoken in many homes. Operation Blue Star continues to affect Sikhs as much as the Holocaust affects Jews.

To meet the needs of Indian Sikhs an all-India gurdwaras bill is under consideration. It envisages a three-tier structure of gurdwara management, a central SGPC, whose authority would extend to all five Takhts and most historic gurdwaras, regional boards autonomous in matters of management, and, locally, sangat-elected committees. Apparently, it will not resolve the question of whether the jathedar of the Akal Takht enjoys precedence of authority over the other Takhts, or what the authority of jathedars should be. It seems to leave local sangats autonomous in many respects, and this would allow tensions of the past to continue between local and more central authority. The definition of a Sikh is also one on which those framing the bill have found it hard to agree. The inclusion of *sahajdharis*, as defined above, is not one which every Sikh accepts.

While an all-India gurdwaras bill is being debated, some Sikhs of the diaspora are beginning to talk about a council of Sikhs which will be the voice of the Panth to the world. How it will be organized, who will have a right to vote or be elected to membership, and what authority it will enjoy, are not matters which have yet been given serious consideration but the day may not be far away when plans for such a body will be laid. When it comes into existence, one hopes that it will be as a result of a felt need on the part of the Panth and not in response to bodies such as the World Council of Churches which would find it convenient to have a Sikh organization with which to confer.[23]

The Sarbat Khalsa has recently been revived. In 1985 a Sikh leader, Harchand Singh Longowal, was permitted by such an assembly to negotiate with Prime Minister Rajiv Gandhi. They reached an Accord, but soon after, Longowal was assassinated. Not everyone was prepared to accept the majority view. In addition, it, and similar gatherings since, did not represent Sikhs worldwide.

Meanwhile, authority remains vested in the Guru Granth Sahib and the uncertainly defined Guru Panth. Occasionally a group of Sikhs will try to elevate someone to leadership of the Panth, perhaps a jathedar of the Akal Takht, but such men have a way of disappearing more quickly than they rise to prominence. There is a saying that 'Every Sikh is a *sardar*'.[24] There is much truth in it. The democratic spirit of the Sikhs and with it a willingness to follow only God is deeply engrained in the Sikh character. The recognition of any other authority lasts as long as the circumstances that gave rise to the need for that authority. Our discussion must, therefore, end inconclusively with perhaps the two Sikh cries:

> *Sat Sri Akal* (Truth is Eternal)

and,

> *Vahiguruji ka Khalsa, Vahigurji ki Fateh*;
> Hail to the Guru's Khalsa, hail to the victory of the Guru.

Both serve to remind the Sikh that authority should remain where it has always been, in God. The One who is Beyond Time, *Akal Purukh*, has not delegated it to any creatures or institutions. The problem for Sikhs, as perhaps for all people of faith, is that of responding to the temporal necessity for organization, without losing sight of eternal reality. Since the death of Guru Gobind Singh in 1708, despite their proximity to Hinduism, not least through marriage ties, Sikhs have not succumbed to the temptations to establish a priesthood or even a professional ministry. They remain very much the successors of the tradition as it existed in the eighteenth century. Only time will reveal whether they will shift the base of authority in the twenty-first century, but it does not appear likely.

FREEDOM

In common with each of the other chapters in this section, this one also has as its subject freedom as well as authority. We addressed the subject of authority first because it is that issue which may have exercised Sikh minds most in recent years. However, we must recognize that Sikhism is a movement which came into existence to offer freedom to men and especially women who seemed to have no prospect of spiritual liberation in a world dominated by the caste system. Hand in hand with this, the Gurus were anxious that human beings, be they Hindu or Muslim, should enjoy social justice. Although Sikhs have always been involved in this search, it has to be admitted that many of the freedoms which concerned the Gurus have yet to be realized. The rejection of caste discrimination and the equality of women with men are still goals to be achieved.

The Rahit Maryada, the Sikh Code of Conduct, indicates that freedom in the Panth is not licence. It is only fully enjoyed when one obeys God's will (*Hukam*). It also suggests that it should be restricted in the cause of panthic unity. The Rahit Maryada was approved in its final form in 1941 and was a result of a series of decrees (*hukams*) and disciplinary codes going back to the times of the Gurus. It was the consequence of anxieties most recently expressed in the late nineteenth century that the distinctiveness of Sikh teachings might be lost by reabsorption into Hinduism. This fear still exists today as Sikhs find themselves wooed or attacked ideologically by militant expressions of India's dominant tradition.

In practice the focus of Sikh criticisms of individual freedom tends to concern members of the Panth who cut the hair and do not wear the turban. These two most obvious forms of conformity are considered evidence of deep-seated laxity. There are Sikhs who would dispute this, insisting that inner spirituality, to use a very Western term, has always been more prominent in the Gurus' message than any insistence on physical appearance. However, whenever groups feel themselves to be under threat there tend to be particular fundamentals to which they rally; uncut hair (often expressed as 'beard') and turban are those to which Sikhs cling. In gurdwara addresses, especially in the diaspora, it is these which preachers proclaim as most important to a Sikh youth who may have too little Punjabi to understand fully what he or she is being told.

Freedom's limit is conformity to the cherished tradition. This Sikh scholars are usually expected to endorse and explain rather than question. Academic freedom has always been a contentious matter in the area of religion and ideology. Socrates may be the first known Western historical figure who was condemned for undermining the beliefs and ethics of the young or the polis in general. They existed in India from at least the time of the Buddha.

During the nineteenth century Sikhs found themselves confronted intellectually by the Hindu Arya Samaj and Christian missions. The outcome was the strengthening of the Panth, which made its response through Khalsa colleges and a flourishing of academic activity inspired by the Singh Sabha movement. Since 1968, when Professor W. H. McLeod published his PhD study entitled 'Guru Nanak and the Sikh religion', some Sikhs have perceived him as the leader of a plot to undermine their religion. In his study he subjected the Janam Sakhis, religious biographies of Guru Nanak, to the same methodology which during the previous century had been used on the New Testament accounts of the life of Jesus. The present situation is one in which some of his own postgraduate students are accused of denying their religion and being intellectually seduced by Professor McLeod. It is clear that he and they have no intention of damaging Sikhism. The clash at an academic level is one of methodology. McLeod often describes himself as a sceptical historian, using 'sceptical' in a value-free way to refer to an academic approach which accepts no historical statement or fact without subjecting it to every possible form of analysis. Critics of his work might ask whether such rigour can be properly applied to faith statements. The religious importance of religious statements can quite easily be overlooked in the process of such examination. Perhaps the best contextualization of Professor McLeod's work has been done by Dr Darshan Singh of the University of Patiala in his PhD assessment of Western approaches to Sikhism.[25] A graduate of Harvard as well as Indian universities, he is aware of the difference between Eastern and Western approaches and of Edward Said's criticism of the so-called orientalist examination of Indian religions. We cannot pursue the matter, which has become an acrimonious argument, but must only add that the sociological, anthropological and historical is not without its risks. In fact, no non-Sikh academic, even working with Sikhs, who studies the religion is likely to be free from suspicion.

There is nothing new in the imposition of limits upon academic freedom. The former Soviet Union and modern-day China may come to mind, but it is unlikely that any studies of a religion or ideology are entirely exempt from it. Even in the late twentieth century it is important to know where a writer on the Christian Reformation is 'coming from' academically, and to be aware of whether a book on Punjab history has been written by a Sikh, Muslim, Hindu or Christian. It may be some time since the promotion of an academic in a British university post in Religious Studies was blocked by denominational considerations, but one is left to ask what influence a preference for theology as opposed to religious studies, or gender, or race, may have upon appointments and internal politics. It is easy to be critical of intolerance among some Sikhs who are demanding some say regarding what is taught in posts which they have financed in whole or in part.

The arguments which surround the work of Professor McLeod relate not only to the study of Sikhism but also to the broader issue of what methods are appropriate in studying religion and how ready a community must be to accept approaches which are alien to it. Sikhism is now a world religion in terms of not only distribution but also scholarly interest. How Sikhs are to respond to the new situation in which they find themselves is one of the important questions for them to answer in the next generation. For what it is worth, the present writers would suggest that Sikhism, in common with other religions, may have more to fear from materialism as a threat to panthic integrity than it has from intellectual rationalism, especially when the majority of young Sikhs growing up in the West are religiously illiterate. However, readers of this chapter who are involved in Sikh studies cannot afford to ignore any of the academic sensitivities expressed above.

NOTES

1. A brief outline of Sikh beliefs and practices and history can be found in W. O. Cole and P. S. Sambhi (1993) *A Popular Dictionary of Sikhism*. Richmond, Surrey: Curzon Press, pp. 9–31.
2. AG, Adi Granth, is commonly used to refer to the Sikh scripture, the Guru Granth Sahib.

All printed versions are identical in format and are 1430 pages long.

3. A Janam Sakhi is a hagiographic account of the life of Guru Nanak. The one most easily available for Western readers to study is probably W. H. McLeod (ed.) (1980) *The B40 Janam Sakhi*. Amritsar.
4. I. Macauliffe (1969) *Valaitvali Janam Sakhi, Janam Sakhi Parampara, Kirpal Singh*. Patiala: Punjab University, p. 33.
5. e.g. AG 466, cremation or burial; AG 1289/90, meat-eating.
6. Gopal Singh, p. 185.
7. Sangat and Panth are sometimes used synonymously of the Sikh community. Nowadays sangat tends to mean the local community or congregation and Panth the community worldwide.
8. Macauliffe, *op. cit.,* vol. V, p. 95.
9. Quoted in McLeod, *op. cit.*, p. 38.
10. John Malcolm, *Sketch of the Sikhs* quoted in W. H. McLeod (1976) p. 49.
11. Khushwant Singh, vol. I, p. 107.
12. Gopal Singh, pp. 347–9; Teja Singh and Ganda Singh, pp. 107–9.
13. Rajiv A. Kapur (1987) *Sikh Separatism*. Vikas. This provides a comprehensive study of the crisis.
14. W. H. McLeod (ed.) (1987) *The Chaupa Singh Rahit-Nama*. Dunedin: University of Otago Press, is probably the most easily accessible example of Rahit Nama.
15. *Rehat Maryada* (1978) SGPC English edition, p. 6 (d).
16. *Ibid.*, p. 21.
17. Many explanations are given for the five symbols which khalsa Sikhs must wear. The *kesh*, uncut hair, is usually regarded as the most important, presumably because it is the most obvious; this is not to diminish the significance of the others. It emphasizes keeping the natural, God-given form.
18. Rehat Maryada, *op. cit.*
19. These are: removal or cutting of hair, eating halal meat, adultery, and the use of tobacco in any form.
20. Rehat Maryada, *op. cit.*, p. 27.
21. *The Spokesman Weekly* (Delhi), 29 June 1981, p. 3.
22. For further discussion and details see *The Spokesman Weekly*, 19 January 1987; 9 October 1989.
23. A World Sikh Conference, Vishwa Sikh Sammelan, is planned for September 1995. This will be the first gathering of its kind. Although the draft agenda does not include the word 'authority', the subject is bound to be discussed.
24. A Sardar was originally a chieftain or leader of one of the Sikh military bands of the eighteenth century. It is now used as a form of address for all Sikh men. (The female equivalent is Sardarani.)
25. Darshan Singh (1991) *Western Perspective on the Sikh Religion*. Sehgal.

BIBLIOGRAPHY

Translations of the Guru Granth Sahib are based on Gopal Singh (1987) *Sri Guru Granth Sahib*. World Sikh Centre; and Manmohan Singh (1962) *Sri Guru Granth Sahib*. Amritsar: SGPC. Extensive sections of the Rehat Maryada are given in McLeod (1990), as listed below.

W. O. Cole and P. S. Sambhi (1995) *The Sikhs: Their Religious Beliefs and Practices*. Brighton: Sussex Academic Press.

M. A. Macauliffe (1978) *The Sikh Religion*, 6 vols. Oxford University Press, Indian reprint.

W. H. McLeod (1976) *The Evolution of the Sikh Community*. Oxford: Oxford University Press.

W. H. McLeod (1989) *Who Is a Sikh?* Oxford: Oxford University Press.

W. H. McLeod (1990) *Textual Sources for the Study of Sikhism*. Chicago: Chicago University Press.

Gopal Singh (1988 edn) *The History of the Sikh People*. World Book Centre.

Khushwant Singh (1977) *A History of the Sikhs*, 2 vols. Oxford University Press, Indian edition.

Teja Singh and Ganda Singh (1989) *A Short History of the Sikhs*. Patiala.

Freedom and Authority in the Life of a Nation

Chapter 8

Freedom and Authority in Northern Ireland

John Greer

A minister was experimenting with an informal approach to his service for children of Sunday school age. 'Can anyone tell me?' he asked, 'what is small, grey, eats nuts and has a long bushy tail?' There was a long silence, and then one small boy put up his hand and said 'I know the answer should be Jesus, but it sounds like a squirrel to me'. This is not really a very funny story, but it does make an important point. Christians and other religious folk are inclined to present Jesus or the Buddha or other authority figures as the answer to questions before the questions are really understood. 'The answer should be Jesus' is certainly the way in which Christians incline to present religious problems, irrespective of whether it is credible and makes sense.

I start this reflection with a confession to make. I have no quick and easy answers for the questions raised by the Irish conflict. I do have a feeling in my bones that in some way 'the answer should be Jesus', but others may well decide that Jesus is the problem, rather than the answer. However Ireland is perceived, it must be recognized that it must enter a consideration of controversial issues. As I struggle for words to clothe my ideas, and for ideas to express my convictions, I become more and more aware that I am walking through a dangerous bog or a minefield where one false step may lead to my being drowned or blown up. But I do not despair for: 'I walk on thorns, but firmly, as among flowers ...'[1] – two lines from a poem quoted by Allan Boesak. What are the thorns? Where are the flowers? Perhaps together we will find them, keep our path clear of the thorns and rejoice in the beauty of the flowers.

At the outset I suggest that instead of attempting to cover 1500 years we may best proceed by looking at freedom and authority in three periods in Irish history, namely:

1. The fifth century, when Patrick planted the Christian faith in Ireland.
2. The sixteenth century, the time of the Reformation.
3. The 20-year period of the so-called Troubles from 1968 to 1988.

Hopefully, through our consideration of the first two of these periods we may understand something more about the third period.

THE PERIOD OF PATRICK

The beginnings of Christianity in Ireland are hidden in the mists of time, but they are particularly linked with the names of Palladius and Patrick. According to Patrick Corish, Professor of Modern History at Maynooth College, one date was firm beyond all doubt. Prosper of Aquitaine recorded in 431 that 'Palladius, ordained by Pope Celestine, is sent to the Irish believing in Christ as their first bishop'.[2] But then Palladius disappears, leaving Patrick the British evangelist in sole charge as the apostle of Ireland, and what we know of Patrick comes from his *Confession* and the letter to the soldiers of Coroticus. In these letters, Patrick speaks of himself in his own words,[3] and we learn from them that

> his mission is highly personal and highly successful. He preached to the limits of human habitation and baptized great numbers of people. Everywhere he ordained clerics to baptize and preach. He was quite fearless. He continually faced plots and dangers, and at least once was taken captive and in danger of his life.[4]

> By the middle of the sixth century, Christianity had become the dominant religion all over Ireland.[5]

Now Patrick believed that he brought freedom from heathenism to the Irish. This is reflected in his *Breastplate* (if Patrick wrote it).

> I summon today all those powers between me and these evils ...
> against incantations of false prophets
> against black laws of heathenry ...
> against craft of idolatry
> against spells of women and smiths and wizards.[6]

Against these Patrick calls on the power and authority of Christ to protect him and free him from all sorts of evil. The Apostles' Creed, which expresses faith in the Holy Trinity, is his standard of belief. The Scriptures are the source of his faith and his doctrine. Christ the true Son is his Lord; Christ who is the one who has forgiven him, and has called him to be a bishop and an evangelist. The faith which liberated Irish Christians like Patrick and brought them freedom was not validated by an ecclesiastical authority such as the Pope but was based upon their own experience. Their faith was not a narrow pietism but a total commitment which led to monastic life for some, though not for all. Indeed, some Christians spent part of their lives in a monastery and other parts in the secular world, an arrangement which made for strong links between the Churches and the wider society. For example, Cu Cuimne, the wise, who died in 747, was educated in a monastery, lived as a layman and returned to the cloister, and Patrick Corish quotes a short poem about him from the *Annals of Ulster*:

> Cu Cuimne in youth
> read his way through half the truth.
> He let the other half lie
> while he gave women a try.
> Well for him when in old age
> he became a holy sage.
> He gave women the laugh
> he read the other half.[7]

Corish reminds his readers of the way in which poems like this became gathered into great 'books of lore'. While much is legend and myth, there are 'islands of authenticity in the bog',[8] and he tells the story of St Moling.

> Once upon a time Moling was at prayers in his church and he saw a lad coming towards him, a goodly lad arrayed in purple raiment.
> 'Who art thou?', says Moling.
> 'I am Christ, Son of God', says he.
> 'I know not that', says Moling. 'When Christ would come to have speech with the Culdees, it was not in purple raiment or in kingly guise that he would come, but after the fashion of hapless men, as a leper or a man diseased.'[9]

So, many centuries before Christian Aid or Trócaire or Tear Fund were heard of, Irish Christians looked for Christ's presence in the poor. They learned to recognize him in the world's needy.

THE REFORMATION IN THE SIXTEENTH CENTURY

The Middle Ages saw developments in the organization of the Church in Ireland. The Synod of Rathbreasil in 1111 established a diocesan episcopate. A later synod at Inish-patrick in 1148 authorized Malachy, the Bishop of Connor and later Archbishop of Armagh, to travel to Rome to receive the papal pallium, which showed that an archbishop held his authority from the Pope. The Synod of Cashel in 1171 laid it down that the Church in Ireland should perform its sacred offices according to the usages observed by the Church of England. This exemplifies how in the Middle Ages every effort was made to anglicize the Church, and when the Reformation swept across Europe reform was an integral part of English policy in Ireland. Henry VIII became supreme head of the Church of Ireland; the monasteries were suppressed; the Prayer Book was imposed in English on a people who spoke Irish. The official *Directory* for public worship, adopted by the English parliament in 1645, was not translated into Irish.

> But perhaps the most serious obstacle in the way of those who wished to bring to Ireland the changes brought by the Reformation in England was the fact that in the eyes of the vast majority of the Irish people the Reformation was merely a further attempt by the English crown to extend its control over Ireland. Because of this, it was easy for the native leaders to convince the Irish people that by fighting for their faith, they were fighting for their freedom, and that the Established Church was another part of the English government, which was not content with ruling their bodies, but wanted to direct their souls also.[10]

Thus the Irish fought for their spiritual freedom, they recognized the authority of the Catholic hierarchy and hoped for the victory of the Catholic monarch, Philip II of Spain, over the Protestant Elizabeth. Elizabeth was excommunicated by Pius V in his papal bull *Regnans in Excelsis*, in which she was declared a heretic and a persecutor of true religion, and she was deprived of her pretended right to the throne. Sixtus V renewed the excommunication, relieved her of all royal rank and released her subjects from all sorts of allegiance.[11] He gave every blessing except money to the Armada that was to attempt to capture England and he supported Philip's view that an attack on England was God's work. I may add that I make reference to the Armada because 1988 was the four-hundredth anniversary of its defeat and of the sinking of the galleass *Girona* 15 miles from where I live, an event which was the subject of a special travel-ling exhibition. Sixtus supported Philip, who shared his hatred and dread of heresy which he regarded as subversive of everything he valued,[12] and who could not bring himself to recognize the rights of heretics to freedom of conscience. Thus the period of the Reformation ended with Western Christendom divided into two irreconcilable factions whose roots and origins are unmistakably theological and cultural; the antagonists sought and fought for freedom for their own view of the world and for authority to control the lives of their enemies. The scene was thus set for the flight of the Irish chiefs, O'Neill and O'Donnell, and for the plantation of their lands in Ulster by Scottish and English Protestants. The English having failed to win the hearts of the natives, the Irish were moved off to the hills and forests or fled into exile, and when the 1641 rising began in the north, it was put down by Cromwell and his soldiers, who were rewarded with large plots of land.

Thus 'by 1648 the religious map of Western Europe, as it would persist for 300 years, had taken shape'.[13] According to Owen Chadwick, 'the ill-temper of unprincipled men was encouraged by the narrow doctrines of the theologians'.[14] These doctrines were so narrowly defined that they excluded one side or the other from salvation. According to the Roman Catholic Church, a man could not be saved without the true and complete faith; and he could not believe the true and complete faith unless he believed the word of the infallible Church.[15] According to orthodox Calvinism, outside the visible Church there was no salvation, and a Christian had to be a member of a congregation where the Word was purely preached and the sacraments rightly administered. Neither of these virtues was to be found in the Roman Catholic Church, and so it was hard to see how a Roman Catholic could in a true sense be a member of the Church of Christ. In such a situation, 'fear trampled upon charity'.[16] In such a situation, Christians were no longer free to choose, and systems of ecclesiastical authority and rigid doctrine controlled the minds of the faithful. But living in such a divided and diverse situation, mutual tolerance eventually became possible. 'The states and churches of a divided Europe found in the end that they must tolerate or die',[17] a lesson which the Churches in Northern Ireland are only beginning to learn.

But before moving to the present day, it is important to stress how the clash of irreconcilable cultures has been perpetuated in Ireland over the past three centuries. According to Lyons,

> different cultures have collided because each has a view of life which it deems to be threatened by its opponents and power is the means by which a particular view of life can be maintained against its rivals. These views of life are founded upon religion because this is a region where religion is still considered as a vital determinant of everything important in the human condition and religion is vital because there have been in conflict three (latterly two) deeply conservative strongly opinionated communities each of whose churches still express what the members of those churches believe to be the truth.[18]

O'Farrell also sees the difference between the Irish and the English as being a dispute between rival world-views: 'In Catholicism the Irish could find the form, means and organisation to preserve and develop their ancient separate identity, their meaning and ultimate integrity.'[19] The Catholic religion became the depository for Irishness, while to be English was to be Protestant. O'Farrell agrees that the heart of the contemporary Irish conflict is religious. In Northern Ireland, 'at the core of everything lay religion, Reformation and Counter-Reformation confronting each other in intolerance as they had done for centuries'.[20]

Freedom and authority in Northern Ireland have thus come to mean freedom for me and for my tradition; freedom to worship in my way, freedom to believe in my God, freedom to march in my territory, freedom to fly my flag, freedom to proselytize for my clan, freedom to keep Sunday as my conscience dictates, freedom to view the world of nature and of grace through my spectacles. Authority in Northern Ireland means having power to practise and to enforce my version of freedom. This is authority in a broad sense: political authority, moral authority and religious authority. The authority over evil which Patrick possessed has now been overtaken and replaced by the more complex authorities of twentieth-century Church and state, which today are often in open conflict. And this brings us to the third and most difficult part of the chapter, which is concerned with the period of the Troubles, from 1968 to 1988. How have our contemporaries in Northern Ireland faced the questions of freedom and authority and what more can they do?

THE TROUBLES IN NORTHERN IRELAND 1968–88

In the first part of this chapter we saw how the British evangelist Patrick planted the Christian faith in Ireland and freed the native Irish from evil powers by the authority of Jesus and by the ministry of the Christian Church. In the second part, we looked at the period of the Reformation and we saw how reform was perceived by the English and by the Protestants as a victory for the cause of freedom. But this was a victory which divided the country into areas settled by the planters, largely in the province of Ulster, and those occupied by the Gaels. What was freedom for the Protestants was tyranny for the Catholics, and the way out of this impasse was the partition of Ireland in 1920 which gave rise to two theocratic states, a Catholic state south of the border and a Protestant state north of the border. Apart from partition there was little in the way of political development for 300 years until it became apparent that in the late twentieth century Northern Ireland could no longer operate as a Protestant state ruled by a Protestant government. This brings us up to the period of the present 'troubles' from 1968 to 1988, and what we have seen in this period is the death pangs of a monopolistic Protestant state and the birth pangs of some form of a pluralist society in which freedom is a reality for both religious/political traditions and in which authority is exercised fairly for all the members of that society. Death pangs and birth pangs are painful periods, since on both sides of the community there have to be concessions, willingness to see other people's points of view, accommodation, and compromise. We must recognize that the achievement of such a mature political outlook may be an impossible dream.

Prior to the exchanges associated with the present cease-fire, the most serious attempt to think these issues through was a series of five documents from 1985 to 1988 published together in 1989 under the title *Living the Kingdom* by an interchurch Group on Faith and Politics:[21] 'Breaking Down the Enmity', 'Understanding the Signs of the Times', 'A Declaration of Faith and Commitment', 'Towards an Island That Works', 'Towards Peace and Stability'. These papers are severely critical of those who absolutize political positions, and the writers argue that the Christian faith

> challenges all exclusive claims of tribe, tradition and political commitment. The Gospel invites us into the space created by Christ, and to find there those who were previously our enemies. It therefore breaks down the enmity between us – enmity caused by different traditions, and national, political and religious loyalties. The Gospel opens up for us a view

of wholeness, justice and living in right relations which sees the whole world as potential brothers and sisters. True politics may therefore be seen in the light of this vision as being the nourishing of humanness in corporate life, of finding ways of human beings living with each other.[22]

The group was equally opposed to those who demanded either a total commitment to loyalism or a total commitment to a united Ireland, and it considered what changes were necessary for the South to face the realities of the North. The group recognized the need for a political framework such as the Anglo-Irish Agreement and it argued that there was a need for movement beyond the Agreement and for the continuation of non-political action between voluntary agencies, community groups and churches.

A recurring theme in *Living the Kingdom* was the danger of an exclusive faith. It asks to what extent the Churches have defended an exclusive faith. It asks how this exclusive faith shows itself. Are Protestants who are 'born again' open to the possibility of the Holy Spirit working through Roman Catholics? Do Roman Catholics place too much emphasis on the 'One True Church'?[23] According to *Living the Kingdom*, Christians from both traditions are called to be signs of the Kingdom. This means 'that we work for new political situations in Northern Ireland in which the identity of both Nationalists and Unionists is respected and in which neither can dominate the other'.[24]

There are numerous other papers, books and pamphlets which have been published in the past 20 years and which can contribute to our understanding of the situation in Northern Ireland, too many even to mention by name. *For God and His Glory Alone*[25] is a particularly important contribution by evangelical Christians which relates some biblical principles to the situation in Northern Ireland. Some passages are noteworthy: 'As Evangelicals, we must accept our share of the blame for any way in which we have contributed to the alienation felt by many of the minority community in Northern Ireland.'[26] The group of evangelicals reject the identification of Unionism or Nationalism with the Christian faith:

> there are Evangelical Christians living on this island whose culture is British and whose political preference is for a continued link with Britain. Equally there are those whose culture is Irish and whose political preference is for a united Ireland. From the biblical viewpoint both are legitimate preferences.[27]

> Because God is a God of Justice, there cannot be anything other than a counterfeit peace when society is built on injustice. Any society which is influenced by Christian principles will be concerned with justice as a priority. Working for peace means working for justice.[28]

This is reflected in the many publications on Christianity in our context,[29] for instance, in *Religion and Politics in Contemporary Ireland* David Hempton explores the roots of the Northern Ireland problem by identifying seven wrong ways to think of the relationship between religion and politics, all of which are dangerous because they have at least a grain of truth in them. These are:

1. The Sin and Sit it out Philosophy: this is the idea that Christians should withdraw from the sinful world but save individual souls.
2. Unrealistic Liberalism: Christian love must not degenerate into wishful thinking and idealism.
3. The Politicization of the Gospel: Hempton is critical of the marriage of pseudo-Marxism and liberalism, and of the marriage in Ireland of religious establishment to a national identity.

4. Triumphalism and Tribalism: politics based on triumphalism and dominion can never produce respect and justice.
5. Equivocation over Violence: this ecclesiastical equivocation must be ended. Those who provoke violence are as guilty as those who engage in it.
6. The Politics of No Responsibility: it is wrong to try to allocate blame. The Churches have failed to educate the Irish people in political, social and moral matters.
7. The Search for the Holy Grail: in our search for answers, there is no rational step which is not open to fatal objections.

In opposition to faulty relationships between religion and politics, Hempton has five suggestions to make of a more positive nature:

● Our theology must be right and must take account of man's sin and God's grace.
● There is a need for penitence on the part of Protestants and Roman Catholics and penitence is both costly and risky.
● Facing up to our history. Irish people must face up to the problems of their own history with honesty and integrity.
● Acceptance of realities such as the border. Violence merely strengthens the resolve of Protestants not to surrender.
● The Churches must direct their attention to the quality of life in Church and society. 'For Christians it is absolutely imperative that grace, penitence, love and forgiveness should overcome violence, triumphalism, moral ambiguity and prejudice.'

We conclude this section with one final comment from Hempton:

> We are like two communities fighting over a loaf which has now become a pile of crumbs. There can be no lasting peace in this province, however ingenious the political initiatives might be, until the sectarian deadlock is broken.[30]

There lies the challenge to those who would make some contribution to the resolution of the issues of freedom and authority in Northern Ireland.

CONCLUSIONS

By way of drawing together the threads of my reflections, I would like to make three final points.

1. This matter is a concern for children from a young age as well as for adults. Dr Maurice Hayes, an eminent Roman Catholic, tells how his 6-year-old daughter played with another small girl. As they played, he heard the other child say 'Let's play Protestants: I want to be a Protestant'. On being asked why she wanted to be a Protestant, she replied 'I want to put her off the swings'.[31] Sectarian attitudes are learned early and penetrate deep. Research by Dr Roger Austin at the University of Ulster has shown how these attitudes and prejudices are learned and transmitted in games played in the school playground. Sectarian rhymes like the following are used to attack the other side's leaders or symbols:

> We're the boys from Londonderry
> F. the Pope and the Virgin Mary[32]

In their autobiographies Robert Harbinson[33] and Bernadette Devlin[34] further illustrate the ways in which 'the historico-mythic consciousness is handed on from one generation to the next complete with an entire environment of symbols ... before they reach the age of reason'.[35]

2. If it is a matter for children, it must also be a matter for schools and teachers, and reference must be made to *Violence in Ireland: A Report to the Churches*,[36] Greer and McElhinney[37] and Greer.[38] The importance of the school has at last come to be realized by educators in Northern Ireland and was made official policy by a Department of Education for Northern Ireland (DENI) Circular in 1982. This circular proclaimed that the whole educational system 'has clearly a vital role to play in the task of fostering improved relationships between the two communities in Northern Ireland'.[39] A number of projects had already adopted this policy before DENI took it on board, but this does not make the DENI policy statement any less welcome. Also to be welcomed is the guide to *Education for Mutual Understanding*[40] and the reference to education for mutual understanding as a required cross-curricular theme for all children in *Education Reform in Northern Ireland: The Way Forward*,[41] a document which set out Dr Brian Mawhinney's policy for education, also 'Cultural Heritage' – another cross-curricular theme. It is, however, a matter of regret that when the Shap Working Party was set up in 1969, its leaders visited Northern Ireland and organized conferences for teachers there, but it did not take firm root. I well remember the visits in the early 1970s by Ninian Smart, Donald Horder, Donald Butler and David Naylor. But somehow the time was not considered right for the world religions approach to RE. An opportunity was lost to promote the 'Lancaster approach' to the study of religion at all age levels, and one can only speculate what effect this approach might have had on education in general and on RE in particular if it had had greater success in the intervening period.

3. 'Freedom and authority in Northern Ireland' is a daunting challenge for anyone to face. Ciaran McKeown, one of the early Peace People, said to a journalist: 'Anyone who isn't confused here doesn't really understand what's going on.'[42] According to Denis Barritt: 'One could say of the people of Northern Ireland that they can find a problem to every solution.'[43] It was Dervla Murphy's views that 'The problem, as it now exists, is plainly insoluble. Can it then do any harm to think in terms of changing it instead of solving it?'[44] A reaction which involves an immediate sense of confusion may be a sign that the real difficulties are being understood. However that may be, I would ask that we stay with the insoluble issues as identified, rather than change them for something easier to handle. Let's walk on thorns, but firmly as among flowers.

NOTES

1. A. Boesak (1984) *Walking on Thorns*. Geneva: World Council of Churches.
2. P. Corish (1985) *The Irish Catholic Experience*. Dublin: Gill and Macmillan, p. 1.
3. J. Duffy (1975) *Patrick in His Own Words*. Dublin: Veritas.
4. Corish, *op. cit.*, p. 3.
5. *Ibid.*, p. 4.
6. *Ibid.*, p. 15.
7. *Ibid.*, p. 18.

8. *Ibid.*, p. 28.
9. *Ibid.*, p. 112.
10. K. Milne (1966) *The Church of Ireland*. APck, p. 34.
11. R. Stenuit (1972) *Treasures of the Armada*. Cardinal, p. 24.
12. G. Williams (1988) 'The most powerful monarch in Christendom'. In *Royal Armada 400 Years*. Manorial Research (Armada) Ltd, p. 136.
13. O. Chadwick (1964) *The Reformation*. Harmondsworth: Penguin, p. 366.
14. *Ibid.*, p. 367.
15. *Ibid.*
16. *Ibid.*
17. *Ibid.*, p. 398.
18. F. S. L. Lyons (1979) *Culture and Anarchy in Ireland 1890–1939*. Oxford: Clarendon Press, p. 144.
19. P. O'Farrell (1971) *Ireland's English Question*. London: Batsford, p. 12.
20. *Ibid.*, p. 302.
21. *Living the Kingdom* (1989) An Interchurch Group on Faith and Politics. For a summary of the argument in *Living the Kingdom*, see R. Boyd (1988) *Ireland*. Geneva: World Council of Churches, pp. 57–64.
22. *Living the Kingdom*, *op. cit.*, p. 5.
23. *Ibid.*, p. 39.
24. *Ibid.*, p. 53.
25. *For God and His Glory Alone* (1988) Evangelical Contribution on Northern Ireland.
26. *Ibid.*, p. 7.
27. *Ibid.*, p. 9.
28. *Ibid.*, p. 12.
29. Denis Barritt and Charles Carter (1962) *The Northern Ireland Problem*. London: OUP; Maurice Hayes (1984) *Why Can't They Be Like Us*. John Malone Memorial Lecture; Dervla Murphy (1984) *Changing the Problem: Post-forum Reflections*. Dublin: The Lilliput Press; Stanley Worrall (1984) *Testament of a Sojourner*. Queen's University Belfast; David Hempton (1983) Religion and politics in contemporary Ireland. *Journal of the Irish Christian Study Centre*, **1**, 23–24; John Morrow (1974) *The Captivity of the Irish Churches*. Audenshaw Paper no. 45; Roy Wallis, Steve Bruce and David Taylor (1986) *No Surrender! Paisleyism and the Politics of Ethnic Identity in Northern Ireland*. Department of Social Studies, Queen's University Belfast; Hans Küng (1986) *Church and Change: The Irish Experience*. Dublin: Gill and Macmillan; John Whyte (1978) Interpretations of the Northern Ireland problem: an appraisal. *Economic and Social Review*, **9**, no. 4; Presbyterian Church in Ireland (1977) *Pluralism in Ireland*; John Hickey (1984) *Religion and the Northern Ireland Problem* (1977). Dublin: Gill and Macmillan; Denis Barritt (1982) *Northern Ireland: A Problem to Every Solution*. Quaker Peace and Service; Eric Gallagher and Stanley Worrell (1982) *Christians in Ulster, 1968–1980*. Oxford: OUP; Ian Ellis (1985) *All Things New*. London: SPCK; *Northern Ireland: A Challenge to Theology* (1987) Occasional Paper no. 12, University of Edinburgh Centre for Theology and Public Issues; Cahal Daly (1984) *Communities Without Consensus*. Dublin: Irish Messenger Publications; Cahal Daly (1983) *Dialogue for Peace*. Dublin: Irish Messenger Publications; Patrick Buckland (1987) *The Northern Ireland Question 1886–1986*. The Historical Association.
30. Hempton, *op. cit.*, p. 30.
31. Hayes, *op. cit.*, p. 13.
32. R. Austin (1989) Playground culture in Northern Ireland. *Ulster Folk Life*.
33. R. Harbinson (1966) *No Surrender*, 2nd edn. London: Faber.
34. B. Devlin (1969) *The Price of My Soul*. London: Pan.
35. H. Grant (1987) Reconciliation in Northern Ireland. *Social Study Conference*, p. 6.
36. *Violence in Ireland: A Report to the Churches* (1970) Belfast: Christian Journals/Dublin: Veritas.
37. J. E. Greer and E. P. McElhinney (1985) *Irish Christianity: A Guide for Teachers*. Dublin: Gill and Macmillan.
38. J. Greer (1987) Bridge building in Northern Ireland. *The Furrow*, **38**, no. 7, 443–8.

39. Circular 1982/21 (1982) *The Improvement of Community Relations: The Contribution of Schools*. Belfast: Northern Ireland Office.
40. *Education for Mutual Understanding: A Guide*. Northern Ireland Council for Educational Development.
41. DENI (1988) *Education Reform in Northern Ireland: The Way Forward*. DENI.
42. C. McKeown (1984) *The Passion of Peace*. Belfast: Blackstaff Press, p. 72.
43. Barritt, *op. cit.*, p. 5.
44. Murphy, *op. cit.*, p. 16.

Although the author's illness has prevented further revision to this text beyond 1990, it remains highly illuminating of the background complexities involved in the 'peace process'.

Chapter 9

Freedom and Authority in Israel

John Levy

In the book of Numbers the story is told of the infamous prophet Balaam, known for his sorcery, who was hired to curse the children of Israel. Far from publicly cursing them, he praised them extravagantly.

> None hath held iniquity in Jacob,
> Neither hath one seen perverseness in Israel.

Pure hyperbole, of course. Ancient Israel did not wholly merit such praise, just as contemporary Israel, subject to intense and legitimate scrutiny, does not deserve equally exaggerated commendation – or the blanket condemnation voiced from some quarters.

The modern state of Israel is a polity blessed in many respects – creative, democratic, pluralistic. Yet it is also burdened by appalling internal dilemmas, and is situated in a tragic region where endemic tribal and national rivalries compound its domestic problems.

Any examination of the multiple establishments within Israel, and the degree of personal and communal free expression within the state, will therefore offer a complex and contradictory picture. The track record of Israel is both commendable and flawed.

THE ISRAEL SCENE: A BACKGROUND NOTE

It is essential to establish at the outset that Israel is not a simple and uniform society. By virtually every benchmark, Israel is a country of abundant extremes and diversities.

Its geographical contours set the scene. Though the whole country is about the size of Wales, the southern 60 per cent of Israel is mainly mountainous desert, its Negev citizens coping with arid, rainless conditions for 50 weeks per year; whilst northern Israel benefits from heavier rainfalls and a milder climate reflected in the greenery of the coastal plain and the Galilee. It can snow on Mount Hermon in the north at the very same time as holiday-makers bask in the desert heat of Eilat, by the Red Sea in the southernmost part of the country.

Israel's historic past has proved equally panoramic. Virtually every empire of the

Western world has either used Israel as the obvious land corridor between Europe, Africa and Asia, or seized the territory and incorporated it into empire. The meanest Israeli towns can display tens of layers of archaeological remains. Bet Shean, a struggling Israeli new town, can show the tourist over 20 layers of history in its 'backyard'. Jerusalem offers the visitor the archaeological record of over 40 civilizations.

Such a rich historic past translates today into a 'societal present' which is truly heterogeneous. Jews have lived *in situ* continuously for over 3000 years. Samaritans, now reduced in numbers to a mere 550 souls, have lived in Israel for 2500 years. Christianity, born out of Judaism, has maintained a varied cultural and religious presence for nearly 2000 years; and Islam has been a major force since the Arab invasion in the seventh century CE. Add the Druse and the Baha'is to the cultural–religious sum and Israel today presents the analyst with an extraordinary and subtle multi-cultural 'model'.

The model is especially complex, for none of these religious communities is cast in a single mould. The Jews have drawn on the traditions of communities formerly dispersed over a hundred different lands. Incoming refugees from Russia, Afghanistan and Ethiopia are significantly different in language, religious tradition and outlook from the Jews of Europe and the English-speaking countries.

Christian practice today falls into 35 denominational streams incorporating most of the Churches of the Western world and the establishments of the Eastern Communion. And whilst Islamic religious practice in Israel is predominantly Sunni, the social structure of the Arab population within Israel offers a spectrum of classes and tribes all in a state of rapid change, confirming once more that Israeli society cannot be superficially categorized.

The Millet system of authority structures

The Ottomans who ruled the area for 400 years (1517–1917) instituted the Millet system, whereby each religious community was permitted significant local autonomy.

Broadly, that same structure prevails today. Each religious community has complete control over all personal matters relating to births, marriages and deaths. In the deliberate absence of a civil, secular system, Jewish citizens of Israel have to use the services of the rabbinate, and Christian citizens the Church of their community of origin, as do Muslim, Druse, Baha'i and Samaritan Israelis respectively within their own communities.

The Government recognizes as having full legal standing the religious calendars of eight communities (Christian holy dates can in fact fall on three, not two, separate dates of the year in the Western, Orthodox and Armenian religious calendars); and the state devolves considerable legal authority to the religious courts of each community over the legal interpretation of disputes or rulings on personal issues.

Official funding for school building programmes and for the erection of places of worship is provided by the government of Israel, on an ongoing basis. To draw a parallel with the UK, the propriety of mother-tongue teaching and of denominational education which is so hotly debated in the UK would be regarded as a necessary and self-evident value in Israel!

The exercise of freedom

Given a society composed of so many interest groups, it is a major task of government to protect and support each authority system and establishment, and to keep good order, both between and within the sectional communities making up modern Israel.

On the whole, Israel has done a professionally creditable job. Despite appalling pressures – not least the strain of building a new nation in the face of unremitting military threats from the Arab world – Israel, i.e. the area within the 1967 cease-fire lines, has remained overwhelmingly liberal, social democratic and tolerant.

There is a clear national commitment to the prophetic values of the past, to the maintenance of a secular, political system, and to a robustly self-critical and democratic social order. The result is that each of the religious establishments can practise its faith freely within Israel; and the private individual can exercise personal freedom of speech and religion without let or hindrance. It is precisely because dissent and non-conformity is tolerated within Israel – a rare Middle Eastern phenomenon – that such cultural pluralism and personal freedom can flourish.

The public benchmarks of dissent are legion. Universal suffrage for all males and females over the age of 18, whatever their community of origin, is the norm. Each election offers multi-party choice – 27 groupings ranging from the CP Left to the near-Fascist Right bid for public favour in the November 1988 national elections. A vocal and independent press, active trade unions, a judiciary which has frequently reined in the executive, an energetic civil rights movement, a conscript army system which encourages the fullest critical examination of issues by officers and NCOs alike (where conscientious objection is virtually non-existent given the physical threats to Israel), and an education system which fosters and supports the fullest range of religious views results in a society which is vibrantly heterogeneous, where the individual citizen in broad terms is neither culturally shackled nor ideologically constrained.

National and locally elected officials in Israel, most particularly Teddy Kollek, Mayor of Jerusalem, have proven that Jewish and affirmatively Zionist politicians can govern Israel in the interests of all its citizens. The Jerusalem administration alone has spent literally millions of pounds repaving the Via Dolorosa, refurbishing many of Jerusalem's churches, providing funds – at the request of individual churches – for new church schools, and building a major exhibition centre on Islamic art – just one of dozens of social, educational, housing and cultural projects in the Arab areas of Jerusalem.

By their actions Kollek and other Israeli politicians have clearly recognized that Israeli society is culturally heterogeneous and have tried to fulfil the 1948 Declaration of Independence which pledged that the new state of Israel:

> will foster the development of the country for all its inhabitants, ensure complete equality of social and political rights for all its inhabitants irrespective of race, religion or sex, and guarantee freedom of religious conscience, language, education and culture, and safeguard the Holy Places of all religions.

PROBLEMS

But whilst fashioning a functioning, broadly peaceful, multicultural society in the Middle East is a significant achievement, maintaining its equilibrium is a continuing problem.

Vesting religious authorities with exclusive rights can all too easily lead to religious authoritarianism and fundamentalist and triumphalist excesses, traits all too evident on the Israel scene. In a region riven by power rivalries, the Israel picture becomes more problematic still.

Authoritarianism: the Jewish communal position

The founding fathers of Israel, most of whom were secular Jews, assumed that a continuation of the Millet system represented a viable *modus vivendi* with their Orthodox counterparts. Wishing neither to impose their secular views on the religious hierarchies, nor to cause offence, they resisted the temptation to establish a parallel secular apparatus for registering births, marriages and deaths. They intended to show due respect. As waves of fundamentalism have gathered strength in recent years and religious interest groups grown more strident, the secular have come to the conclusion that they have in fact created their own religious Golem (monster).

The Jewish situation graphically illustrates the problem. In Israel today, over 81 per cent of the total population is Jewish, nearly 20 per cent being described as strictly Orthodox, and 50–60 per cent as religiously traditional.

All religious power in the Jewish community is vested in the hands of the Orthodox establishments. The Ministry of Religious Affairs, the Ashkenazi and Sephardi chief rabbis, urban chief rabbis and their religious councils are all drawn from Orthodox circles – and are almost entirely male.

Though rigorous debate over all issues is the hallmark of Orthodox Judaism – and there are a number of outstandingly visionary and independent thinkers amongst the Orthodox rabbinate in Israel – the Orthodox establishment in action has proven ultra-conservative and ever more aggressive and socially intrusive in its broad demands.

By law, an Orthodox Jewish rabbi has to handle all issues relating to births, marriages and deaths, even if the Israeli citizens involved are wholly secular in outlook. Liberal and Reformed congregations exist in Israel for worship, but their rabbis have no legal authority and the ideas of the Progressives are anathema to the Orthodox establishment.

Orthodox women feel as discriminated against as Progressive Jews. Denied representation on elected local religious councils, some have taken their legal battles to the higher, secular courts. Judgements on the whole range of marriage and divorce issues brought before the religious courts have further distressed both Orthodox and secular women in Israel. The male rabbinate establishment has shown itself to be male-centred, anti-feminist and illiberal.

Religious revivalism – a conspicuous feature of all the communities in Israel – has been given powerful new direction with the formation of a clutch of Jewish religious political parties in recent years. All their political platforms concentrate on demands for stricter public observance of sabbath, festival and religious moral disciplines. In the Knesset (Parliament) and at local demonstrations, Orthodox groups have lobbied for a ban on El Al flights on sabbaths and festivals, for cinemas, football matches and road traffic to be banned on such days, for advertising campaigns featuring glamorous models to be suspended, and for the legal definitions of 'who is a Jew' for the purposes of immigration registration and marriage to be ever more narrowly circumscribed.

No doubt acting with the best of motives, the Orthodox establishment has in practice bitterly divided Israel, and set Orthodox and secular on a collision course. Inevitably, the arms of the secular state – Parliament, the legal system and the police – have had to be activated to calm inflammatory situations.

One incident involved a Jewish belly-dancer who discovered that all her bookings in Jerusalem were cancelled as a result of pressure on local hoteliers by the Jerusalem rabbinate. She took her complaint to law and the courts ruled against the rabbinate. It transpired that the rabbinate had attempted to stop belly-dancing in local hotels by threatening to withdraw the kosher certificate of hotels hiring such dancers. The courts ruled that such threats far surpassed the legal authority of the rabbinate, which purely covers supervision of kosher catering facilities.

The Orthodox rabbinate lost the 'belly button battle' – but won the war with El Al over flying schedules. Other points of contention will inevitably emerge in future.

It must be stressed that the religious communities of Israel are neither monolithic in thought or action nor wholly reactionary. The political mobilization of the devout is, however, proving tragically divisive. Far from offering the Jewish public an inspirational lead, many of the Orthodox and their rabbis are widely perceived as exploitative, as authoritarian, and as limiting the freedoms and civil rights of the Jewish citizens of Israel.

Strident triumphalism

The rigid interpretation of religious norms, which is not a phenomenon just limited to Jewish Israelis, is aggravated by a more dangerous current still in the Middle East – a crude triumphalism which affects all the faith communities in the region.

On the Jewish side, triumphalism has emerged in the form of a superstitious primitivism, a crude religiosity which attributes any disaster or mishap to a lack of scrupulous religious conformity. Following the death of a group of school children whose bus was struck by a train on an unmanned crossing, Rabbi Peretz, a leading Sephardi rabbi/politician, remarked that their death was the result of a general lack of sabbath observance in Israel.

Equally bizarre and, it must be added, marginal was the public comment of the Sephardi Chief Rabbi of Bat Yam, a town near Tel Aviv, that 'Hitler destroyed the Ashkenazi Jews of Europe because of their atheism. Hitler was an emissary of the Almighty and was ordered to spare Sephardi Jews because of their loyalty to Torah.'

Triumphalism has also taken shape in the politico-religious fanaticism of a small but determined segment of the ultra-Orthodox. Believing the cause of Israel to be absolutely just, some have opted for the most militant response to Arab terrorism. Arab violence has been met with equal ruthlessness and violence. The underground cells of such Jewish religious militants are tiny in number. Their willingness to attack Arabs, or Jewish Israelis in the peace camp dubbed by them as traitors, clearly poses a direct challenge to the democratic order in Israel.

Other militants – often men and women newly returned to Orthodox practice – have pressed for total Jewish control of the Old City of Jerusalem; and, in the case of Birkhat HaCohanim (the Temple Mount Faithful), for the replacement of the Muslim shrines on Temple Mount by a rebuilt Third Hebrew Temple.

Their activities have produced calamitous clashes between Jews, Christians and Muslims in the Old City of Jerusalem. The Jewish majority emphatically condemns their actions but this determined minority clearly believes that 'God is on their side'.

Muslim fanaticism

Islamic triumphalism presents a similar threat to the balance of good order.

In recent years, the Islamic revival has been as evident in Israel as in other parts of the Middle East. New programmes of mosque building and the presence of large numbers of young women, as well as men, in traditional clothing rather than Western styles of dress reflects the general trend towards newly rediscovered religiosity.

This return-to-faith in itself is to be welcomed. However, support for the Iranian Islamic revolution and for its politico-religious triumphalism is far more alarming. In both Israel and the territories governed by Israel, Islamic fundamentalists are politically on the march.

In the major Israeli town of Umm El Fahm, 11 of the 15 seats in the March 1990 local elections were won by the new Islamic Movement. In Nazareth, the largest Arab town in Israel, one-third of the seats were won by the Movement. Their ideology is similar to the platform of Sheikh Ahmed Yassin and the Hamas-Islamic Resistance Movement – which has formed in the Gaza Strip. Sheikh Yassin's words make chilling and unambiguous reading:

> The land of Palestine is an Islamic trust left to the generations of Muslims until the day of resurrection. It is forbidden for anyone to yield or cede part or all of it.

> The solution to the Palestine problem will only take place by Jihad/Holy War. Initiatives and an international conference only waste time.

> It is not enough to have a state in the West Bank and Gaza. The best solution is to let all – Christians, Muslims and Jews – live in Palestine in an Islamic State.

> The Zionist invaders were never a people. The Jews are not a people.

> Degradation was decreed for the Jews wherever they may be because they kindled the anger of Allah.

Such statements deepen the confrontation lines between Arab and Jew.

Christian extremism

Today Christians in Israel are hopelessly enmeshed in the religio-political conflict of wills.

Like Jews and Muslims, the Christians of the Holy Land have produced their idiosyncratic triumphalisms. The tourist sees a spectacular panorama of denominations spanning the divergent practice of Churches of the West and the dozens of Church establishments forged in the East. In practice, personal and ideological rivalries have marred Church history in the Holy Land – the poaching of members being the very least aspect of this competition. The state of Israel has had to cope with repeated acts of petty vindictiveness – the competing triumphalisms of Ethiopians unilaterally changing locks on passageway doors to frustrate the Coptic Christians; Greek Orthodox and

Armenian monks openly fighting in Manger Square over the 'privilege' of clearing up the litter after the Christmas celebrations; armed Armenians at loggerheads over the appointment of a new Orthodox Patriarch.

It has been a major charge on the Christian Affairs Office of the Ministry of Religious Affairs in Jerusalem to ensure that all the conventions of Christian religious practice – and there is a detailed corpus of guidelines and timetables – are followed to the letter; and, when they are contravened, to calm inter-Church tensions.

The outbreak of the Intifada in December 1987 stilled most of these rivalries. Political events have put pressure on Christians in the Holy Land, most of whom are Arab. The pressure on individual Christians and on their Church authorities has been enormous. The fear of fundamentalist Islam, crude intimidation and the injury or deaths of Arab Christians in the rising have created a new Jewish–Christian divide in the Holy Land.

Christians today are frightened. An increasing number of Christian religious sites have been damaged by Muslim fundamentalists. This is particularly true in the Bethlehem area where, for example, the Carmelite monastery walls have been daubed with 'Islam will win' slogans and a PLO flag suspended from the cross; and similar incidents have taken place in Gaza.

In early April 1990, over 200 masked Palestinian Muslims broke into the Greek Patriarchate, and grabbed the Patriarch Diodorus, one yelling 'Traitor! You have sold our property.' Others hoisted the PLO flag on the Patriarchate roof. Not surprisingly, a major confrontation and disturbance followed shortly thereafter at a hospice in the Christian quarter which had been sold to a fundamentalist Jewish group.

Notwithstanding the protection of Christian sites and Christian religious practice afforded by Israel, many Palestinians are now fearful that the threat voiced in Lebanon 'to get the Sunday people once the Saturday people have been dealt with' may be realized by Israel. Many are selling up and leaving the Middle East. Others with varying degrees of stridency now seek acceptance by the Palestinian Arab national camp. Demands for 'peace and justice for the Palestinians' are repeated almost like a catechism.

One clear outcome of such polarization is the disastrous deterioration in Jewish–Christian dialogue. With so little mutual trust, and disagreement on so many points of principle, many of the Christian–Jewish frameworks in Israel have virtually ceased to function.

WHAT THEN OF FREEDOM AND AUTHORITY?

Middle East conflict inevitably undermines the attempt to fashion a multicultural order in Israel, though it has not succeeded in stifling this rare condition. Nothwithstanding external threats, most casual visitors to Israel note the surprising absence of tension within Israel and a normalcy in everyday life.

The images of war are equally prevalent, however. Armed soldiers, male and female, in every setting in Israel, are omnipresent. Conflict between Israel and the Arabs and the pressure from inter-Arab rivalries in the region directly impinge on every citizen in Israel, for as the country has universal conscription (other than for Muslim citizens of the country), everyone is forced to confront profound existential questions. The harsh reality is that Arabs and Jews in Israel are affected by their world to a degree not experienced by the average individual citizen in the UK. Six Arab–Israeli wars in 43 years, and endless rounds of terror, violence and the involvement of outside powers – some openly threatening Israel with annihilation – force the private Israeli to consider the local situation as a personal concern.

The responses of Israelis to these problems and dilemmas are as numerous as the range of traditions in the country. There are reactionary and progressive ideas, the benign and the unremittingly hawkish, voices urging a suspension of civil rights and steadfast defenders of the democratic *status quo*, voices urging the 'beating of swords into ploughshares' and others offering harsher prescriptions to those threatening to drive Israel into the sea.

Inevitably, any incident in the tragic cycle of violence, Arab killing Jew, or Jew Arab, only deepens the distance and mutual suspicion between Arab and Jew.

How then can the multicultural equilibrium be safeguarded? The fragile response has to be that as long as Israel remains a heterogeneous society and the arguments of its citizens and establishments profoundly contradictory, in democratic interplay, there remain firm grounds for hope.

Alongside the rancorous voices advising the mailed-fist approach, there are many others urging greater sensitivity – the rabbi arguing that 'it does not help to uproot your neighbour's tree', the right-wing Minister of Justice placing severe limits on new powers of control and detention requested by the army; and the chief Israeli military legal officer reminding soldiers that they operate under an unequivocal moral obligation to act responsibly and cannot, like the Nazis, claim the exemption of 'simply obeying orders'. Such moral imperatives are frequently given expression in Israel even though, tragically, the moments of collision and breakdown occur.

As long as Micah's prophetic charge to Israel, 'What doth the Lord require of you – only to do justly, to love mercy and to walk humbly with your God', remains the social imperative in Israel, there is at least the hope that personal liberty and freedom and the network of religious, cultural and ethnic authorities within Israel will each remain true to their own witness. Then the words of Balaam will fully reflect on the state of Israel: 'How goodly are thy tents, O Jacob, thy dwelling places, O Israel.'

FURTHER READING

Bergen, Kathy, *et al.* (1991) *Justice and the Intifada: Palestinians and Israelis Speak Out*. New York: Friendship Press.
British Council of Churches (1982) *Towards Understanding the Arab Israeli Conflict*. London: BCC.
Ellis, Marc H. (1990) *Beyond Innocence and Redemption: Confronting the Holocaust and Israeli Power. Creating a Moral Future for the Jewish People*. New York: Harper and Row.
Jakobovits, Immanuel (1984) *'If Only My People ...': Zionism in My Life*. London: Weidenfeld and Nicolson.
Lipman, Beata (1988) *Israel: The Embattled Land. Jewish and Palestinian Women Talk About Their Lives*. London: Pandora.
Marx, Emanuel (ed.) (1980) *A Composite Portrait of Israel*. London: Academic Press.
Nakhleh, Khalil and Zureik, Elia (eds) (1980) *The Sociology of the Palestinians*. London: Croom Helm.
O'Brien, William V. (1991) *Law and Morality in Israel's War with the PLO*. London: Routledge.

Rubinstein, Amnon (1984) *The Zionist Dream Revisited: From Herzl to Gush Emunim and Back.* New York: Schocken.

Said, Edward (1980) *The Question of Palestine.* London: Routledge.

Ye'Or, Bat (1984) *The Dhimmi: Jews and Christians under Islam.* London: Associated Universities Press.

The text of this chapter was completed before the formal peace negotiations between Israel and the PLO got underway. Though the end product might well be quite different if writing on it were to begin now, the picture conveyed remains authentically that of a critical enthusiast for Israel.

Part Two

Religious Education

Chapter 10

Freedom and Authority in Religious Education

John Hull

In relationship to religious education (RE), we are creators; in relationship to religion, we are creatures. We make RE; in religions we learn that we are made. We thus have authority over RE but religion has authority over us. Religion is revealed; RE is only enacted.

This is the contrast which seems to establish the difference between theology and education as a whole, and between religion and RE in particular. Theology (we often think) is given; education is contrived.

The purpose of this chapter, however, is to challenge this distinction. Both parts of it are exaggerated: religion is more of an artefact than we sometimes think, and RE less. The contrast between the two sides of the antithesis can only be obtained by falsifying each. The argument will show not only that the distinction is false, but that the appeal of the distinction itself, its taken-for-granted quality in much religious thinking, springs from a kind of falseness. This falseness in turn affects the kinds of authority which are attributed to religion and RE.

ALIENATED AUTHORITY

I can be alienated from my friend but not from my enemy. Alienation implies a bond. In alienation that which we ourselves have produced is estranged from us. In extreme forms of alienation, we are actually made by those objectified realities which stand over against us, and the height of alienation is when this curious inversion of the truth is actually affirmed in conscious thought. In such situations, the alienated products of our own creativity claim authority over us.

Leaving political structures aside, the three principal modern forms of modern alienated authority are the commodity, the media and religion. The commodity occupies a central position in modern consumer societies. Commodities attract our desire and mould our desire at the same time. They both define and enshrine the pleasures which make life worth living. They appear before us as if created by nature to perfectly match our needs.[1] The media also possess authority to define the significant. A great deal of

this authority is obtained through the apparent objectivity – we should say the objectivization – which gives them the quality of natural presentation. The rises and falls of
temperature, governments and share prices are all announced in the same factual
manner. This is what things are like.[2] The intentions and interests behind the production
of commodities and commercials are disguised and forgotten.

Beside these characteristically contemporary forms of alienation is the third, the
classic example of human inability to recognize human productivity: religion. There is,
however, a significant difference. In the commodity and the media the externalized
authority is not made explicit. Our attention is not drawn to it because its power lies in
its unexamined naturalness. With religion, on the other hand, the objectivization of
authority is not only highly articulate but self-proclaimed and self-defined. Ideations
such as revelation and inspiration crystallize the apparently non-human structure, giving
it an *a priori* quality, a sort of numinous, analytic[3] quality.

The very fact that the commodity and the media conceal the source and nature of
their authority while the religions affirm theirs, often in shrill tones, is in itself not
without significance. In spite of the contrasts between them, these forms of modern,
alienated authority are essentially complementary and interlocking. Together they create
a complex which is so all-pervading that we may speak not only of examples of alienation but of alienated existence.

DIALECTICAL THINKING

Consciousness depends on contrast. We know that we sleep because we awaken. Before
the contrast there is the world of undifferentiated one-ness. At first the baby does not
have a world; he or she *is* a world.[4] This and that appear. Self and not-self emerge.
There is speech and speaker, thought and thinker. We shall call this quality of thought
its dialectical aspect.

The dialectical quality of thinking has been emphasized by modern philosophy
(Hegel) and psychology (Piaget). Piaget saw patterns of thought as passing through a
series of equilibrations when a balance between inner and outer worlds had been
achieved. In the work of Hegel, dialecticity had become a principle being worked out in
the history of human culture and spirituality, but Piaget emphasized that dialectical
qualities of thinking do not arise merely at the ideational level but are the result of
interaction between the growing person and the world. For Piaget, dialecticity was
genetic, developmental and environmental, being necessarily concrete before it could be
abstract. Even in its abstract form it remains the linguistic refinement of concrete
experience.

In their emphasis up⟩n work, the mutuality of the exchange between human beings
and environments, and the impact of this exchange upon patterns of thinking there is
much in common between Jean Piaget and Karl Marx.[5] Hegel had already shown that
social contrasts such as that between the lord and the serf could be tolerated by being
denied or rationalized, and had interpreted this as a sort of denial of dialecticity. The
consciousness of the serf, even if it became a happy consciousness through religion,
was false because the true impact of the disparity of power between the serf and lord
had been denied.[6] Nevertheless, it was the Marxist understanding of the relationship
between ideas and work (praxis) and the application of this to the psychology and soci-

ology of politics which has most in common with the approach of Piaget, and no doubt both Marxist and Piagetian influences are significant in the changed relationship between subject and object which is such a feature of recent developments in method, whether in the natural or the social sciences.

The results of this change in scientific method in recent decades are well known. Facts are already embedded within theories; observation and interpretation are intermingled. The impact of a dialectical relationship between the knower and the known has been so great that for years philosophers of science have been describing any other view as a kind of naive objectivization.[7] It can now be seen that the positivistic science, especially of the nineteenth century, with the inexorable logic of its accumulation of facts, its ignorance of its own social and cultural function and its claims of normative knowledge, was in itself a striking example of alienation.[8] That which had been created by human beings stood over against the human mind as an unanswerable truth. Again we see how it is that when dialecticity is denied, that which stands over against human life as an unqualified authority becomes suffused with sacred power. Science became a religion, and evoked the commitment of total loyalty from its worshippers.[9]

NON-DIALECTICITY

Dialectical thinking is healthy because the mind is situated in a world. Not only does that keep thinking material, relative and incarnate but it retains the possibility that the relationship between mind and world will itself become an object of perception, thus making it possible to think about thinking. A mind enclosed within itself is given over to stereotypes, illusions of absoluteness, and egocentricity. As the literature on cognitive pathology shows, mental processes which lack the dialectic are incapable of realistic self-criticism or of methodological enquiry.[10] Instead, they revert into brooding, fantasizing[11] and repetition. It remains true, however, that non-dialectical thought possesses authority. It is authoritative just because it is non-negotiable, and it is non-negotiable because it exists in a world filled with nothing but mirror images of its own projections.

As examples of non-dialectical thought we may take racism, tribalism, all forms of national totalitarianism, and certain mental illnesses such as schizophrenia. It has often been pointed out that all of these conditions, whether collective or individual, have common characteristics. They tend to exaggerate space and to fracture time.[12] They tend to offer a strong sense of identity by marking a sharp boundary beyond which there lies the other – the alien other.[13] They concentrate goodness within whilst evil is expelled to the outside. They are all naturalistic, presenting themselves as rooted in biology, be this natural evolution, or the mystic realities of blood and soil, and they tend to arise as simplifying reactions to crises.[14] If the crisis should deepen, they become forms of 'delirious perception',[15] taking on qualities of absolute succour and ultimate demand, infused with a sort of generalized moral value which produces an inner sense of righteousness which justifies an ever more devout commitment to an ever more elevated authority. The delirious quality will become ecstatic in paroxysms of violence.

REIFICATION AS A PROCESS OF NON-DIALECTICAL THINKING

Reification is the cognitive result of projection. In projection, we attribute to others the emotions and intentions we ourselves have; in reification, ideas which are the products of our personal and social lives become independent of us. A reified idea has a false life of its own. There may, of course, be a real object which corresponds to the reification. In reification, however, perception becomes deductive, i.e. controlled by the inner world of the perceiver. Reification is the cognitive aspect of alienation which thus describes the situation of the one whose life has become more or less ruled by reifications. The objects of reification are absolute, one-dimensional, fascinating or even hypnotic, and the relationship of the thinker to them is non-dialectical. Although the concept of reification has some use in the interpretation of cognitive disorders such as schizophrenia, it is mainly used to describe concepts which have a social base. Reification is typically the product of a social group, a collectivity.

There is always an element of falseness about reification, possibly self-deception. This may take the form of inversion (as when that which we have made is thought of as having made us) or of taking the part for the whole. In the latter case, the reification has something in common with a fetish, although the latter is a concept drawn from religious studies and psychoanalysis, while the former is drawn from the sociology of knowledge and cognitive psychology.[16]

THE PART-WOMAN AND THE PART-GOD: AN EXAMPLE OF NON-DIALECTICAL IMAGERY

The pornographic image has a fetish-like quality. The part is taken for the whole, and there is an addictive aspect, in that arousal becomes increasingly difficult without pornographic aid. The pornographic image also has definite features of reification: it is a stereotype, it is depersonalized, and it represents a kind of abstract perfection with whom there can be no real relationship. Relationship is unnecessary to fulfilment, and the pornographic image offers its devotee a fulfilment which is both authoritative and egocentric.

Relations with the part-God have a similar intensity. In the fetish-like image of God the part is taken for the whole, there will be no development of the relationship, and there will be powerful impulses towards repetition. In their reified form, the images of God perform social functions which are concealed from the devotee; for example, in adoring God the devotee is adoring his or her race, nationality, tradition or identity. It is a noticeable feature of relationships with reified images that there is a powerful sense of otherness – the masturbator before the pornographic image 'forgets' that he or she is masturbating, so effective is the sense of erotic otherness, and the worshipper of the reified and fetish-like God-image has a similar sense of ecstatic otherness which produces nothing but a state of inner aesthetic spirituality, exhausting itself in egocentric bliss. In both cases the reified authority will have blissful qualities which will be (in the case of religion at any rate) defended in the name of individualism.

It should also be noted that the blissful egocentricity which is characteristic of the pornographic image and the reified divine image is also a characteristic of the relationship between the modern consumer and the beautiful and desirable artefact. This has been frequently discussed in the literature on the sociology and psychology of shopping.

The falsity of pornography can be seen in contrast to the true nature of human sexuality, which is not called intercourse for nothing. It is one of our profound forms of mutuality and takes place in concrete relationship to the world, where each is the world to and in the other. Wherever woman is worshipped without actual relationship (or man as the case may be) the result may well be pornographic. A similar thing happens in the religious realm wherever God is worshipped apart from the kingdom of God and the mission of God.

AUTHORITY IN DEVELOPMENTAL PERSPECTIVE

Up to this point we have been examining false forms of authority springing from alienated existence. We have described these forms of authority as the reified expressions of social realities often fed by individual needs, sparked off by a combination of personal and social crisis. We have noticed that these alienated forms of authority are non-dialectical, and we have argued that loss of dialectical quality is a feature of reified authority.

It would be a mistake to believe that one can pass directly from 'false' authorities to a 'true' authority. While it is true in general that all false authority is non-dialectical, there is no sharp break between the dialectical and the non-dialectical. Authority, like dialecticity, takes many forms. Moreover, just because the non-dialectical does exercise a strange kind of authority over us, we cannot necessarily conclude that the dialectical is devoid of authority. Perhaps mutuality has its own authority. By thinking about authority in terms of non-dialecticity and alienation, however, an attempt has been made here to point to an essential feature of all authentic authority, namely, its mediated quality is not denied. Authority is false when it is experienced as confronting the self in an external, objectified manner. It is the process of reification which abolishes mediation and gives authority its mysterious numinosity.

Mediations may be social and political, or they may be autobiographical and religious. Education operates through the mediations, and is itself one of them. The approaches to authority within any religious tradition will be many and various, and it would be possible to study the way in which historical factors in the development of doctrine have mediated the doctrines of authority, or the authority of the entire doctrinal system, in certain ways. From the point of view of the educator, however, the mediations exhibited within the religious tradition itself remain at the level of content. In order to give us a theory of education and an actual teaching technique, we must turn from theological mediations *per se* to the social and individual context. In the first few pages of this chapter, various aspects of modern culture were taken as mediations of authority. We must now turn to human development itself as an important mediating influence.

AUTHORITY AS A COMPOSITION

The study of authority has attracted the attention of cognitive psychologists. This is because the way in which authority is construed is generally reckoned as involving cognitions regarding truth, kinds of evidence, credulity, autonomy and other attributes which are relevant to styles of cognitive operations. One of the most influential workers in this field is the American William G. Perry, whose studies of the development of epistemological reasoning in American college and university students lies behind much of the work in justice reasoning done by Lawrence Kohlberg and in faith development by James W. Fowler and Sharon Parks.[17]

Perry was particularly interested in the impact which their studies made upon students in higher education and how students developed not only in academic but in ethical maturity. Perry distinguishes nine basic positions with respect to authority. The fourth position is subdivided into 4A and 4B, and between each position there is a transitional period. Each position and each transition is illustrated by a typical response, so altogether there are 20 typical statements (bearing in mind that there is a transitional statement between positions 4A and 4B). Each of the positions (including 4A and 4B) is given a label; thus there are ten labels. The whole process is grouped into three broad phases of development.

The first developmental phase is called *dualism modified*. Before this phase even begins, we have the first position, which could be called 'dualism unmodified' or 'uncritical dualism'. The dualism which Perry has in mind is that of an absolute distinction between the knower and the known, such that knowledge is absolutely transcendent, it is objectified over against the knower as being authoritative, unchangeable and simply true. Authority, in other words, is absolutely external to the self; self and truth are at opposite poles. Perry labels position one 'basic duality' and illustrates it with the following statement: 'authorities know, and if we work hard, read every word, and learn right answers, all will be well'. The transition from this is 'but what about those others I hear about? and different opinions and uncertainties? Some of our own authorities disagree with each other, or don't seem to know, and some give us problems instead of answers.' We see that the breakdown of absolute authority begins with exposure to conflict and contradiction.

The second position is labelled *multiplicity pre-legitimate*. We observe that characteristic of this first phase is the appearance of multiple authorities. The experience of pluralism is vital in educating people in authority-reasoning. The first few positions are arranged according to the way in which the student handles the experience of multiplicity. At first, the multiplicity is regarded as being deceptive: 'True authorities must be right. The others are frauds. We remain right; others must be different and wrong. Good authorities give us problems so we can learn to find the right answer by our own independent thought.' We notice that the student finds an educational explanation for the difficulties that he or she is meeting. The good teacher, it is now thought, does not want us to accept the right answers on authority, but to work them out for ourselves. The introduction of problems and multiple possibilities is a pedagogical device, a way of making us think. Behind this, however, there remains the one single true authority all the time. The transitional case is 'but even good authorities admit they don't know all the answers yet'. The position begins to break down when the educational theory is contradicted by the self-confessed ignorance of the teachers. The student wonders whether this is, in turn, just an educational ploy or whether the teachers really mean it.

In position 3, *multiplicity subordinate*, a way has been found of organizing the conflict which goes beyond interpreting it as mere pedagogical tactics. What organizes the multiplicity is the concept of progressive knowledge, or an ongoing research programme. The position is called 'subordinate' because the multiplicity is still held to be subordinate to the residual image (from the first position) of an absolute and unified authority which will triumph in the end. We might call this a kind of eschatological view of authority: 'Then some authorities and differences of opinion are real and legitimate temporarily, even for authorities. They are working on them to get to the truth.' This third position begins to break down when there is what we might call a sort of eschatological delay. The conviction gradually dawns on the student that the eschatological explanation does not provide for a working approach to life's problems. It is too remote. 'But there are so many things they don't know the answer to, and they won't, for a long time.'

The fourth position straddles the end of phase 1 (*dualism modified*) and the start of the second phase (*relativism discovered*). The fourth is transitional, but it is divided into a first part and a second part with its own transitional period. During this important stage a new way of organizing conflict emerges. All hankering after an absolute and final truth is abandoned, at least in the form understood by the student at the first phase. A reaction sets in which takes the thinker to the opposite pole: acute individualism, or subjective relativism. Perry uses the expression 'solipsism', suggesting that a revival of egocentricity has occurred, in which the mind falls back upon itself, the external authority having failed, it turns inwards to its own isolated experience. The label for position 4A is *multiplicity (solipsism) co-ordinate*. Here the multiplicity is no longer made subordinate to a final, absolute truth, but various views are co-ordinated by a theory of individual subjectivity. 'Where authorities don't know the right answers, everyone has a right to his or her own opinion. No one is wrong.' The transitional is 'but some of my friends ask me to support my opinions with facts and reasons' or it may take the more rebellious form: 'then what right have *they* to grade *us*?'

Just as the first phase dealt with the different ways in which diversity was handled, so the second main phase (from position 4A onwards) is concerned with how relativity is handled. The same techniques are used as had previously been used for the organization of diversity. Thus we find, first of all, *relativism subordinate*. Now relativity is no longer co-ordinated according to simple or naive individual's subjectivity, as in 4B, but in accordance with a new principle, that of evidence. 'In certain courses, authorities are not asking for the right answer. They want us to think about things in a certain way, supporting opinion with data. That is what they grade us on.' In other words, the authority is no longer the simple, naked authority of an absolute, converging truth, but is the authority of evidence. Thus there are different kinds of authority, just as there are different kinds of evidence. This leads into the next position when it is generalized: 'but this way seems to work for most courses and even outside them'.

This tendency to generalize the contextual nature of authority is fully articulated in position 5: 'then all thinking must be like this, even for them. Everything is relative but not equally valid. You have to understand how each context works. Theories are not truth but metaphors to interpret data with. You have to think about your thinking.' With this fifth position, the second phase, *relativism discovered*, comes to its climax and begins to break down with the transitional 'but if everything is relative, am I relative too? How can I know I am making the right choice?'

With position 6 we commence the final phase of the development of what I am calling authority-reasoning. This final phase is called *commitments in relativism developed*. Here a synthesis is attempted between the idea of an absolute authority unrelated to the self, and the opposite idea of individual relativism. The focus now turns towards the authority of commitment, or the nature of commitment to authoritative truth. The problem now is how commitment is to be handled, and the positions deal with various ways in which commitment is transformed. Position 6 is labelled *commitment foreseen* and the example is 'I see I am going to have to make my own decisions in an uncertain world with no one to tell me I am right'. The transitional is 'when I decide on my career or marriage or values, everything will straighten out'. Once again, we have a kind of eschatological deferment, what Erik H. Erikson would have called 'the moratorium'. The young adult at this stage is still naive about the nature of fully mature adult life. It is still seen as a period of stability on the far side of commitment.

Initial commitment is the label given to position 7 with the example 'well, I have made my first commitment' with its transitional 'why didn't that settle everything?' The eschatological hypothesis has once again collapsed, and we have now reached the point where, as Robert Kegan puts it, the self emerges from the position where it *is* an administrating institution to the position where it *has* an administrating institution.[18]

This is why position 8 is labelled *orientation in commitments*: 'I have made several commitments; I have got to balance them. How many? How deep? How certain? How tentative?' Here, instead of authorities external to the self being co-ordinated by some means or other, beyond the control of the student, a variety of authorities are being administered by the student herself or himself. The transition from stage 8 is marked by 'things are getting contradictory. I can't make logical sense out of life's dilemmas.'

We may compare the stage reached by position 8 with the crisis which Erikson suggests as being characteristic of adult middle life. He describes it as the struggle between generativity and stagnation, which leads to the strength or virtue of being able to nurture or care if it is successfully resolved.[19] Perry's final stage is labelled *evolving commitments*: 'This is how life will be. I must be whole hearted while tentative, fight for my values yet respect others, believe my deepest values right yet be ready to learn. I see that I shall be re-tracing this whole journey over and over again, but, I hope, more wisely.'[20]

It would be easy to criticize Perry's interesting scheme by pointing out how it enshrines the characteristic student values of America in the 1960s. Without denying the importance of some such critique, we must at the same time be careful not to evade the force of Perry's conclusions by a too-facile relativization. We would be left with the thought that if the scheme of Perry is relative to his own culture, then what developmental view of authority is mediated by our own culture? The central suggestion made in this present chapter is that we need to take the kind of scheme put forward by Perry and to use it as an instrument for the criticism of our own approaches to authority, as mediated through our own religious and social institutions, especially those typical of our kind of late twentieth-century industrial capitalism. Only then will we have the possibility of a worthwhile educational theory.

Moreover, we have the interesting possibilities of applying Perry's scheme to religious traditions. Do all religious traditions encompass all nine positions? Is the authority of a religious tradition relatively content-free, i.e. mediated principally by cognitive and cultural structures rather than by specific doctrinal formulations? Do specific religions, or sub-religions within major traditions, tend to cluster around one position rather than another?

RELIGIOUS APPLICATIONS OF AUTHORITY-REASONING

In the ten or fifteen years which followed the work of Perry, considerable progress was made in clarifying the way in which cognitive structures mediate understandings of authority. In the 'faith development' theory of James Fowler, the six major stages are dissected by seven aspects which run right across the stages. One of these is 'locus of authority' and the criteria for the allocation of various understandings of authority to a given stage of overall development are set out in the *Manual for Faith Development Research*.[21] In the first stage 'authority is external' and may be regarded as a form of attachment to the principal parent-figure. Authority is thus an aspect of dependence. In stage 2, the older child is able to negotiate with authorities to achieve a more favourable balance of power, which springs from the child's stronger sense of self, insight into social roles, and grasp of language. Authority, however, is still external. In stage 3 authority is grounded in the tacit conventions of society. Social approval is a principal factor in determining whether authority will be accepted. The guidance of significant others is sought, and the criteria which are valued are of an interpersonal kind, such as honesty, charm or integrity. Authority is based on trust.

In stage 4, authorities are accepted or rejected on the basis of rational principles, and there is an awareness of ideology, world-view, and the need for coherence within one's own valued system of commitment. Indeed, compatibility with one's own system of belief is a principal criterion for the selection of authority. Previously, acceptance of authority was tacit, now it becomes explicit. Authority may reside in ideas, systems, institutions and traditions, as well as in persons. Authority in this fourth stage is internalized, since the person can arbitrate between competing claims for authoritative status.

There is a tendency in stage 5 not only to hold multiple sources of authority, but to relate these in complex patterns through the increased capacity for inter-contextual perspective-taking. It is within this dialectic of multiplicity that the locus of authority evolves within the stage 5 self. The uncritical subjectivity of stage 3 is mediated through the rationality of stage 4 into a new kind of critical subjectivity. In stage 6 this is actualized in a critical relationship between self-chosen but universal principles and a transcendent ground.

In comparing the scheme of Perry with that of Fowler, one must remember that Perry is dealing only with college students, and we may take his work as having to do with the interchange between Fowler's stage 3 'synthetic conventional faith' and stage 4 'individuative reflective faith'. We find this more fully developed in the work of Sharon Parks, who has taken the middle phase of Perry's scheme (positions 4A and 5, 'relativism discovered') as suggestive of an intermediate stage between Fowler's 3 and 4. In general, Parks combines Perry and Fowler to produce four basic stages in the evolution of authority. In the first of Parks' positions, we find *authority-bound/dualistic* forms of cognition, in which 'The person's knowing is inextricably bound up with the power of the trusted Authority'.[22] The dualism lies in the tendency in this first stage to sharply divide truth from falsehood, us from them, and the little tolerance for ambiguity. Parks emphasizes that many adults do not receive permission from their religious groups to go beyond this form of knowing all their lives.

Parks agrees with Perry that the second phase in the composition of authority may be called *unqualified relativism*. This leads to the third stage, *commitment in relativism*, while she calls the fourth stage *convictional commitment (paradoxical)*. Parks develops in some detail the idea that these forms of authority-reasoning are paralleled by a series of forms of dependence. Corresponding to the authority-bound stage, we have *dependent/counter-dependent*. This exposes the link between uncritically accepted external authority and total trust or unexamined dependence upon another. This corresponds to Fowler's stage 3 'synthetic conventional faith', since authority is conceived mainly in interpersonal terms. The bounds of the authority will usually be quite clearly defined. The trusted person or the group represented by that trusted person will be the locus of trust and source of authority. The sense of what is authoritative rests on a felt dependence upon a trusted group.

When this kind of absolute dependence collapses during the critical years of late adolescence, especially during higher education, its place may be taken by 'counter-dependence'. One pushes against the pattern of authority; one resists the role of the authoritative other in order to break free. The capacity to create a new kind of authority is still lacking, however, and so in this phase of counter-dependence the authority of the other is still paramount, although in negative tension.

Sharon Parks emphasizes that dependence is a health-giving mode of human relationship. She rejects as a typical aspect of Enlightenment rationality the idea that maturity involves a move from dependence towards autonomy.[23] Nevertheless, she insists that dependence, while a permanent axis of adult development, passes through several modes of composition. In each of these modes, it is related to a similarly evolving mode of authority.

So it is that we pass into the second phase, where inner dependence is associated with 'unqualified relativism'. By *inner dependence* Parks means that during this period while the various sources of authority outside the self are not denied or excluded, as is vainly attempted during the period of counter-dependence, the inner voice of the self is accepted as one of the multiple sources of authority. There is a new capacity to care for and respect the self, which is conjoined with other sources of authority. This then passes into the third form of dependence, which is *inter-dependence* corresponding to 'commitment in relativism'.

Sharon Parks' treatment is interesting because of the way in which a developing sense of authority is shown to be mediated through aspects of trust, friendship, confidence and the need for some form or other of dependence. She uses this insight to criticize Fowler's direct transition from external, uncritical authority to internally validated self-composed forms of authority.[24] The locus of authority does not shift in one, complex movement from outside to within, characterized by greater adjudication of more complex alternatives, but passes through an intermediate stage of relativism. During this stage of late adolescence or early adulthood, the authority of self-chosen commitments is knowingly weighed against other recognized authorities, so that authority is controlled by personal loyalty to the chosen and trusted group in the presence of a known and understood relativity. It is not quite the same as Fowler's 'synthetic conventional authority' (Fowler's stage 3), and nor is it quite the same as his stage 4, 'individuative reflective' authority. Parks emphasizes that this in-between stage is the time when the mentor, the guru, the counsellor/friend is especially important in the life of the student or young adult. Through this evocation of personal loyalty, the possibility of commitment within relativity is secured for the maturing self. Parks has thus deepened our understanding of the way in which patterns of authority are grounded in emotional development and need for security.

AUTHORITY AND MODERNITY: THE CONTEMPORARY EDUCATION PROBLEM

'Today it would seem that among many Christians the process of growing into mature human beings is estranging them from the faith.'[25] Many adults get trapped in a sort of magical faith in which complete security was offered through mere repetition. Segundo remarks that if this security is challenged through education, the result would be a sense of deep anxiety.[26] Cognitive developmental psychology does illuminate the sequences through which authority is composed by the self. It is less illuminating on the problem of arrested development, although Fowler's idea of institutional sponsorship up to but not beyond a certain stage is an interesting suggestion, which he has developed in his studies of congregational conflict.[27] We need the resources, however, of a psychoanalysis and critical social theory if we are to use the rest of the material to form an effective theory of RE today. The American Jesuit W. W. Meissner has drawn upon psychodynamic theories of personality development to shed light on the nature of adult acceptance of authority. 'The patterns of protection, well-being and authority inherent in family structure find their natural extension and elaboration in religion.'[28] The conflicts of the anal period of early childhood are particularly significant. The child comes to realize more sharply his or her dependence upon superior powers, and there may be a narcissistic compensation which may take the form of an all-powerful Heavenly Father. This 'idealizing projection' is extremely important in the history of adult religious authority. Heinz Kohut has studied in some detail the way in which early narcissistic wounding (i.e. some kind of break in the relationship between the child and the mother which inflicts a sense of deprivation upon the child) may be met by *either* an attribution of grandeur to the self *or* the idealization of the parental image.[29] In the former case, the self is holy, just and righteous, while weakness and evil are expelled beyond the boundaries of the self. This becomes important in forms of tribalism and nationalism. Its religious form is when the tribe or nation with which the self identifies is glorified as the perfect source of authority. The situation when through projection the other is idealized, while the self is seen as poor, sinful and unworthy, is equally important for religion, and may be particularly observed in certain kinds of Christianity.[30] Kohut emphasizes that although there are pathological forms of narcissistic compensation, there are also normal, healthy and life-giving forms of narcissism.[31] The idolization of the grandized self may indeed prevent me from having a genuine respect and affection for my actual self, while if my worship of God springs from my own need I may not be able to pass beyond the projection of my need into the One who is to be loved for intrinsic reasons. Nevertheless, without a general sense of living within a benevolent and supportive world which may well include a loving God, I may lack the optimism and confidence which can inspire real creativity, but fixation upon the totally adorable power of the all-beautiful other can lead me into self-accusation and excessive passivity. By opening the bounds of the self to relationships with structures beyond the self, the way is prepared for a rich accession of meaning, which goes far beyond the infantile authoritative dependence and becomes a resource for mature life. The psychoanalytic approach enables us to distinguish the types of religious authority which flow from the oral period, the anal period and the super-ego period, and is thus an essential complement to the cognitive theories of Perry, Fowler and Parks.

Max Horkheimer was one of the first to create the bridge between the authority of the family understood in psychoanalytic terms, and that of society. When the child eternalizes the authority of the parent, it is the entire authority structure of the parental culture which is being digested. Today, the authority of the school has largely taken the place of parental authority in the task of defining centres of power, truth and meaning:

> The spiritual world in to which the child grows in consequence of such dependence as well as the fantasies with which he peoples the real world, his dreams and wishes, his ideas and judgements are all dominated by the thought of man's power over man, of above and below, of command and obedience.[32]

Thus it seems natural that the world of adult life should be experienced in this way. It is natural for some to command, while others obey. It is because of their central role in the formation and maintenance of this view of social power that ideas of God have such a fetish-like quality. One asserts them, affirms them, denies them, blasphemes them, and adores them, but it is difficult to think them.[33]

It is at this point that the far more complex and subtle theories of contemporary social critics such as Claude Lefort[34] and Cornelius Castoriadis[35] become helpful. The discourse or rhetoric which maintains the modern sources of authority has become more and more transparent. The rhetoric of freedom grows more strident as the sense of helplessness before the vast impersonal forces of money grows deeper. Even the destruction of the ozone layer and the greenhouse effect are spoken of as if they were meteorological phenomena, not consequences of human intervention. Lefort remarks 'The discourse on liberty always comes back to support the discourse on property, just as the discourse on justice comes back to support the discourse on order'.[36]

We see thus that in the study of modern education, authority and freedom are not to be poised against each other, as in the classical reason of the Enlightenment, but are to be seen as joined together in the contemporary rhetoric of industrial power. The tacit authorities continually reinforce our alleged freedom, while actually contributing to our increased helplessness. Unable to handle their own multiplicity, and the victims of their own social function in the maintenance of the bourgeois historical enterprise, Western religions exemplify more and more the characteristic features of false consciousness.

THE ROLE OF RELIGIOUS EDUCATION

In the opening pages of this chapter, reference was made to the non-dialectical as being a pathological quality in the authority-reasoning of adults. If we look again at the stages of normal authority-reasoning described by the cognitive developmentalists, we see that it would be possible to describe the earlier stages as being non-dialectical. The egocentricity of children's thinking is necessarily of this nature, but if adults thought like children, they would be insane[37] to think like children, but the task of education is to enable healthy children to become healthy adults. This means that non-dialectical forms of thinking must give way to dialectical relationships, and at this point we have to realize that the normal development through the stages is today severely interrupted by the forms of alienation and false consciousness which have been described. We need to examine our methods of RE in the light of this predicament.

If children are brought before the objectified and extrinsic authority of a sacred text in a way which leaves no scope for humour, disagreement, fantasy and other forms of child-like anticipation of adult dialectical thinking, the result may be a fixation into reified, fetish-like relationships. These will be thrown off by the adolescent during the period of counter-dependence and may only be resumed at the cost of adult integrity, as often happens in adult conversion experiences when they are of the infantile type.[38] Those whose introduction to sacred texts has been of this kind, but who are unable to pass successfully through counter-dependence, may well find themselves in adult life fixed and frozen in infantile forms of congregational life, where non-dialectical worship and resistance to open and critical education will create an atmosphere which makes learning and adaptation increasingly impossible. Such brittle and dogmatic faith will become increasingly tribalized in its relations with the outer world and increasingly compartmentalized in its interior institutions.

This is why it is important that RE syllabuses should continue to be multicultural. In 1988 RE in England and Wales passed through a period when an attempt was made to reduce its dialectical qualities in the interests of tribalized religion and national capitalism. We can interpret the horror of 'mish-mash', an expression frequently used to denigrate the multifaith approach, as being the horror of the non-dialectical mind for the freedom and openness of the dialectical.[39] Luckily, through a providential conjunction of ignorance and incompetence on the one hand, assisted by some shrewd religious educational drafting on the other hand, we seem likely to have escaped the worst consequences of this brief tribalistic revival even if it continues to linger.[40] We must, however, go on insisting that there is no such thing as Christian-based RE or pure and simple Christian collective worship in our maintained schools. The law requires that RE should *both* reflect Christian traditions *and* take account of the teaching and practices of the other principal religions. In this reflection and this taking account of we may well be able to renew an emphasis upon learning religion which will encourage pupils to reflect upon and to take account of what they learn. The absurd vagueness and indirectness of the expression 'wholly or mainly of a broadly Christian character'[41] offers a chink of hope, although not a very large one, for maintaining collective worship in a more or less educational context. Whether this possibility will be realized is doubtful. If the intentions of those who insisted upon Christian collective worship are realized, we will have a new kind of non-dialectical worship, in which religion will fulfil with almost embarrassing candour its role in the maintenance of the authority of the powers that be. If, as seems more likely, the whole thing collapses under the weight of its own administrative nuisance-value, we shall probably see a return to collective worship as the reification of school authority expressed in mainly moral terms. In either case, the task of a religious education which advances human freedom will be impaired.[42]

In the long run, and this is what lies behind these reflections about the role of reified authority in late industrial capitalism, the only true authority in today's world is the authority of human poverty and wretchedness. Our theology and our religious education are, after all, not to be so sharply contrasted as at first we thought. They have this in common: they are both functions of the people with whom we stand in solidarity.

NOTES

1. W. F. Haug (1986) *Critique of Commodity Aesthetics*. Cambridge: Polity Press, pp. 72ff. Compare J. Hugh Davidson (1987) *Offensive Marketing*. Aldershot: Gower Publishing Company, p. 58.

2. A classic criticism of the role of media in modern culture is to be found in Max Horkheimer and Theodor W. Adorno (1972) *Dialectic of Enlightenment*. New York: Herder and Herder (first published in German, 1944), especially ch. 4, 'The culture industry: enlightenment as mass deception', pp. 120ff. A more recent treatment is provided by Alvin Gouldner (1976) *The Dialectic of Ideology and Technology: The Origins, Grammar and Future of Ideology*. New York: Seabury Press. For a critique of the role of nature and the naturalization of the social in contemporary culture, see Max Horkheimer (1974) *Eclipse of Reason*. New York: Seabury Press, especially ch. 3, 'The revolt of nature', pp. 92ff. For the image of the natural and its exploitation in emotional marketing see Davidson, *op. cit.*, p. 195.
3. Religious authority of this type is said to be self-authenticating. Reference is made to nothing beyond itself. Instead of connecting (synthesizing), such religious authority is analytic, i.e. true by definition. It is this quality of being suspended, of shimmering in the air, which gives authority its numinous power, and also marks it out as being alienated. For a general study of alienated religion, see Gregory Baum (1975) *Religion and Alienation*. New York: Paulist Press.
4. This way of describing it is fully discussed in Robert Kegan (1982) *The Evolving Self: Problem and Process in Human Development*. Cambridge, MA: Harvard University Press.
5. For the compatibility of Piaget and Marx, the most important work is that of Lucien Goldmann. See, for example (1976) *Cultural Creation in Modern Society*. St Louis: Telos Press, including 'Introduction' by William Mayrol, especially p. 11.
6. G. W. F. Hegel (1931) *The Phenomenology of Mind*. ET J. B. Baillie (rev. edn 1931). London: George Allen and Unwin, pp. 234–40.
7. Imre Lakatos and Alan Musgrave (eds) (1970) *Criticism and the Growth of Knowledge*. London: CUP, pp. 91 ff.
8. Horkheimer, *op. cit.* pp. 58ff.; Jurgen Habermas (1971) *Knowledge and Human Interest*. Boston: Beacon Press; Cornelius Castoriadis (1984) *Crossroads in the Labyrinth*. Brighton: Harvester Press.
9. Thomas S. Kuhn (1962) *The Structure of Scientific Revolutions*. Chicago: University of Chicago Press; Joseph Gabel (1972) *False Consciousness: An Essay on Reification*. Oxford: Basil Blackwell, pp. 11ff.
10. Sigmund Freud (1958) Psychoanalytic notes on an autobiographical account of a case of paranoia (The case of Schreber, 1911). In The Standard Edition of the *Complete Psychological Works*, vol. XII, London: Hogarth Press, pp. 1–82; Ludwig Binswanger (1975) Introduction to Schizophrenie. In *Being-in-the-world: Selected Papers*. London: Souvenir Press, pp. 249–65; Gabel, *op. cit.*; David T. Bradford (1985) Therapy of religious imagery in paranoid schizophrenic psychosis. In Moshe H. Spero (ed.) *Psychotherapy of the Religious Patient*. Springfield, IL: Charles C. Thomas, especially pp. 168ff.
11. See, for example, Otto Rank's description of 'Living in reminiscence' in (1964) *Will Therapy*. New York: W. W. Norton (German original 1929), p. 39; Sigmund Freud discusses the vague, dream-like quality of inhibited thought (1959) in 'Inhibitions, symptoms and anxiety'. In *Standard Edition*, vol. XX. London: Hogarth Press, p. 117.
12. Binswanger, *op. cit.*, p. 303; Gabel, *op. cit.*, pp. 38ff., 79ff.
13. Compare the concept of 'pseudo-speciation' in the work of Erik H. Erikson, e.g. (1975) *Life History and the Historical Moment*. New York: W. W. Norton, pp. 176–80.
14. Ninian Smart (1983) 'Religion, myth and nationalism'. In P. Merkl and N. Smart (eds) *Religion and Politics in the Modern World*. New York: New York University Press, pp. 15–28.
15. Gabel, *op. cit.*, pp.14ff.
16. The basic work on reification is still Gyorgy Lukacs (1971) *History and Class Consciousness*. Cambridge, MA: MIT Press. For the concept of the fetish, see Freud (1946) *Totem and Taboo*. New York: Random House. For the influence of Emile Durkheim, who combined both concepts in his anthropological work, see Gabel, *op. cit.*, pp. 36–8. For the functions of inversion, see Jorge Larrain (1979) *The Concept of Ideology*. London: Hutchinson, pp. 46–142.
17. William G. Perry (1968) *Forms of Intellectual and Ethical Development in the College Years: A Scheme*. New York: Holt, Rinehart and Winston; Lawrence Kohlberg (1984)

Essays on Moral Development, Vol. II: *The Psychology of Moral Development.* New York: Harper and Row; James W. Fowler (1981) *Stages of Faith.* San Francisco: Harper and Row; Sharon Parks (1986) *The Critical Years: The Young Adult Search for a Faith to Live By.* New York: Harper and Row.

18. Kegan, *op. cit.,* pp. 221–54.
19. Erik H. Erikson (1981) *Insight and Responsibility.* London: Faber and Faber, pp. 130ff.; and On generativity and identity: from a conversation with Erik and Joan Erikson. *Harvard Educational Review,* **51**, no. 2 (May), 249–69.
20. See Perry, *op. cit.,* ch. 5, 'The developmental scheme', and the foldout chart (inside back cover). Kohlberg, *op. cit.,* provides a convenient summary chart on pp. 433ff. and it is from this chart that the illustration of student attitudes has been taken.
21. Romney M. Moseley, D. Jarvis, and J. W. Fowler (1986) *Manual for Faith Development Research,* revised edn. Atlanta, GA: Emory University, Center for Research in Faith and Moral Development.
22. Parks, *op. cit.,* p. 45.
23. *Ibid.,* p. 57.
24. *Ibid.,* p. 85.
25. Juan Luis Segundo (1973) *The Community Called Church.* Maryknoll, NY: Orbis Books, p. vii.
26. *Ibid.,* pp. 37–9.
27. James W. Fowler, *op. cit.,* pp. 286-91, 294-6.
28. W. W. Meissner (1984) *Psychoanalysis and Religious Experience.* New Haven and London: Yale University Press, p. 139.
29. Hans Kohut *The Analysis of the Self* (The Psychoanalytic Study of the Child, monograph series no. 4). New York: International Universities Press.
30. *Ibid.,* p. 27 note, p. 106 note.
31. *Ibid.,* p. 299.
32. Max Horkheimer (1972) *Critical Theory: Selected Essays.* New York: Seabury Press, Continuum Books, p. 106.
33. *Ibid.,* p. 290.
34. Claude Lefort (1986) *The Political Forms of Modern Society: Bureaucracy, Democracy, Totalitarianism.* Cambridge: Polity Press.
35. Corneilius Castoriadis, *op. cit.;* and *The Imaginary Institution of Society.* Cambridge: Polity Press, 1987.
36. Lefort, *op. cit.,* p. 209.
37. Gabel, *op. cit.,* p. 43.
38. Leon Salzman (1985) Religious conversion and paranoid states as issues in the psychotherapeutic process. In Spero, *op. cit.,* pp. 212ff.
39. John M. Hull (1991) *Mishmash Religious Education in Multi-Cultural Britain: A Study in Metaphor.* Derby: Christian Education Movement.
40. This interpretation is developed in my (1989) editorial, Agreed syllabuses since the 1988 Education Reform Act. *British Journal of Religious Education,* **12** (Autumn), 1–5. See also my booklet (1989) *The Act Unpacked, the Meaning of the 1988 Education Reform Act for Religious Education.* Birmingham Papers in Religious Education no. 1. Middlesex: CEM.
41. Education Reform Act 1988 I sect.7(i).
42. For more recent developments, see John M. Hull (1995a) 'Can one speak of God or to God in education?' In Frances Young (ed.) *Dare We Speak of God in Public?* London: Mowbray, pp. 22–34; and (1995) 'Collective worship: the search for spirituality'. In *Future Progress in Religious Education* (The Templeton London Lectures). London: Royal Society of Arts, pp. 27–38.

Orthodoxy and Openness: the Experience of Children

Chapter 11

Orthodoxy and Openness: the Experience of Buddhist Children

Peggy Morgan

INTRODUCTION

The headings used in this section indicate an emphasis in the study of religious traditions which is even now not always apparent. It is an emphasis first and foremost not
on systems of thought but on believers and their experience, whether they are adults or
children. The emphasis was made seminally by W. Cantwell Smith when he distinguished between people of faith and the cumulative traditions (Smith, 1963). To
understand people's faith and experience, it is, of course, usually necessary to consider
the great systems of thought and practice within which they locate themselves,
Buddhism in this case. That is why there is a section in this book on the classical traditions and the material found in their texts and histories on the theme of freedom and
authority. The writers of these sections often illustrate their points with reference to
contemporary use of scriptural material amongst religious communities. This necessary
backwards and forwards movement between text and context, classical and popular
traditions, systems and persons is one that is greatly facilitated by a partnership between
the historian and the anthropologist, the textual scholar and the phenomenologist, the
university department and the local faith community. Many teachers have of necessity
worked from the human to the theoretical side. They have been presented with the challenge of understanding the particular faiths of the children in their classes and schools,
with its mixture of culture and religion, family adaptation and orthopraxis, and then
moved into the general and theoretical study of the history and texts of the religious
traditions to support the local and particular.

The first stage of particularity in the case of Buddhism is to recognize that the
Buddhist tradition has always transplanted easily into the conventions and lifestyles of
the many cultures into which it has been taken. This is entirely in keeping with its
emphasis on change as part of the world in which we live. Gautama Buddha taught in
the vernacular language of his area of India and encouraged his followers to do the
same as they 'went forth'. Languages involve language worlds and translation in the
broadest possible sense. Starting where people are when you are teaching them the
Dharma is an important Buddhist method which reaches its full articulation in the

Mahayana doctrine of *upaya kausalya*, skilful means (Pye, 1978). There is also historical as well as geographical particularity in the cultures in which Buddhism has
flourished. For example, Indian Buddhist life in the time of the Emperor Ashoka was
very different from that in the twentieth-century Indian Buddhist communities founded
by Dr Ambedkar. So the generalizations must always be qualified by saying not only
'Theravada Buddhists', but 'Sri Lankan Theravada Buddhists', or even 'Sri Lankan
Buddhists in this century'; and then they must be qualified again with 'Sri Lankan
Buddhists from this village', 'this Sri Lankan family living in London' or 'one Sri
Lankan Buddhist that I met'. There are, of course, continuities between these as well as
discontinuities. Buddhist viharas, monasteries and *dharma* centres in the West often
have a strong ethnic connection even when most of those living there or supporting
them are British Buddhists. For example, the conventions at Amaravati are very Thai,
those at Samye Ling very Tibetan, and those at Throssel Hole very Japanese.

HELP IN NURTURE

There is an old Sri Lankan saying that Buddhism is not established in a country until it
has an indigenous sangha. Sangha is used here to mean the community of world-
renouncers, bhikkhus and bhikkhunis. The idea has been present in the Western
transplantation of Buddhism too, and it is relevant to the nurture of children as
Buddhists. This was brought home to me some years ago in a conversation with a
friend. He told me that he had almost become a Buddhist thirty years ago, but since he
was married with a young family he thought that he would not be able to nurture his
children in his chosen religion because there was at that time no monastic sangha within
the country and that the living of the faith in a rounded sense was therefore not possible. Because of this he decided to remain a Christian and bring his children up within
what he saw as a total cultural package. He had been attracted by the Tibetan Buddhist
tradition, but what he articulated would also be understood by Theravada and Zen
Buddhists. A great deal of the responsibility for passing on the tradition for Buddhists
lies with the monastic sangha, and it is therefore with the provision of teaching for children at monasteries and viharas that I shall begin.

Viharas that are linked with national Buddhist groups, such as the Chiswick Vihara
for Sri Lankans and the Wimbledon Vihara for Thais, nurture the children of the families that support them in various important ways. First of all they offer a language and
culture link with the national community from which the parents come. This is important for the personal history and identity of both the parents and children. Religion in
this context is a part of culture. Buddhism can be seen as a reinforcing of cultural,
ethnic identity. From the children's point of view this is not irrelevant, as it is their
ethnic identity which 'labels' them in many of their interchanges in day-to-day life
rather than their Buddhism. The religion is taught as it would be in, for example, Sri
Lanka. At the Chiswick Vihara the teaching follows the syllabus and course of exami-
nations developed in Sri Lanka by the Young Men's Buddhist Association. As Richard
Gombrich points out (1971, p. 53), the impetus for the founding of 'Buddhist Sunday
Schools' and the Young Men and Young Women's Buddhist Associations in Sri Lanka
came from Col. Olcott and the pattern of Christian schools. There is here then, an
interesting case of double adaptation, firstly in Sri Lanka and then here. The contents of

graded teaching books are topics such as 'The Life of the Buddha', 'Jataka Tales', some history of Buddhism and verses and suttas appropriate for lay Buddhists. Although the core of the community are Sri Lankans, there are British Buddhist families who go along and there is a very open and welcoming atmosphere at all the viharas. The children seem to enjoy the teaching and this is probably as much to do with atmosphere as style or content. They like the stories and can retell them in a lively way (Cush, 1990, pp. 44ff.). Religion here is what you are born into and what develops with the routine practices of giving alms to monks, making offerings of flowers, incense and light before an image of the Buddha, taking refuge and reciting the precepts.

There is a sense, for the children, of a world apart from the weekday world of secular British schooling, where their concerns are more often with getting a good education so that they can become established within British society in material and professional ways. These are, however, perfectly appropriate goals for Buddhist lay-people and there is therefore no great sense of clash between these traditional vihara schools and everyday school. There is an affirmation of education in general, especially where the members of the monastic sangha are also learned. Literacy has always been important for Buddhists, because the scriptures are important. When I have heard comments specifically on RE in schools, it seems to be that religion is not taught very much at all. This is sometimes remarked upon with surprise by both Buddhist parents and children, who thought that there would be a strong Christian-derived moral teaching in British schools, with which they would be very happy (see also Bowker, 1983, p. 186). Morality for Buddhists is the foundation for all accomplishments and superior to intellectual learning for its own sake. Any difficulties with the explicit language world of other religions as taught in schools are usually handled very sensitively by Buddhists, as the following example shows.

> One day Chloe's teacher had tried to explain to her class at school about God. She had said he was a loving father in heaven who cares for everybody. Chloe asked her father that evening, 'what is God, Daddy?' Daddy replied that God was the life, the energy in every-thing: in the trees, in the bricks of their house, in Snowy the cat and in all people. 'But, Daddy, the teacher said that God was a father in heaven.' Chloe said. Daddy replied that it helped many people to think of God like that, but that other people found it more helpful to talk about the way in which they and everything else were all part of nature. That was why they showed respect for everything. Chloe thought about it very carefully and thought how wonderful it was to have this energy flowing through her life and everything else.
>
> (Morgan, 1982, p. 2)

MUST I BE LIKE THE BUDDHA?

The story of Gautama Buddha's life and enlightenment is a standard part of traditional Buddhist education. Buddhist children, however, seem to accept that his way and goal is extraordinary and includes an ideal which will not be attained by them for a long time. Some of the favourite materials for teaching are the Jataka Tales, the stories of the preparation for enlightenment in a long chain of lives based on the high ethical ideals of Buddhism. The most popular stories teach patience, trustworthiness, self-sacrifice and generosity. There are also suttas which encourage the right relationships within families, such as respect for parents. This is the social side of Buddhism, what Spiro (1982) calls kammatic Buddhism. It is illustrated by the introduction to a little book I picked up at one of the viharas called *Buddhism for Primary*. This is written by a Sri Lankan and printed by the Singapore Buddhist Mission. Its introduction relates well to our theme.

> Modern living has become so fast and complex that there is a strong tendency for young people to go astray without proper sense of purpose in life. There is therefore an urgent need for them to be given some moral education that will guide them along the correct path in life, thus helping them to live in peace and harmony, not only with themselves but also their fellow beings ... they will grow up and become good, useful and responsible citizens of our country.
>
> (Pemaloka, 1983, p. 1)

Lesson one in the book is called 'An Obedient Prince'. It says, on the theme of obedience, 'A good child is an obedient child. Nobody likes a disobedient child. A disobedient boy or girl is like a piece of charcoal. An obedient child will be like a bunch of nice sweet-smelling flowers' (Pemaloka, 1983, p. 5). The prince who is the subject of the chapter is Rahula, Gautama Buddha's son, who may or may not, historically, have been obedient. What we do know, and what is at the heart of the religious teaching of Buddhism, is that Gautama Buddha disobeyed his father by going out of the palace grounds with his charioteer and later left the palace stealthily to go on his own religious quest. There is a tension here between two religious ideals. One is to preserve the fabric of society with all its social conventions and the other is the radical choice of those on a path to enlightenment which might go against all social norms. The story of Prince Vessantara, as well as that of Gautama Buddha himself, is another case of radical challenge to normal loving behaviour. Vessantara gave away his wife and children in the exercise of his great generosity (Cone and Gombrich, 1977). Buddhists are not alone, of course, in experiencing such tensions. They are there in the Abraham story and in Jesus' words about leaving home and family for his sake. Westerners often see Buddhism as a religion on the level of meditation and enlightenment only, but when most Asian Buddhist parents send their children to the vihara for teaching it is to reinforce culture and social behaviour, not to challenge it. This is well understood by the monastic sangha, who depend on moral hard-working and generous householders to maintain their own conventions of world renunciation. If one asks the children about the clashes, who they want to be like and whether there are problems, they are able to handle the levels even though they are not unpacked for them formally in the teaching. Yes, of course, they wish to be on a Buddha-like path to enlightenment, but that will be after many lives. Meanwhile they talk about harmlessness, respect for others, especially in the family, caring for all living beings, kindness and generosity as the appropriate goals. The need for obedience to parents will not be expressed in such a heavy way as the text of the book quoted above, but more as it reported of Wimala: 'Wimala is fond of her family and is glad to obey the rule that children should honour their parents, help them and live by the family ideals' (Ascott, 1978, p. 8). This is all completely in keeping with the traditional perceptions of the faith. The articulation of Chula (aged 13) moves further towards a more general position: 'Buddhism teaches that you shouldn't do things just because it is the fashion to do so, or because others are doing it, or because people tell you to. You should do what is right' (Cush, 1990, p. 43).

NOT BECAUSE THE BHIKKHU SAYS SO

As one can sense from the schoolbook passage about Rahula quoted above, the style of teaching in traditional Buddhist cultures may be different from styles of teaching in the West today. There is no doubt, however, that there is change and adaptation to the different perceptions and expectations of the children here. Buddhists articulate their faith in terms of reason and experience and have no vested interest in being tied to rigid authority structures if these are not part of the culture in general. Children like Chula seem to be encouraged to think why they act in certain ways and to see good social relationships as of mutual benefit. They are not encouraged to be rigid in either their thinking or behaviour but to be mindful of and flexible with regard to the feelings of others. Despite their ascetic style of life there is almost always a great warmth in the way bhikkhus and bhikkhunis relate to children.

In the monasteries where the majority of monks, nuns and families are Western anyway, that shift has not had to take place. Children seem to have a natural rapport with members of the sangha and often comment on how much they smile and laugh and seem to like children. In the spring 1988 edition of *Rainbows*, the children's magazine distributed from Amaravati Buddhist Centre, there is a photograph of a young boy sitting next to a bhikkhu in a companionable way and smiling up at him. Underneath there is a poem called 'A Spiritual Friend' (p. 10).

> A Spiritual Friend ...
> is the one who you can depend on,
> One who knows you like you know yourself.
> One who you can ... fight with, play with
> scramble in the hay with,
> One you can do nothing and be quiet with.
> One who can laugh and cry with,
> and one who you are never shy with.
> Such a friend is the one you can trust
> with all your heart,
> And to be such a friend to others ...
> Our sisters and our brothers,
> Our fathers and our mothers,
> Brings a happiness which will never depart.

TO DO IS TO UNDERSTAND

One of the things Buddhists seem to talk about most often in relationship to the bringing up of children is the need for them to develop respect for other people and for the world in which we live. This is taught in a variety of practical ways. One is the formal set of actions expected in relationship to monks and nuns and in shrine rooms. Children seem to understand that the 'hands together' gestures and bows or prostrations that are taught are not about the status of the image of the Buddha or the authority of the people outside themselves but about their own attitudes. This was illustrated particularly vividly to me in a vignette of family life in a Western Zen Buddhist household:

> In the evening when everyone was home and they came into the kitchen for supper, Chloe liked the way they all stopped chattering and moving about and stood quietly for a moment with their hands in front of them. Food gave them life and it was respectful to think for a

moment about eating it, to pay attention to where it had come from and how it had been prepared. It also gave Chloe time to look up at the picture of the face of the Buddha on the wall above the table. He looked as though he was thinking very carefully about what he was doing too.

(Morgan, 1982, p. 2)

It is interesting that in the children's activity room at Amaravati Buddhist Centre there is not only provision for all the constructive activities of making and doing that we associate with good primary school education in the West, but also a small shrine, which in fact forms a focus to the room. Here the children learn what are seen as conventions of the religious life which encourage giving, respect, quiet and attentiveness. The activities and perceptions which have flowered from this are well documented in *Rainbows*. There are family days, family weekends and an annual family week at Amaravati which are Buddhist in the implicit rather than the explicit sense. Buddhists do not have a monopoly on the appropriateness of giving or on the development of loving kindness, for example. The stories that are told and the activities that take place are culturally eclectic but seen to be dharmic, the truth about the way things are, rather than Buddhist in a narrow sense. This is a concept and emphasis that we shall come back to later.

I'M A VEGETARIAN SOME OF THE TIME

One of the dominant themes in *Rainbows* and expressed strongly in the words of a 7-year-old Sri Lankan Buddhist is 'What I like best about Buddhism is that we do not hurt animals' (Cush, 1990, p. 43). The sense of closeness and concern for all nature and the teaching of non-harming (see below) is well expressed in the popularity of the animal Jataka Tales, which most children seem to like and remember. People who are not Buddhists always expect Buddhists to be vegetarian, and a teacher with only theoretical knowledge may be surprised to see a Buddhist child eating meat at school. This kind of perception of how a child ought to be practising his or her religion can be the negative side of thinking that we are well-informed. What being well-informed really means is knowing the kind of framework and presuppositions within which believers work out their own lives, and then attending to the individual cases against the background of a given tradition. Any teacher should enjoy discussing examples in an open-ended way with the child, and from my experience there will be a whole range of possible responses on the meat-eating topic. Here are some examples:

Buddhism does not have any dogmatic rules about what you can or cannot eat.
You can eat meat if it has not been killed specially for you.
I do not like vegetables and my mother says it is important that I have meat to grow strong.
You cannot get a proper meal here without meat.
Fish is not the same as meat.
People eat meat in Tibet.

It is not difficult to identify different kinds of answers here, although whether children are or are not able to do this depends on their age and the way in which they discuss their religion elsewhere. The first answer seems to state something about the style and orientation of Buddhism as a religion, perhaps over against other religious traditions.

The second answer is one that comes out of the historical tradition as observed by the monastic sangha. Buddhists may want to add that if you buy meat in a shop there is a strict sense in which it has been killed for you, the consumer. This was spotted by a 13-year-old interviewed by Denise Cush (Cush, 1990, p. 41). The third and fourth responses are of a practical kind and linked to the desire to transplant their way of life as fully as possible. The fourth answer assumes teaching about a hierarchy of life which is an important part of Buddhism and the fifth links with the fact that in Tibet it was not possible to grow enough vegetables to feed people, but there was reflection on the principle of non-harming and as few lives were taken as possible, which meant killing one yak, which would feed more people than ten chickens. Many Tibetan Buddhists in the West, however, are changing because they find it is possible to live on a good vegetarian diet here.

The above do not, of course, exhaust Buddhist responses to the question. Many Buddhists apply the precept of non-harming very strictly and are not only vegetarian but vegan. For further background against which to continue the discussion with Buddhist children see Kapleau (1986) and Ruegg in Gombrich and Balasooriya (1980).

HOW TO BE HAPPY

The issues of *Rainbows* seem to me to resonate with the perception that non-harming (*ahimsa*), generosity (*dana*), loving kindness (*metta*) and compassion (*karuna*) given out to the world return as happiness to the giver and that lack of compassion brings sadness and isolation. In the discussion of vegetarianism above, the first Buddhist precept of non-harming is mentioned. This is linked again to the suffering of animals in the autumn 1987 edition of *Rainbows*. First, there are these words written under an illustration of a standing image of the Buddha: 'The Buddha looked with a kind heart equally on all living beings, therefore we call Him "The Compassionate One". To develop compassion in our lives is skilful.' On the next page there is a story about deer in the forest with empathetic questions about the life of deer. After this there are two illustrations of fishing and with them these comments along with more questions such as 'do you like fishing?'

> When a fish meets the fishhook if he is too greedy, he will be caught.
> When his mouth opens and takes the bait his life is already lost.
>
> A bite!
>
> A flame-coloured fish has swallowed bait and hook.
> The boy pulls away and his catch comes out of the water.
> Peter looks at the fish and suddenly his heart is sad.
> He realises that he has hurt the fish very much and caused it to die.

Here is another variation on the same theme.

Figure 11.1

Figure 11.2

Taking Care of Animals

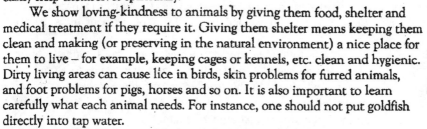

WE CAN BE KIND TO ANIMALS by helping them to be well and happy. Animals do not always have a very pleasant life. They often feel great fear or anger. They live in a world of instinct and cannot easily help themselves spiritually.

We show loving-kindness to animals by giving them food, shelter and medical treatment if they require it. Giving them shelter means keeping them clean and making (or preserving in the natural environment) a nice place for them to live – for example, keeping cages or kennels, etc. clean and hygienic. Dirty living areas can cause lice in birds, skin problems for furred animals, and foot problems for pigs, horses and so on. It is also important to learn carefully what each animal needs. For instance, one should not put goldfish directly into tap water.

We should also be careful about what kind of food we give animals. It is not kind to give pets the wrong kind of food, such as cakes, sweets and chocolate. (If in doubt you can always ask your vet).

If we have a dog, then it's good to train it well so that it does not annoy or threaten people, or make gardens and pavements dirty.

We can also be kind to animals by letting them be free, if we know they can live safely outside. We can avoid killing them unnecessarily, just because we don't like them. We can be enormously cruel to insects, for example, forgetting that they too have a right to live, just like us.

If we are kind to animals, the animals may become friendly to us.

BEING KIND is seeing all living beings as ourselves.
When others are hurt, I know what it is like,
 because I too have been hurt.
When others are killed, a part of me dies.
When others are happy and do good things,
My heart is full of joy and I'm also happy.

LIVING BEINGS are: People, animals, birds, insects, plants, flowers, fish and sea creatures – all things having life force.

Can you think of some ways that we can be helpful
 to living beings?
In which ways do you already help any living beings?

Figure 11.3

There is not only an emphasis on what human beings can do for and with animals but often a piece of teaching about what we can learn from a tree or a dog. Everything is potentially one's teacher. This does not, though, override the importance of the more formal and abstract sets of teachings that are a central part of the tradition for Buddhists. Following the story of the fish and linked with the questions which follow it, there is a list of the five precepts written by one of the children. These lay precepts and the moral perfections, particularly those of giving and compassion, feature regularly in the work done at Amaravati. *Rainbows* often contains straightforward simplified versions of the precepts and perfections of children, as in the Spring 1988 edition. These are also listed in most basic books on Buddhism (Morgan, 1987). Figure 11.3 on p. 123 is a version presented in the form of a poem by a 10-year-old.

The most important help for following any of the teachings for Buddhist children seems to be the example of the people with whom they spend their time. First and foremost these are their parents and after that the teachers at the *dharma* centres and also the Buddha. In some ways children's experience reverses the normal doctrinal hierarchies of the faith, when the Buddha is the paramount example.

It is important to mention at this point that it is possible to find quite different models from those in the descriptions given above. The journal of Nichiren Shoshu Sokka Gakkai in the UK has a children's page and members' children are very involved in the movement (Cush, 1990, p. 99). The example they look to is Nichiren, not Gautama. The use of the mantra 'Nam-myoho-renge-kyo' as a help is paramount. Here are the words of a 7½-year-old who began the practice of chanting at 2½:

> When I moved in, the children on the streets were bullies to me, but then I started to chant daimoku and they became my friends. My friend Kelly was having a lot of illness so I encouraged her to chant Nam-myoho-renge-kyo. Now she can chant and she gets less illness. I am very happy for her.

This is such a very different approach from the others that I have been describing that it merits more space than is available here, and having alerted the reader to its existence I shall move on.

THE DHAMMA (DHARMA) SCHOOL PROJECT

The greatest tensions that I have heard expressed about being a Buddhist and living in an environment dominated by secular and materialistic attitudes have been amongst Western Buddhists, both parents and children. This is perhaps because they have self-consciously chosen an alternative faith rather than continued to practise a way of life and culture into which they were born. Their dissatisfaction with much in Western schooling is being currently expressed in the Dhamma School project. It is necessary to say once more that I have not found that the Sokka Gakkai groups fall into the range of what follows.

The traditional Buddhist affirmation of education mentioned earlier is sometimes expressed with qualifications. Here are some voices from the World Federation of Buddhists, from Thich Nhat Hanh writing in the Vietnamese context, from Stephen

Batchelor giving a Buddhist perspective and from those involved in the Dhamma School project, whose school opened in 1994. These seem to give an appropriate ending to my own reflections.

> Since critical reflection is an important part of human potential, and essential for spiritual growth, we endorse the broadest possible expression of literacy and educational opportunity.
>
> (World Federation of Buddhists, 1984, section 3.6)

> The education that is needed for the present time is one that can wish away from the innocent minds of the young generation all the dogmatic knowledge that has been forced upon them with the pursuit of turning them into mere tools of various ideologies and parties. Such a system of education will not only liberate us from the prison of dogma but will also teach us understanding, love and trust. These qualities ... are the prescription needed for the revival of our society that has been paralysed by suspicion, intrigue, hatred and frustration.
>
> (Hanh, 1967, p. 57)

> In numerous respects, Buddhist training complements secular education. However, many of the questions it asks and the goals it pursues are at odds with the questions and goals of secular society. On many fundamental issues Buddhism presents a challenge to the secular world. It challenges its emphasis on egoistic self-interest, material gain, power and fame; its short-sightedness in seeking merely the rewards of this brief span of life; its failure to appreciate the fundamental inter-connectedness of all living organisms and systems; its exploitation of non-human forms of life; and, above all, its loss – even denial – of spiritual insights and values.
>
> (Batchelor, 1989, p. 10)

> A variety of ideas and reflections have been articulated which touch on key issues, especially the need to give the school a strong spiritual dimension, while avoiding the pitfalls of religious dogmatism which so often lead to stultification and separatism. In this context, it was felt that a Buddhist framework which was too narrowly defined, either in culture or ethnic terms, could be detrimental to the flowering of free enquiry and universal responsibility which lie at the heart of all genuine education.
>
> We are living now at a time of great change and turbulence in the world, when all the forces of wisdom and compassion need to be summoned forth to deal wisely with the energies which have been unleashed. It is at times such as these that concerns of self, grudges, complaints and animosities need to be transcended. Our own petty interests must be replaced by a vaster and more generous vision. One of our most valuable resources for a more enlightened world lies in the proper nurturing and education of our children. The actualisation of this vision of global responsibility, through skilful education and service, is one of the noblest responses we can make to the current world crisis.
>
> (*Forest Sangha Newsletter*, 1991)

REFERENCES

Ascott, J. (1978) *Our Buddhist Friends*. Nutfield: Denholm Press.
Batchelor, S. (1989) *Education in a Pluralist Society: A Buddhist Perspective*. Geneva: World Council of Churches Interlink Project.
Bowker, J. (1983) *Worlds of Faith*. London: BBC.
Cone, M. and Gombrich, R. (1977) *The Perfect Generosity of Prince Vessantara*. London: OUP.
Cush, D. (1990) *Buddhists in Britain Today*. London: Hodder & Stoughton.
Gombrich, R. (1971) *Precept and Practice*. London: OUP.
Gombrich, R. and Balasooriya (1980) *Buddhist Studies in Honour of W. Rahula*. Bedford: Gordon Fraser.

Hanh, Thich N. (1967) *The Lotus in a Sea of Fire*. London: SCM.
Kapleau, P. (1986) *To Cherish All Life*, 2nd edn. Totnes: Buddhist Publishing Group.
Morgan, Peggy (1982) *Buddhist Stories*. Oxford: Westminster College.
Morgan, Peggy (1987) *Buddhism*. London: Batsford.
Pemaloka, Ven. (1983) *Buddhism for Primary*. Singapore Buddhist Mission.
Pye, Michael (1978) *Skilful Means*. London: Duckworth.
Smith, Wilfred Cantwell (1963) *The Meaning and End of Religion*. London: Macmillan.
Spiro, Milton (1982) *Buddhism and Society*, 2nd edn. California University Press.

Rainbows, the Children's Journal. Great Gaddesden: Amaravati Buddhist Centre.
Forest Sangha Newsletter. Amaravati Buddhist Centre.
There was a report on the opening of the Dhamma School in Brighton in the April 1995 issue of the *Forest Sangha Newsletter*.
The Buddhist Directory of Groups and Organisations. The Buddhist Society, 58 Eccleston Square, London.

Chapter 12

Orthodoxy and Openness: the Experience of Christian Children

Brian Gates

It is estimated that by the year 2000 approximately a third of the world's population under the age of 15 years will be at least nominally Christian, and a fifth more actively so: more than 436 million. Already, the majority of them are no longer from the Western world.[1] In the UK, at least until recently, it has been taken for granted that those children who chose not to call themselves Christian would be the exceptions. This supposition was based on extrapolations from what was known about the religious allegiance of the adult population, together with evidence of Sunday school enrolments, baptisms and confirmations.[2] However, no such claim can now be substantiated.

Church attendance figures for England, as revealed by a census taken on an October Sunday, amount to no more than 14 per cent of the under-15 age group. These 1.2 million comprise 38 per cent Free Church, 34 per cent Roman Catholic, and 28 per cent Church of England.[3] Extending the figures to include those claiming Church membership, rather than regular attendance, the picture for Britain as a whole emerges as: England 16 per cent, Scotland 24 per cent, and Wales 25 per cent. Sunday school attendance, which remained a national custom for the majority of children until the 1950s, is now the norm for but a few.[4]

AGENCIES OF FAITH TRANSMISSION

These changes in the extent to which Christian belonging is a majority condition for children and young people in Britain are not always appreciated by politicians or even Church leaders. They reflect, or are reflected in, changes of practice in all the agencies of faith transmission – the Churches themselves, the home front, the wider cultural context and formal educational provision.

Within the Churches, the decline in Sunday school enrolments may indeed correlate directly with the secularization of the weekend and the increasing variety of alternative activities to engage children's attention. At the same time, there has been a policy shift, from within many of the Churches, against setting Sunday school as a priority.[5] Evidence of their long-term effectiveness, in rate of retention of those attending Sunday school into adult membership, was thin. Instead, therefore, of making special efforts to promote a provision which in effect separated children from the adult community, there was a deliberate move to integrate them more directly into the life of the Church by making them welcome in the main liturgy.[6] However rich the quality of learning resources typically available for children who are actually involved in church or Sunday school,[7] they are now a less comprehensive minority than used to be the case. Without doubt, one result of this is that, in sharp contrast to the childhood experiences of their own parents, those who themselves became parents in the 1980s and 1990s, for the most part, never received this minimal exposure to Christian education in Sunday school or church service, a pattern now being repeated with their own offspring. This leads Philip Cliff to comment that 'it takes only two generations to de-Christianise a people'.[8]

Christianity has nevertheless continued *within the home*, but as a more diffuse presence than earlier in the century. It is found through contact with grandparents and other older friends and relations, and this irrespective of the now 19 per cent incidence of children born out of 'wedlock'.[9] It also remains in the self-identification of adults with the established Church of England or some other variant of Christianity, now down to 65 per cent, but significant even in the absence of formal membership or attendance.[10] Rites of passage continue to have a Christian face, though less predominantly than once was the case. In England and Wales, of all marriages, those in church are down to 53 per cent, and in Scotland 57 per cent.[11] Similarly, in the case of death, although in recent years there has been the major change to a majority preference for cremation rather than burial, there has been no comparable shift away from Christian officiation.[12] Most children pick up perceptions of Christianity from its presence on all these domestic fronts.

Direct church contact and exposure to Christianity as an element in extended family routine are both reinforced and qualified in the *wider cultural context*. Uniformed organizations, such as Scouts and Guides, have a membership of well over a million young people. They are less likely than once was the case to meet on church premises. Yet the beliefs and values which they commend, whilst not being necessarily Christian in an explicit sense, often still convey a positive feel for that tradition. This is less obviously true in other forms of leisure activity. Sport, enjoyed by large numbers of young people, whether as active participants or as spectators, for the most part does not have Christian sponsorship. More likely, Christianity may feature incidentally, as in a continuing ritual, such as the singing of 'Abide with Me' in the soccer cup final, or less predictably in the response to some tragedy on the terraces. A daily diet of four or five hours spent on television and video viewing, together with ubiquitous pop music, are new in human history and quite widespread in their blanket cover. They are not generally seen or heard as purveyors of the Christian Gospel, more as perversions of it. Yet, from time to time, they may expose injustice and do more than their bit to feed the hungry. Indeed, they may well in their lyrics reveal the ambiguity of Christianity, as of any institutional religion, as a force for compassion or cover for hypocrisy. Children register all these images, and begin to do so long before the days of formal education.

Changes are no less apparent in the *contribution of schools* to faith transmission. Since its inception in 1870, the national educational system of England and Wales has officially been a partnership of Church and state. Sensitivity to Christianity has therefore been 'written into' Church and county schools alike. There has always been a conscience clause to safeguard the rights of teachers who believed differently. Even so, for most of a century, it has been a fair assumption that the majority of teachers would have a working knowledge of, and basic sympathy for, Christianity.[13] Now, however, there is no reason to suppose that teachers personally will have any greater degree of Christian involvement than the adult population generally.[14] Whether consciously, or unconsciously, this is likely to be communicated to the children whom they teach.

In the 1970s, recognition by educationists generally that religious beliefs are contentious led to a shift in judgement about the most appropriate shape and content for any direct religious education (RE). The mixed condition of belief and unbelief amongst teachers and pupils alike made nonsense for them of an obligatory daily act of Christian worship.[15] Similarly, the teaching of religion had to take account of its plurality in the world. Thus, the Bible-based syllabuses which had formerly been agreed as a means of responding to Christian diversity gave way to ones which sought to identify core versions of the major faiths now found within the nation.[16] At best, children on this basis might have their appetites whetted for wanting to understand more of Christianity. They would not, however, be catechized.

In practice, however, the best is rarely achieved. The main reason is that teachers generally have not been helped to take on this task, either as generalists in the primary school or as secondary school specialists. Successive reports have exposed the dearth of RE provision; time and resources have not been given to it.[17] Children's school-based experience of Christianity, as well as of other faiths, has accordingly been patchy.

Church schools continue to exist as part of the state educational system, though the proportion of such schools had dropped to 31 per cent, and that of children whom they teach to 22 per cent in 1991.[18] With few exceptions, they are linked with the Anglican or Roman Catholic (RC) Churches; there are more Anglican than RC primary schools, but more RC than Anglican secondaries. In common with all other maintained schools, their public funding is conditional upon their delivery of the National Curriculum. Accordingly, in the appointment of teachers, academic and professional qualifications have been as significant as Christian allegiance, or even more so, most noticeably at the secondary level.

Historically, there has been a difference of emphasis between the two Churches which has affected policy on both admissions and RE. Schools linked with the Church of England, in keeping with its claim to be the established Church of the nation and not a denomination, have defined their catchment and curriculum boundaries in relation to neighbourhood and national need. Thus, especially at the primary level, parental engagement with the Church of England has not usually been a precondition for entry, and RE has been more generally Christian than denominationally specific. By contrast, RC schools have normally been for children from RC families and the RE has entailed preparation for life as an adult Church member.[19]

More recently, this difference of emphasis has become further complicated. In keeping with the Anglican priority to serve the whole neighbourhood, children from diverse religious backgrounds have been admitted and adjustments made to reflect this in the curriculum.[20] Similarly, in some RC schools and dioceses, a distinction has been drawn between general RE and specifically Catholic initiation and, in accord with the Vatican's commitment to dialogue with other religions and to racial justice, boys and girls from minority faith communities made deliberately welcome.[21] Crude economic pressure to maintain the size of pupil intake has been an additional factor in all this.

In consequence, children's experience of Christianity in a Church school setting is almost as varied, in both content and quality, as it is in county schools.[22] Taken altogether, the cumulative impact of the various agencies of faith transmission is far from co-ordinated. Christianity as experienced from church, at home and in the wider cultural context is set alongside that which comes from school. Thus, any understanding bringing all these ingredients into a coherent and consistent whole depends greatly on the individual journeying of each child becoming adult.

Apprehension at the consequences has led some Christians to establish independent Christian schools, whose teachers and entire curriculum are bent on Christian nurture for all their pupils.[23] There is no question of the enthusiasm and integrity of the proponents of such schools. What is questionable is the feasibility of creating such in more than a tiny number of instances. However worthy, lack of public funding on the one hand, combined with the difficulties of finding appropriately qualified teachers on the other, make the venture a precarious one. Moreover, such a strategy belongs more with that end of the Christian tradition which would keep itself apart, than that which affirms the entire world as derived from God.

From this overview of the various agencies of faith transmission, it is clear that the nature of what is shared, as well as the degree of explicitness shown in the sharing, are both likely to vary enormously in the impact they have on individual children. Ironically, the very strength of Christian institutional presence, as perceived by the leaders of the other religious communities, may actually carry with it a substantial weakness. In effect, so diffuse is the range of responsibility for Christian education and nurture that there is little co-ordination or agreement amongst the Churches, locally or nationally, as to priorities and procedures for achieving them. If that is at all true for the Churches, how much more does it apply to all the other shaping agencies. It is all too easy for any one agency to assume that each or all of the others is/are taking necessary initiatives, when actually there is galloping confusion or a gaping silence.

CHILDREN RESPONDING AS CHRISTIANS

Even amongst boys and girls who are being actively nurtured in the Christian faith there will be great diversity of experience as to what this entails. The source itself will likely be the self-conscious initiative of other Christians, but they may, for instance, be parents, friends, teachers, leaders, listeners, enthusiasts, neighbours from round the corner or even off the television.

That other Christian may denominationally be charismatic Roman Catholic, Plymouth Brother, Baptist, Methodist, Quaker, United Reformed, evangelical Church of England or Anglo-Catholic, Greek or Russian Orthodox, Elim Pentecostal or House Church Movement; and there are others. The location may be a parish divided by the issue of the ordination of women or another blighted by prurience in the press, there may be a lively congregation with lots of other young people or it may be rhythmically staid, it may even be a special youth camp like Spring Harvest or Green Belt designed to show that being Christian can be passionate and engaging of large numbers. There may equally be an ethnic dimension, as in an Afro-Caribbean Assembly of God in north London or the Serbian Orthodox Church in Bournville.

One mode of Christian expression to which the child responds may powerfully predominate: a series of stories from the Bible; a collection of pictures, verbal or visual, which vividly convey some sense of Godness; some songs or simple gestures which reveal deep feelings of trust, courage, thankfulness, sorrow or wondering in the face of the best and worst that life has thrown up; exemplary actions of caring and tenderness, of power being deployed for the poor and weak, of forgiving and being forgiven. More probably, instead of just one of these modes predominating, there will be a mixture of several. Either way, the precise combination and substance of what is conveyed will reflect that the Christian Gospel comes in many different personal guises, each with both cognitive and affective dimensions.

Crucial for Christian education and nurture must be the ambition of one Christian for another that they will come to be discerning in the faith for themselves. Anything less is to be Christian without personal conscience, the direct opposite to the life modelled in Jesus of Nazareth. For conscience involves knowing and being known. 'Conscienczation', which has a close kinship with Christian education, involves growing not only in self-awareness but also in sense of responding to an accompanying more-than-ness which is there in every moment.[24] For this to happen at all effectively presupposes that the various elements in the process of Christian initiation, in whatever forms of individual local expression they take, will be richly shared and understood. But it must also be recognized that the outcome of that process is not fully controlled by any of its participants. For the Christian faith is itself transformative for all concerned, whether as child or adult, in so far as they find themselves responding to that source of illumination which is at the same time in their midst and beyond.

The extracts which follow are intended to give a glimpse of the rich complexity of children responding to that challenge to make sense of Christianity. From talking with boys and girls who are actively Christian, it is evident that many of them find it feasible to hold their faith deeply and yet to be open and discriminating with it. Here are just three examples taken from research involving 340 boys and girls between the ages of 6 and 16 years; they were each similarly interviewed over a period of two hours. Although the conversations ranged much more widely, what follows focuses on three particular aspects: superstition, attitudes towards other religions, and beliefs in God and Father Christmas.

Ruth, aged 7, is from a Church of England background, but has been a member of the Salvation Army's junior club for the last six months. She is encouraged in her Christian faith by her mother and father.

Questioned about whether she knows any ways of getting good or bad luck, she tells me:

I've got a lucky Cornish pixie at home. If you put it on, you get good luck and when you take it off, you don't ... I never get told off on Sundays if I wear it.
How do you think it works?
I just suppose there's a thing that makes it work: magic.
Does crossing fingers help?
No, it doesn't really. My sister was playing in the garden and she was too fed up with the sun. So she said something like ... if I cross my fingers it will rain. She crossed her fingers and it wouldn't do anything.

Magical belief is clearly in evidence in what Ruth says, but it is qualified by appeal to experience.

Ruth is aware that different kinds of Churches exist, but sees them as sharing a common belief in Jesus. By contrast, people of other religions do not believe in Jesus. She sides with the Christians because, if they believe in Jesus, they know what's right and what's wrong, because Jesus can tell them. People that don't believe in Jesus, don't believe the things that are right.

How can Jesus tell them what's right and wrong?

Well, he comes into their heart, and they can use their brain to help them think.

How can she tell?

You feel that Jesus is in your heart and this helps you do the right thing all the time.

Again experience is critical, along with the use of reason.

As for Father Christmas, Ruth identifies him as giving presents at Christmas, and sometimes seen in big supermarkets. What does he represent?

The baby who was born in a manger. The kings brought presents, so we get presents and Father Christmas brings them ... He comes at night time on Christmas Eve and he puts a star on each of the chimneys of the ones that are asleep and the good ones. Then on Christmas Day he comes and brings all the presents to the good children.

He can get to them all in one night can he?

Well, I suppose there are lots of Father Christmases.

How does he get inside?

He comes down the chimney; if the fire's not alight, that is.

Is this the same Father Christmas as seen in the shops?

No, because the ones that live in the shops are men dressed up as Father Christmas, and they don't have the real fur coat on.

Do you think there really is a Father Christmas?

Yes, because otherwise you don't know who brings you your presents.

What then is the difference between Father Christmas and God?

Well, God loves you, and so does Father Christmas, but God, really, he's with you all the time, and Father Christmas only comes at Christmas.

How do you know that God is with you?

I don't really know, but I feel it ... I've got a Bible at home, and I read it every night, and every time I read it, I feel that God's with me, loving.

Adrienne, aged 10, is from a Roman Catholic family and attends the local church primary school. Though she is highly articulate about her faith, she considers that she was too young to be confirmed a year ago.

She is familiar with children's luck-bringing routines, like touching wood and crossing fingers, but says she does not believe in anything like that. Though she reads her stars, and finds coincidences in what is predicted, she regards them as just for fun. In fact she senses some tension between superstition and Christianity:

it's a thing that people invented when they didn't believe in Christ at all. You could have the odd superstition here and there, like if a black cat passes in front of you, but you mustn't be terribly superstitious – living your life as a bag of nerves or something like that ... I think you can't be a very good Christian and too superstitious ... You believe in so many ridiculous things. To be a Christian you should have whatever is coming to you.

All Christians, according to Adrienne, believe centrally in Jesus, although there are minor variations between different groups such as Protestant, Anglican and Roman Catholic. As for other religions,

they're much the same, they're all waiting for a saviour. The only difference with our religion is that it believes the Saviour's already come. We don't know which is the proper religion, but it's just in Scripture. And all these other religions, they've got Scriptures as well. You don't really know which religion is true, but the one you believe in, you believe in it because you think it's true, but you don't really know.

How do you know which religion to believe?

If you're born into a religion, like I was born into the Catholic religion, you don't just

think about it really. I used to wonder when I was small, which religion to believe, but now I believe in this one ... You can always change your religion.
Do you think that your religion is more true that the others?
You can't say that any religion is any more true than anybody else's, because you don't know which one is true. But if you believe in a religion, you think it is more true, and you don't really know.

Adrienne's diffidence about how to check alternative claims to religious truth does not show itself when she speaks of Father Christmas and God.

There isn't any Santa Claus any more. Originally, as St Nicholas, he used to go round to poor children and give them presents.
What does he stand for?
He's a symbol of being happy and being kind to people. I think now he's been too commercialized and you don't get the same sort of feeling about Father Christmas any more.
What's the difference between Father Christmas and God?
Well, Father Christmas – he has the same sort of feeling as God does and Christ, and coming to give presents and this sort of thing. There is a connection between God and Christ and Santa Claus, but, you know, Santa Claus is different, in a way, to Christ.
Is God real?
Nobody knows if he is real, but Scripture tells us that he is and he was, and he always will be. I believe you've got to think that there is somebody superior to you, somebody whom you should worship ... be thankful to, or in some cases, put the blame on. I think without God in the world you're sort of lost ... There wouldn't be any union, people wouldn't be so kind.
How do you know God's real?
Well, there again, you don't know that he's real, you just have to depend on Scripture and everything that's been passed down through the ages. So many things prove that God's real, and I believe that he is.
Is God he or she?
God isn't a he or a she. He's not, you can't talk about what sex he is, because there's no sex for God ... He's just there ... he has no body and no shape. The only thing that tells us whether God is he or she is Jesus Christ, he was a man. Of course he was a man, because no woman would be able to suffer the pain he went through, I suppose. I don't think a woman (could have done it), not in that time, anyway. Because now, with Women's Lib and everything, and equality, it wasn't the same in those days. I mean women were not as strong characters; they were sort of frail and just only in the background in life. It was a man's world, definitely, I don't really think a woman would have made much of an impression on the people of those times.

Patrick, aged 15, is a regular attender at the local United Reformed Church in his hometown in the north of England. He is both sharp and humorous in talking about his faith.
Is he superstitious?

Occasionally ... Just to prove to myself that it's not true, I walk under ladders and nothing has happened to me yet. Occasionally you do get luck or bad luck, but there is no formula by which you can get it.
Is there any difference between religion and superstition?
Well some superstition comes from religion, and vice versa, to a large extent.
Are all religious people superstitious?
No. It depends on how you look on your religion. Some people have got rather a naive view of religion which ties on to superstition. But if you can, while not losing faith in your religion, still question it to a great enough extent, you can see that these superstitions have got very little to do with it.

Are there different ways of being Christian?

> It depends what you believe and to what extent you believe the Bible or to what extent you are prepared to question. If you believe that the Bible is absolutely literal truth from beginning to end, that makes you a fundamentalist. I know one fundamentalist that goes to a Methodist church.
> *So are all Methodists fundamentalists?*
> No, and neither are all fundamentalists Methodists. Jehovah's Witnesses and Seventh Day Adventists are fundamentalists ...

Patrick is comparably discriminating about other religions in relation to Christianity.

> I'm afraid that I've got a slight mental block in myself, which prevents me questioning to too great an extent the Christian religion ... But I can look objectively at Judaism; I can look objectively at all other religions, and at other variants of Christianity, and I can see through them. I was once very attracted towards Buddhism, where there's no God and you go on and on through successive lives trying to make yourself better, and eventually you reach a stage where you can sort of will your spiritual self to separate from your physical self, you're so perfect and your spiritual self goes to Nirvana. Nirvana is sort of idyllic non-existence so to speak, and I thought that was quite convincing.
> *You no longer think so?*
> Well, I think some of the other things they suggest in Buddhism are not particularly convincing, e.g. they pray, but I can't decide who they pray to, since they don't believe in God.
> *So there's only one religion which is true?*
> Well, all religions are true to a certain extent. All will agree, for example, on a basic moral code, and a lot will agree that there is one God. I don't really think, looking at it objectively, that any one religion is more true than another.

And what of Father Christmas?

> Parents like to tell their young children that Santa brings their presents down the chimney because they like their children to be child-like and have a belief in the supernatural. Then slowly children begin to question this belief and all of a sudden Santa disappears.
> *For adults, what does Santa Claus stand for?*
> A means to the end of getting the children to believe that it's not them who buy the presents, but someone else. If you like, Santa is a benevolent old gentleman – a diminutive form of God.
> *And for you?*
> I stopped believing in Santa when I was 7; having seen a picture of ten Santas in London, the whole idea was spoiled, commercializing the concept.
> *What's the difference between Father Christmas and God?*
> Father Christmas brings along presents to little children at Christmas-time, whereas God works over a broader field. Santa is just an invention. You could say God is too, or alternatively you could say that God exists – whether I do or not – and therefore that he can't be just an invention.

In the accounts given by these three young people of their Christian faith, we see something of the complexity of the process of Christian education and nurture in a context which is Christian, secular and multifaith.

The Christianity which informs them and which they seek to understand is itself multi-form. In its institutional diversity, it has a personal presence in the parental faith community to which they each have an individual sense of belonging. At the same time, it has a more diffuse reality mediated by a Christendom heritage typified by the figure of Father Christmas, now largely secularized. These different forms of Christianity are mutually challenging of each other, and to the child or adult in their midst. They all require interpretation, if understanding is to grow.

There is further challenge from the alternative belief systems, however imperfectly understood, in the shape of other world religions or rejections of all religion. Diversity here is potentially even greater. It may be apparent in the local neighbourhood. It is certainly advertised on the television. Again, interpretation is called for if any of these other beliefs is to be fairly understood. And such understanding is a precondition for any intelligent conversation which may subsequently take place between the Christian, of whatever ilk, and the convictions which come as challenge. None of the three young people has eyes closed to these complexities. Nor do their responses provide any prompt to favour a more exclusive approach to Christian education. Their faith is no less strong for being tolerant of others. And although psychogenetic development creates certain constraints on children's capacities for understanding, it is evident that reason is already engaged, from earliest years, in making sense of faith, fact and fantasy.

NOTES

1. See David B. Barrett (1982) *The World Christian Encyclopaedia*. Oxford: OUP; and subsequent updates in the *International Bulletin of Missionary Research*. More briefly, but with interpretative reflections on the global strengths of the Christian churches: John Taylor, (1990) 'The future of Christianity'. In John McManners (ed.) *The Oxford Illustrated History of Christianity*. Oxford: OUP, pp. 628–65.
2. e.g. Geoffrey Gorer (1955) *Exploring English Character*. London: Cresset Press, ch. 14; or, even a decade later, the Gallup Poll social survey conducted for ABC Television (1964) *Television and Religion*. London: University Press. The extent of disengagement from institutional Christianity was already a matter of contention amongst sociologists of religion in the 1960s; see, classically, the progressive secularization case as argued in Bryan Wilson (1967) *Religion in Secular Society*. London: Watts, as compared with the picture of greater organic continuity presented in David Martin (1967) *A Sociology of English Religion*. London: Heinemann.
3. See Peter Brierley (1991) *'Christian' England*. London: MARC Europe.
4. The current condition is lamented in Church of England General Synod Boards of Education and of Mission (1991) *All God's Children? Children's Evangelism in Crisis*. London: National Society.
5. See Philip B. Cliff (1986) *The Rise and Development of the Sunday School Movement in England 1780–1980*. Redhill: National Christian Education Council, ch. 17.
6. This shift of emphasis was most in evidence in the Church of England and Free Churches; it was the subject of a European consultation: see John Sutcliffe (1974) *Learning Community*. Redhill: Denholm House Press; amongst Roman Catholics, because of their children's traditionally lower confirmation age, church-going links already predominated over Sunday school. The question of how churches might best acknowledge the interests of children was directly addressed in two successive reports from the British Council of Churches: *The Child in the Church* (1976) and *Understanding Christian Nurture* (1981). London: BCC.
7. See *Partners in Learning: Christian Worship and Learning Resources for All Ages*, available from 2 Chester House, Pages Lane, Muswell Hill, London N10 1PR. This is ecumenically produced material, covering the whole of the Church's year on a week-by-week basis.
8. Cliff, *op. cit.*, p. 322.
9. Central Statistical Office (1995) *Social Trends 1995*. London: HMSO. In 1971 only half of these children were registered in the name of both parents; in 1993, three-quarters of them were.
10. This diffuse presence of Christianity is continually picked up in attitude surveys, such as E. Jacobs and R. Worcester (1990) *We British: Britain under the MORIscope*. London: Weidenfeld and Nicolson, ch. 6. Its significance is commented on by Anthony Dyson, 'The

Christian religion' and Kenneth Thompson, 'How religious are the British'. In Terry Thomas (ed.) (1988) *The British: Their Religious Beliefs and Practices 1800–1986*. London: RKP: pp. 103–32 and 211–39. Indeed, the phenomenon of 'believing without belonging' is the central theme of Grace Davie (1994) *Religion in Britain Since 1945*. Oxford: Blackwell.

11. Central Statistical Office (1993) *Social Trends 1993*. London: HMSO, section 11.7.

12. J. Tony Walter (1990) *Funerals and How to Improve Them*. London: Hodder. The significant development of alternative funeral celebrations for humanists is not yet widely pursued.

13. 'The schools ... are the most important source of religious teaching ... the central figure for teaching Christianity is a lady in a primary school. By a happy chance for Christianity, those who teach in primary schools are amongst the most well-disposed to the faith and most strongly practising of all social strata. Their place as religious educators is very little disputed outside the ranks of the intelligentsia and is a major reason why religion is regarded as "a good thing" and the right way to keep the young on a decent path': Martin, *op. cit.*, pp. 88–9.

14. Church sponsorship of teacher education and training has been of enormous significance since the inception of publicly funded schools in 1870. Arguably, however, the potential opportunity to maintain a rich exposure to an explicitly Christian vision has been only partly taken up. The closure of many of the smaller Church colleges or their absorption within larger institutions, together with diversification into liberal arts degrees on the part of those which remain, has more commonly concealed Christian self-consciousness from student teachers than celebrated it in their presence. Surveys by the Culham Institute have remarked this from the responses of academic staff as well as students in those colleges which remain: see John Gay, B. Kay, G. Perry and D. Larenby (1986) *The Future of the Anglican Colleges: Final Report of the Church Colleges Research Project*. Abingdon: Culham College Institute. That challenge is explored in Trevor Brighton (ed.) (1989) *150 Years: The Church Colleges in Higher Education*. Chichester: WSIHE; and is currently the subject of an initiative called Engaging the Curriculum, which is designed in an open way to raise the profile of Christian beliefs and values across the whole curriculum, including that of student teachers. A termly bulletin is available from Professor Adrian Thatcher, College of St Mark and St John, Plymouth.

    Not surprisingly, for the majority of the students, the rest of initial teacher education provision has generally shown no greater attention to Christianity, nor commonly to other religions: see Brian E. Gates (1990) 'Religious studies in polytechnics and colleges of higher education'. In Ursula King (ed.) *Turning Points in Religious Studies*. Edinburgh: T & T Clark, pp. 76–88.

15. Cf. John Hull (1974) *School Worship: An Obituary*. London: SCM Press.

16. Brian E. Gates (1973) Varieties of religious education. *Religion: A Journal of Religion and Religions*, **3**, 52–65; and Religious Education, a proper humanism. *London Educational Review*, 55–61.

17. RE Council of England and Wales (1994) *Time for Religious Education and Teachers to Match*. Lancaster: RE Council of England and Wales.

18. Culham College Institute (ed.) (1992) *Church of England Schools and Colleges Handbook 1992–3*. Redhill: School Government Publishing Company, pp. 114–15.

19. The distinction is clearly characterized in Durham Report (1970) *The Fourth R*. London: SPCK.

20. Robert Waddington (ed.) (1984) *A Future in Partnership*. London: National Society.

21. The theoretical distinction is drawn in Richard M. Rummery (1975) *Catechesis and Religious Education in a Pluralist Society*. London: Shand. In application it is found in National Catholic Commission for Racial Justice (1975) *Where Creed and Colour Matter*. London: National Catholic Commission for Racial Justice; and Richard Zipfel (ed.) (1984) *Learning from Diversity*. London: Catholic Media Office.

22. See the findings in Bernadette O'Keeffe (1986) *Faith, Culture and the Dual System: A Comparative Study of Church and County Schools*. Lewes: Falmer Press.

23. See Bernadette O'Keeffe (1992) 'A look at the Christian Schools Movement'. In Brenda Watson (ed.) *Priorities in Religious Education*. Lewes: Falmer Press, pp. 92–112; and Terry McLaughlin (1992) 'The ethics of separate schools'. In Mal Leicester and Monica

Taylor (eds) *Ethics, Ethnicity and Education*. London: Kogan Page.

24. Gerhard Ebeling (1963) 'Theological reflections on conscience', in *Word and Faith*. ET: London: SCM Press, ch. 17, provides a striking prompt for an explicitly Christian interpretation of Paulo Freire's term for critical consciousness, as also for the notion of reflective practitioner which has come into vogue more recently.

Chapter 13

Orthodoxy and Openness: the Experience of Hindu Children

Robert Jackson and Eleanor Nesbitt

INTRODUCTION

The following discussion is based on a series of three studies of 8–13-year-old Hindu children living in Britain. These were conducted as part of the Religious Education and Community Project based at the University of Warwick.[1]

From 1983 to 1989 we were engaged in research among Hindu children in the 8–13-year-old age range in Britain. Our central concern was the transmission of Hindu tradition to the growing generation. From a study of the 'formal nurturing' of Hindu children in community-run supplementary classes nationwide (1983–84), we moved on to ethnographic research among Hindu families in Coventry. Our aim was to observe and document not only the formal transmission of mother tongue, prayers and stories in such classes but especially the 'informal nurture' of children in Hindu practice and belief. This happens unselfconsciously in the home, as well as in temples and other public venues, and during special events such as life cycle rites and festivals. Research was carried out in a two-year ethnographic study conducted in 1986-87 and a further study of 15 months carried out in 1988–89. Since the studies were of particular diaspora Hindu communities, a number of points should be taken into consideration to reduce any tendency to generalize about the transmission of values to Hindu young people.

First, the studies were of children from particular ethnic backgrounds. Britain's Hindus number at least 360,000 (some estimates are considerably higher), of whom around 70 per cent are of Gujarati linguistic and cultural origin, whether their immediate family background is British, African or Indian. Around 15 per cent are of Punjabi ethnic origin, while the rest have cultural roots in different states of India such as Bengal, Maharashtra and Tamil Nadu. Our findings relate to families whose origins are in the Western Indian states of Gujarat and Punjab. Their mother tongues, cuisine and devotional orientations reflect these regional backgrounds.

Second, the religious practice of the families reflected membership of various groupings within the tradition. Caste is one such grouping, while sampradaya, guru-led spiritual movement, is another. Sometimes caste and sampradaya were coterminous, as in the Punjabi Valmiki movement (Nesbitt, 1990a, b, 1991, 1994). Sometimes membership of a sampradaya was effectively drawn from one or a small number of castes with the same ethnic origin, although only some caste members belonged to the movement. An example is the Pushtimarg, the 'Way of Grace', a movement inspired by Vallabhacharya (fifteenth to sixteenth century CE) and his successors, who encouraged devotion to the infant Krishna (Michaelson, 1987). Adherents are Gujaratis from the Lohana and certain other castes. Another Gujarati sampradaya is the Swaminarayan religion, consisting of followers of Sahajanand Swami and several successions of gurus (Williams, 1984). Two very different movements, which attract non-Indian devotees as well as Hindus from different ethnic backgrounds, are the Sathya Sai Baba organization (Taylor, 1987) and the International Society for Krishna Consciousness (ISKCON), otherwise known as Hare Krishna (Knott, 1986a). The former group runs children's classes known as Bal Vikas (literally 'child development') based on a well-developed published programme of 'Education in human values'. Such movements have long been a vital feature of the Hindu tradition, especially being a means to mediate philosophical ideas and teachings to ordinary people. There is no doubt, however, that their growth in popularity in recent years in the UK is a very significant factor in the way British Hindus are adapting to life in a pluralistic and predominantly secular cultural environment (Knott, 1986b; Williams, 1988).

As well as sampradaya and caste, it should be noted also that certain gurus (spiritual teachers) from India not associated with any particular sampradaya exert an influence on a significant number of British Hindus, especially through their periodic visits to Hindu communities in Britain. Swami Satyamitranand Giri is one such who, at the time of our research, had a substantial following among Gujarati Hindus in Britain.

Third, the age range of the children was such that certain moral issues which might be potential sources of conflict within families were not apparent. The young people were sufficiently distant in age from marriage, for example, for it not to be a matter of contention with parents.[2]

A further preliminary point needs to be made in relation to the term 'Hinduism'. As already referred to in Chapter 4, Wilfred Cantwell Smith in his critique of the concept of religion calls Hinduism 'a particularly false conceptualisation' (Smith, 1978, p. 63). The term 'Hinduism', though adopted and used since the early nineteenth century by insiders as well as outsiders, is essentially a Western construct. It was the introduction of the concept of Hinduism, and the presence of Westerners talking, writing and asking about Hinduism, which led Hindus to try to define true and false Hinduism, which they did (and still do) in different ways.

Thus, for example, Bankim Chandra Chatterjee (1838–94) distinguished between the 'false and corrupt Hinduism' which Europeans denounced and 'true Hinduism' which, in his case, involved devotion to God and a humanistic ethic (King, 1978). For Swami Vivekananda (1863–1902), on the other hand, true Hinduism was the monistic philosophy of Advaita Vedanta, which Bankim had rejected as part of false Hinduism. Many more examples could be cited. For our purposes Hinduism (or our preferred term 'the Hindu tradition') is an umbrella term for a great number of practices and beliefs each of which belongs to some of the millions of people who for historical reasons are called Hindus. Some of these – *puja* (making offerings to an object representing a god), *karma* (the cosmic law of cause and effect which encourages ethical behaviour and the acceptance of misfortune), *dharma* (right conduct appropriate to one's situation) and caste, for example – are characteristic of Hinduism since they are found among most groups of Hindus. Others are less so, whether the teachings and practices of a particular guru-led movement such as Pushtimarg or a local or regional festival whose mythology and associated ritual may be unknown elsewhere. Nevertheless, what is unknown to many Hindus is part of Hinduism if it is familiar to some Hindus.

There are obvious problems in discussing concepts such as 'authority' and 'freedom' within such a loosely knit tradition. Some Hindus would appeal to what they see as the essence of the tradition. T. M. P. Mahadevan, for example, referred to what he saw as the defining characteristics of Hinduism: allegiance to the Vedas, belief in an all-pervading God and emphasis on non-violence (Mahadevan, 1977). In contrast, the ethnographer's observations of what count as sources of 'authority' within particular groups and subgroups (ethnic, caste, sectarian, etc.) would reveal a wide variety of examples; see Donald Taylor's discussion of different types of authority within the Sathya Sai Baba movement in Britain, for example, in Burghart (1987).

What we have attempted to do in this chapter is to look at our data on Gujarati and Punjabi 8-13-year-old Hindu girls and boys, whether involved with religious movements or not, and from a range of castes to see whether there are any predominant values, concerns or goals and, where possible, to make tentative observations about the sources and types of authority which played a part in achieving them. Such observations are not, of course, explanations for the perpetuation or rediscovery of values. The process of value transmission is complex and involves factors associated with the establishment and maintenance of what we have loosely called 'cultural identity', whether it be religio-ethnic identity, caste identity or identification with a religious movement. The three principal concerns which emerged were the perpetuation of Indian languages, the values underpinning family life and other relationships and the ideal of vegetarianism. In each case there are interacting influences at work, sometimes internal to communities, sometimes from other related communities and sometimes from the surrounding secular and Christian culture.

Although teachers in supplementary classes often consciously aim to foster self-discipline and an enhanced self-esteem in the children through increased knowledge of their own culture, neither parents nor teachers, in the main, present such aims explicitly to children. Instead the younger generation gains a conscious cultural identity as part of a peer group whose ethnicity, religion and mother tongue they share. Much of what they learn is via a 'hidden curriculum'. Such concepts as *karma* and *dharma* are implicit without, for the most part, being named.

The balance of authority and freedom for members of Hindu society, both adults and children, varies from one situation to another. Despite the speed and magnitude of social change, Hindus regard flexibility as a positive feature of their ancient tradition and tend not to react with alarm to other value systems.

LANGUAGE AND SUPPLEMENTARY SCHOOLS

Increasingly Hindus are setting up supplementary classes for their children, and for those who attend they provide authoritative teaching which may on occasion override the custom of the home. The majority of Hindu children probably do not attend any of these classes which teach mother tongue or a Hindu curriculum but they merit attention since they have a considerable impact on those who do attend. They are a phenomenon distinctive of the diaspora and they highlight the priorities of Hindus generally in perpetuating their culture in a predominantly non-Hindu society. Of the eleven organizations whose classes we observed, some were non-sectarian. Others were guru-led movements (Jackson and Nesbitt, 1986, p. 1993).

Our study of Hindu supplementary classes indicated that the conscious aims of the organizers varied but overlapped, with some emphasizing the teaching of mother tongue or Hindi and others stressing religious instruction of various sorts. In practice it proved impossible to separate the concern for language and the concern for religion.

The Gujarati classes run by the Vishwa Hindu Parishad in Birmingham and Bolton and Coventry's Gujarati Education Society would, among others, include stories from the *Mahabharata* and *Ramayana* epics. Proceedings would start with a prayer. Conversely, classes teaching hymns and prayers at the Sri Sanatan Mandir in Leicester and elsewhere, though conducted in English, involved the use of much Indian language, as the hymns and prayers were in Sanskrit, Hindi or Gujarati.

The emphasis on language is in line with Hindu elders' feelings. When asked what they felt that children should learn about Hindu religion, parents tended to say 'Gujarati' or, if they were Punjabi, 'Hindi'. The insistence of Hindu Punjabis on their children learning to read and write Hindi rather than their mother tongue is comparable to Muslim Punjabis' emphasis on Urdu. In practice it also contributes to the children's sense of distinctness from the Sikhs, for whom Punjabi, in Gurmukhi script, is the preferred language of literacy.

Hindus in Britain are a minority in a diaspora situation. Not surprisingly, formal nurturing is primarily concerned with the retention of culture rather than with learning from other faiths. Hence the emphasis on language, whether Gujarati or Hindu, as essential to a Hindu lifestyle, to understanding devotional and liturgical material and for communication with other relatives, especially grandparents. While language classes teach their pupils an elementary literacy, oral language is primarily passed on in the home. This is also the case with the other two strands of Hindu tradition which emerged prominently from our research, namely the expression of the values underpinning family life and the emphasis on vegetarianism. These were evident in both formal and informal nurture. The inseparability of mother tongue from values will also be clear in what follows.

VALUES UNDERPINNING RELATIONSHIPS

Family role and values

Elders' concern to instil moral qualities, such as respect for others, was general, regardless of people's regional or sectarian background. This meant, as our interviewee at the Vishwa Hindu Kendra in Ealing stressed, addressing others and referring to them by relationship words appropriate to the relative ages of the parties concerned – 'brother' or 'sister' for someone of the same generation, and 'aunty' or 'uncle' for an older person. This would show affection as well as respect, especially with the addition of the honorific suffix *ji*, whereas the English style of referring to, say, an older man as 'Mr Gupta' or 'Ashok' would be perceived as, in the first instance, cold, and in the second disrespectful. For a child to talk to a parent about 'your friend' or 'my friend' rather than using a relationship term such as *masi* (mother's sister) or *bhai* (brother) can unwittingly cause concern. To a parent who has not been brought up in the West this would be confirmatory evidence that the child had internalized the apparent individualism and distance of Western interaction and lost the sense of being related, with all that this implies of love and obligation.

Hindu children, like others of South Asian origin, are brought up with a strong sense of family responsibilities implicit in particular relationships. The role of brother or sister, son or daughter, maternal uncle or paternal aunt involves particular duties and privileges. These become apparent on special occasions, in all of which children are involved, and so are reinforced. For instance, there are two annual festivals, Bhai Bij or Bhaia Duj, which takes place soon after Divali, and Raksha Bandhan (or Rakhri as Punjabis know it), on both of which Gujaratis and Punjabis celebrate the unique bond between brothers and sisters. Of these Raksha Bandhan, which falls on the full moon of Shravan, usually in August, is celebrated in almost every family. Girls and women tie a decorative thread around the right wrist of their brothers, their cousin-brothers (first cousins) and anyone else whom they regard as brother. They mark the boy's forehead with a dot of red powder and put a traditional sweet in his mouth. Boys then give their sisters some money. Children understand from an early age that a brother's duty is to protect his sister throughout her life.

Children also learn by seeing older relatives performing certain obligations because of the specific relationship in which they stand. Thus a Punjabi brother's care for his sister will include providing for her son's *mundan*. If their parents have died it will also be his responsibility to send the *saugi* (literally raisin), the food which she is allowed to eat before dawn on the fast day of Karva Chauth. Similarly, in many families it is the bride's mother's brother whose duty it is to give her the set of scarlet and ivory-coloured wedding bangles which she wears on the wedding day. It is the bride's brother's wife who may be expected to play a supportive role as her escort on the day, and the bride's younger sisters who play practical jokes on the bridegroom and extract money from him.

Children learn these and other roles through observation of the event, and its replay on video, and by their own involvement and enjoyment. Enjoyment should not be overlooked as a factor in cultural transmission.

Ritual and festivals apart, our interviewees articulated clearly the gender-differentiated family roles which lay ahead of them. Quotations from just two, a 12-year-old Punjabi boy and a 9-year-old Gujarati girl, sum up the expectations of all:

> You've got responsibilities. When I grow up my parents will be old. Then they can't take care of themselves. They need someone to take care of them. Then my two sisters will marry, won't they, so it'll be up to me.

> I'm not looking forward to being married. I want to stay at home and look after my parents when they're old. If I married I would have to live in a different house and only visit sometimes.

As these examples show, individuals' *dharma* (right conduct) is particular to their gender, relative age and the relationship (e.g. eldest son, youngest daughter-in-law) in which they stand to someone else. Thus children may see their father's parents and older relatives enjoying a degree of authority which his younger sisters-in-law, for example, would not have.

As a model for ideal behaviour, preachers, teachers and elders cite the *Ramayana* epic. Rama is held up as the ideal son and husband, Lakshman as the exemplary brother and Sita as the perfectly obedient, accepting, self-sacrificing wife. Other ideals of wifely devotion and filial duty abound in Hindu tradition but are familiar to only a minority of children.[3] Their mothers read stories on the occasion of particular fasts (see below). These also describe virtuous wives, but have only an indirect influence on the children, as they seldom hear or understand them.[4]

Reputation

Probably children learn most from older people's praise and criticism of individuals. As children grow older they become increasingly aware of the need to maintain and enhance their family's reputation. The family includes a network of relatives much wider than the nuclear family. Gossip in the immediate community, particularly of fellow caste members and people with roots in the same region of the Indian subcontinent, is presented as a force always to be borne in mind. Adolescent girls realize that even their imagined misconduct will be the subject of gossip which will damage the family's standing. Members of the community observe how they dress and whether they are seen associating unnecessarily with boys. In most British Hindu families concern for family honour is less prominent and less restrictive on young people than in some other communities of South Asian origin. Nonetheless, it is a more powerful determinant of behaviour than in the wider British society. Hindu children are subject at the same time to pressure from the media and from their peers, Asian and non-Asian. Some of these pressures run counter to the demands of family honour. Adolescents and young adults, especially girls, feel the resultant tension, whereas younger children usually do not experience these dilemmas. In attempting to avoid activating gossip, or hurting parental sensitivities, and in negotiating some personal space in a tightly meshed social fabric, youngsters may learn skills which can fit uneasily with strict adherence to truthfulness.

VEGETARIANISM

Diet, and more specifically vegetarianism, was the third issue to emerge clearly from adults' conversation about their concerns and from children's accounts of their tradition. Many mentioned this as the most distinctive feature of Hinduism. The avoidance of beef was a recurring theme. What Hindus eat and their ideas about food are a significant strand in Hindu tradition. As one Gujarati girl said, by implication contrasting Hindus with Sikhs: 'If you're Hindu being religious or not shows in your food, what you cook, not [in not] cutting your hair.' The range of reasons which children gave for avoiding beef or non-vegetarian food illustrates the complex of interlocking criteria for their behaviour and assumptions. Children described the cow as holy, as a mother, as associated with 'god' and Krishna and as the giver of milk. They had heard these explanations from their elders and seen pictures of Krishna with a cow. Some children mentioned the nastiness, from the animal's point of view, of being killed. In the words of a Gujarati boy: 'Would you like to be killed, because really you might one day be a chicken?' The effect on the killer or consumer of the murdered animal was also mentioned: 'If you eat pork, right, you'll be like a pig.' This may determine a person's future birth. In the words of a Punjabi girl:

> My uncle told me, if there was an animal and I killed it and ate it myself, then in my next life I would be the animal and the animal would be the person who killed me, and I'd see how I liked it.

This family, like many others, has been influenced by the strongly vegetarian teaching of the International Society for Krishna Consciousness (ISKCON). Children's home diet and attitude to meat-eating often depend on the family's allegiance to a spiritual teacher or to a religious movement. This will involve a particular selection and interpretation of scriptural texts to which devotees will make reference. So another boy, much influenced by ISKCON, pointed to the caption beneath a calendar picture of Krishna: 'If one offers Me with love and devotion a leaf, a flower, fruit or water, I will accept it' (Bhagavad Gita 9:26; Prabhupada, 1972, p. 478). This was the verse from the Bhagavad Gita which he argued was evidence that Krishna intended us all to be vegetarian.

In the Arya Samaj a teenage girl, clearly drawing on accepted teaching, named Jesus as an example of a vegetarian. Here we have an instance of Hindus finding support in the scripture of another faith without first-hand knowledge which would in fact have weakened their argument. This sort of appeal to authority shows a circularity of argument. All enlightened teachers are vegetarian. Jesus was such a person. He must have taught and practised vegetarianism.

Children reported that their parents and grandparents had become vegetarian in response to the teaching of a spiritual teacher. Some mentioned Sathya Sai Baba, the South Indian miracle worker whose followers regard him as an incarnation of God. Stories told by leading devotees would combine with love for Sathya Sai Baba and the wider Hindu regard for vegetarianism to reinforce children's vegetarian convictions. So, for instance, in a Bal Vikas summer camp they heard a guru recount Sathya Sai Baba's response to a question about vegetarianism: 'Who is closer to me, my pet elephant Sai Geetha who eats only sweetmeats, or the tiger in the jungle who eats flesh?' Some children referred to older relatives who had become vegetarian through contact with Darshan Das, a Punjabi who drew both Sikh and Hindu adherents and was murdered in 1987. The teaching of the guru of a North Indian spiritual movement, Radhasoami, which is based in Beas, Punjab, was also mentioned in this context (Juergensmeyer, 1982). We heard also of children who had become vegetarian because of the teaching they received in supplementary classes.

No doubt the high value set on vegetarianism by the Hindu tradition generally predisposes Hindus to accept the instructions of gurus and teachers, and it is a part of the expected behaviour of many, but by no means all, castes, but research revealed no tight correlation between, say, being a brahmin and avoiding meat.

THE IMPACT OF SOCIETY

Hindus in Britain are keen to ensure a continued Hindu religious identity but this resolve has not been hardened by the degree of trauma that Sikhs suffered in 1984, when their holiest place was forcibly entered by Indian troops and thousands of coreligionists lost their lives in North India, nor by any challenge as high profile as that posed to Muslims by Salman Rushdie's *Satanic Verses* or by the ramifications of the Gulf war. By comparison Britain's Hindus, though a minority, have felt relaxed, secure within a tradition that has survived several millennia, which has adapted to many changes and takes for granted a diversity of paths, gurus and incarnate forms of the divine. Christianity and 'the English god', as one child called Jesus, fit easily into this outlook.

Methods in formal teaching also show openness to changes in the wider society. The very existence of organized classes is itself a response to an alien environment. As much of the language teaching shows, however, where methods are backward-looking and rigid, children tend to lose interest. Yet to revolutionize the teaching of Gujarati and Hindi by looking outward and appreciating the methods of language teaching which are in use in maintained schools is not feasible given the limitations of time and funding and the teachers and textbooks available.

Nevertheless, many of those supplementary classes, whose prime concern was the transmission of Hindu teaching, are showing the impact of the wider society and, particularly, of the day schools which children attend. So supplementary class teachers, themselves educated in a more traditional, authoritarian way (many of them in India or an African country), mentioned the importance of introducing drama and of involving youngsters in discussion. They also often provided English translations, or at least Roman transliterations, of prayers and dealt with questions about the Hindu tradition and arranged marriage with which children were confronted by peers and teachers at school.

To take the example of one movement, the Arya Samaj in Ealing had a deliberate policy of encouraging the active participation of children and young people in its regular devotional programmes, sometimes, for example, allowing children to conduct the *havan*, the ceremony consisting of chanting Sanskrit verses around a fire on which ghee (clarified butter) and *samagri* (fragrant substances) had been poured. Another very different organization, the Sathya Sai Baba movement, has a highly developed programme of 'Education in human values' in which role-play and discussion of ethical behaviour are essential to Bal Vikas education (Jackson and Killingley, 1988, 1991; Jackson and Nesbitt, 1993).

Despite this apparent lack of defensiveness or exclusiveness, neither British Hinduism in general nor the supplementary classes for children show Christian influence comparable to that in, say, Trinidad's Hindu population (Vertovec, 1987). There, initially last century, Hindus were an underclass of indentured labourers who had almost no contact with India or with the texts of the tradition. Today's classes for Trinidadian Hindu children approximate to Sunday school and include a creed. Hindu children in Britain, however, show their own synthesis of the dominant culture and home tradition. At one level this is the celebration of Christmas with a decorated tree, family parties and the exchange of colourfully wrapped presents.[5] Young Hindus also tend to show familiarity with the Christian nativity story.

At another level this synthesis is detectable in children's use of words and symbols from surrounding Christian culture to explain to the outsider aspects of Hindu practice. For example, when asked to explain what he thought was the significance of a coconut used in *puja*, a Punjabi boy used the analogy of the christingle about which he had learned at school. Describing the naming ceremony (*namkaran*) of a baby, a Gujarati girl called it a christening and referred to the girls closest to a bride at a Hindu wedding as bridesmaids.

Asked to say what was happening in a picture of a religious leader applying red powder to his devotee's forehead with the tip of his finger, a Punjabi boy said: 'He's baptising, [using] red dye on his forehead. People do this on special occasions like when people get confirmed in Christianity.' Children's accounts of prayer also suggested the possible influence of Christian practice. In addition to mentioning the recitation of sacred syllables and verses (mantras) in Sanskrit, from which they derived a sense of peace and confidence, some spoke of spontaneous prayer attributed to English. One young Gujarati teacher, a guru in the Bradford Bal Vikas, said that he taught the children the prayer attributed to St Francis of Assisi and encouraged them to pray 'from the heart'.

The impact of secularization on Hindu children is less easily detectable. The children all took for granted the existence of God and the value of prayer. Parents are more saddened by the thought of any erosion of such Hindu family values as respect and duty than by the possibility of changing attitudes to ritual and the deities. Rejection of family values, which had been previously taken for granted, much more obviously and radically affects others than partial erosion of ritual practice. Individualism is more of a threat than either agnosticism or Christian teaching.

Hindu children are growing up in a community which is characterized by the pragmatism and compromise necessary for survival in a climate which is physically, religiously and socially very different from the environment in which family tradition evolved. Hindu tradition has accommodated diversity over the centuries and over a subcontinental terrain characterized by contrasts.

CONCLUSION

From the data we have collected it would be rash to make firm judgements about sources of authority in the nurture of British Hindu children. It would be even more rash to generalize about British Hindu children themselves, especially those outside the age range we studied. Nevertheless, the authority of tradition, especially as transmitted by parents and other family members, seems crucial in the formation of young people's religious and ethnic identity. The influence of supplementary education further emphasizes this traditional authority for some children.

Language teaching (whether informal oral transmission in the home or formal teaching in supplementary schools) not only reinforces ethnic identity but consolidates religious identity. In the case of Punjabi Hindus, emphasis on learning Hindi marks a religious boundary between them and Punjabi Muslims and Sikhs. The adoption (or at least the ideal) of vegetarianism, too, can signify the distinction between Hinduism and other religious traditions.

It is primarily through interactions within the family that roles and obligations are learned and reinforced, through participation in ritual activity in festivals and rites of passage and, to a much lesser extent, through the stories that may accompany such events.

Spiritual movements, through the charisma of their gurus and through the content of their teaching, their use of sacred texts and their educational materials, are a source of authority for an increasing number of British Hindu children (Knott, 1986c). Although the ideal of vegetarianism was sometimes learned from parents and supplementary teaching not linked to a sampradaya, most of the examples we encountered were rooted in spiritual movements, especially, but not exclusively, Pushtimarg, Radhasoami, ISKCON and the Sathya Sai Baba organization. It is noteworthy that three of these groups worldwide transcend ethnic boundaries and so represent a form of authority that could play an important part in reshaping British Hindu tradition. It has to be remembered, however, that in giving allegiance to the spiritual movement families we studied in no way renounced their ethnic roots. Families might adopt as much from a religious movement as they needed while participating fully in groups such as temple committees, satsangs (religious gatherings) or caste associations which represented other strands in their Hindu inheritance.

Young Hindus are inevitably influenced by the surrounding culture, especially of the school and of the media. Individualism seems much more of an influence than secularization, and potentially can be a source of conflict within families. Christianity, mainly learned about in schools, seems not to be an erosive influence. The inclusive and tolerant nature of the Hindu tradition can sometimes allow stories and aspects of Christian practice and custom to be absorbed into personal and family life without being a threat to it.

NOTES

1. The Religious Education and Community Project was an umbrella term for a series of linked studies at the University of Warwick under the direction of Robert Jackson. These have now been subsumed in the Warwick Religions and Education Research Unit (WRERU). For funding we are grateful to the University of Warwick Research and Innovations Fund and the Leverhulme Trust. The latter supported 'Hindu Nurture in Coventry' and 'Punjabi Hindu Nurture' and is currently funding a longitudinal study of the same young Hindus. WRERU also produces curriculum material (e.g. Jackson 1989a, b; Jackson and Nesbitt, 1990), its most recent materials being published by Heinemann as the Warwick RE Project. Further details are available from the Director, WRERU, Institute of Education, University of Warwick, Coventry CV4 7AL.
2. For a more general discussion of moral issues (including marriage and the family, peace, conflict, minority rights and environmental issues), see Jackson and Killingley (1991).
3. The stories of Savitri's devotion to her husband and Shravan Kumar's devotion to his parents are recounted by Jaffrey (1985), pp. 9–20.
4. For a version of the story which is told on Karva Chauth, see Jaffrey (1985), pp. 73–9.
5. For more critical response to this phenomenon, see Alibhai (1987) and Baumann (1992).

REFERENCES

Alibhai, Yasmin (1987) A White Christmas. *New Society*, **18**, 15–17.
Baumann, Gerd (1992) 'Ritual implicates "others": rereading Durkheim in a plural society'. In Daniel de Coppier (ed.) *Understanding Rituals*. London: Routledge, pp. 97–116.
Burghart, Richard (ed.) (1987) *Hinduism in Great Britain*. London: Tavistock.
Jackson, Robert (1989a) 'Religious education: from ethnographic research to curriculum development'. In J. Campbell and V. Little (eds) *Humanities in the Primary School*. Lewes: Falmer.
Jackson, Robert (1989b) *Religions Through Festivals: Hinduism*. London: Longman.
Jackson, Robert and Killingley, Dermot (1988) *Approaches to Hinduism*. London: John Murray.
Jackson, Robert and Killingley, Dermot (1991) *Moral Issues in the Hindu Tradition*. Stoke on Trent: Trentham Books.

Jackson, Robert and Nesbitt, Eleanor (1986) Sketches of formal Hindu nurture. *World Religions in Education*, Shap Working Party Annual Mailing, pp. 25–9.

Jackson, Robert and Nesbitt, Eleanor (1990) *Listening to Hindus*. London: Unwin Hyman.

Jackson, Robert and Nesbitt, Eleanor (1993) *Hindu Children in Britain*. Stoke on Trent: Trentham.

Jaffrey, M. (1985) *Seasons of Splendour*. London: Pavilion.

Juergensmeyer, M. (1982) *Religion as Social Vision: The Movement Against Untouchables in 20th Century Punjab*. Berkeley: University of California.

King, Ursula (1978) True and perfect religion: Bankim Chandra Chatterjee's reinterpretation of Hinduism. *Religion*, **7**, 127–48.

Knott, Kim (1986a) 'Bound to change? The religions of South Asians in Britain'. Unpublished paper, Community Religions Project, University of Leeds.

Knott, Kim (1986b) Hinduism in Britain. *World Religions in Education*, Shap Working Party Annual Mailing, pp. 10–12.

Knott, Kim (1986c) *My Sweet Lord*. Wellingborough: Aquarian Press.

Mahadevan, T.M.P. (1977) *Outlines of Hinduism*. Bombay: Chetana.

Michaelson, M. (1987) 'Domestic Hinduism in a Gujarati trading caste'. In Richard Burghart (ed.) *Hinduism in Great Britain*. London: Tavistock, pp. 32–49.

Nesbitt, Eleanor (1990a) Religion and identity: the Valmiki community in Coventry. *New Community*, pp. 261–74.

Nesbitt, Eleanor (1990b) Pitfalls in religious taxonomy: Hindus and Sikhs, Valmikis and Ravidasis. *Religion Today*, **6**, 1.

Nesbitt, Eleanor (1991) *'My Dad's Hindu, My Mum's Side Are Sikh': Issues in Religious Identity, Arts, Culture, Education*. Oxford (Westminster College): National Foundation for Arts Education.

Nesbitt, Eleanor (1994) 'Valmikis in Coventry: the revival and reconstruction of a community'. In R. Ballard (ed.) *Desh Pradesh: The South Asian Presence in Britain*. London: Hurst.

Prabhupada, A. C. Bhaktivedanta Swami (1972) *Bhagvad-gita As It Is*. London: Collier Macmillan.

Smith, Wilfred Cantwell (1978) *The Meaning and End of Religion*. London: SPCK.

Taylor, Donald (1987) 'Charismatic authority in the Sathya Sai Baba movement'. In Richard Burghart (ed.) *Hinduism in Great Britain*. London: Tavistock, pp. 119–33.

Vertovec, S. (1987) 'Hinduism and social change in village Trinidad'. Unpublished DPhil thesis, University of Oxford.

Williams, R. B. (1984) *A New Face of Hinduism: The Swaminarayan Movement*. Cambridge: Cambridge University Press.

Williams, R. B. (1988) *Religions of Immigrants From India and Pakistan: New Threads in the American Tapestry*. Cambridge: Cambridge University Press.

Chapter 14

Orthodoxy and Openness: the Experience of Jewish Children

Clive Lawton

There are an estimated third of a million Jews in Great Britain. Most of them are from the Jewish tradition called Ashkenazi, the Central and Eastern European tradition which is most easily characterized in the popular imagination by that arising out of the 'Fiddler on the Roof' environment. Most of those Ashkenazim arrived in Britain at the turn of the century and thus the majority of Jews in Britain are now third- or fourth-generation British.

Those Jews found an already established Jewish community of Sephardim (those originally from Spain and Portugal who had come to Britain often via Holland, Italy or France). Some of these families constituted the famous names of British Jewry like the Rothschilds or the Montefiores. They established an infrastructure, originally unwillingly, to accommodate their 'country cousins' from Eastern Europe. The settled Jews were in part embarrassed by the newcomers' outlandishness but did not fail to see them as their responsibility and so set up many of the structures and institutions we know now to assimilate them into British life.

In return, this huge wave of Ashkenazim breathed new life into a community that was in deep danger of losing its identity in its desire to become acceptable to a rather unaccommodating British ruling class. Some speculate that had those Jews not arrived fleeing the pogroms of Eastern Europe, there might have been little left that was identifiably Jewish about those families by now.

A smaller proportion of present-day Jewry is from Central Europe, arriving before and after the war, escaping the ravages of the Holocaust, and a still smaller number are Sephardim of Oriental origin who arrived with others from the Third World during the 1950s, 1960s and 1970s.

Recent demographic and statistical studies of the Jewish community (for example those carried out by the Board of Deputies of British Jews) suggest that it is still true that about 70 per cent of Jews affiliate to a synagogue of some sort. This does not necessarily imply a very high level of religiosity but it does suggest a very high level of desire to belong.

The thing to which all Jews who so identify want to belong is Jewish history and culture – or, put differently, they want to be part of the Jewish destiny.

The practical result of this is that most Jews who identify as such want their children to have some sort of Jewish education. At the same time, Jews are intensely concerned about their ability to integrate into and contribute to the wider society and it is only a very tiny proportion of British Jews who do not seek a balance between Jewish and Western, secular education of the prevailing humanist, technological type.

The most common way of obtaining Jewish education for one's children is to send them to 'Hebrew classes' or 'religion school'. This normally takes place for at least two or three hours on a Sunday morning and, in some cases, on a couple of midweek evenings as well. As the title 'Hebrew classes' implies, a significant part of the time is devoted to achieving a mastery of Hebrew, at least so that the child can handle the liturgy competently. This frequently means an ability to read Hebrew without necessarily understanding it or, if translation is undertaken, it is often done in the most rote and unproductive manner.

In addition, on the curriculum at this kind of provision is information about aspects of Jewish practice, details of festivals and their observances, Bible stories and homilies, Israel education, moral and ethical instruction and, of course, an attempt to develop a sense of loyalty and association to the synagogue community to which that particular set of classes or school is attached.

These are not forums for open discussion. First, the children are fairly young and their level of knowledge from which they can discuss any matter is fairly low. Second, there is a certain desperation on the part of those running and teaching in these classes that with such limited time they cannot spend time on children 'just discussing'. Finally, they are institutions established to nurture young Jews in the hope that they will replicate and perpetuate the practice of their parents or – better still – their grandparents!

The leadership of the Jewish community has grown increasingly frustrated with this model of education. Typically, children start at about 5 or 6 and finish with Barmitzvah for boys or Batmitzvah for girls, i.e. at 12 or 13 when they are traditionally considered old enough to take on the full designation of 'sons/daughters of the commandments'. Clearly, while these are good years for drilling in a lot of information, they are dreadful for obtaining anything like a mature level of commitment to a religious community that will see one into adult life.

The frustration with this age pattern is not new. The impetus behind the Liberal (Reform) Jewish movement in the nineteenth century doing away with Barmitzvah and introducing a 'confirmation' at 16 was largely to do with the recognition that if Liberal Judaism was to be ideologically, rather than practice, based, then passing-out parades at 13 did not make any sense.

Nowadays, nearly all sections of the Jewish community have realized that in order to keep the adherence of their young, they need to nurture an ideological commitment in which patterns of practice can be embedded. Thus, the 'Sunday schools' have teenage centres, GCSE classes, youth extension programmes and the like in an attempt to retain the young people until something more mature can be attempted with them than the mere transmission of information and patterns of behaviour, i.e. to be able to move beyond skills, beyond understanding, to a carefully guided evaluation.

However, Barmitzvah age has a firm hold on the Jewish sense of maturation and many Liberal communities are finding themselves under pressure to reintroduce Barmitzvah, albeit with many striving to retain confirmation at 16 as well. However, commitment to Barmitzvah (and Batmitzvah to a lesser extent) has a more pragmatic basis as well, even if it is rarely articulated.

The desire on the part of Jewish parents for the children to gain security (a constantly elusive Jewish dream) results in the very high aspirations that Jewish parents have for their children. Add to this a tradition that lays great stress on learning and scholarship and it is not surprising that in this more secular world Jews still express this commitment to learning but this time as a means of gaining acceptance and security in a non-Jewish world. Barmitzvah as a closing ceremony on a young Jew's formal Jewish education comes at about the right time for him to start to concentrate on his GCSE exams!

Thus the programme of Barmitzvah and Batmitzvah education offers perhaps a once in a lifetime opportunity for many Jews to pursue some Jewish studies with a definable and desirable end in view – to celebrate one's coming of age with confidence and pride. As a result, much time and probably too much stress has been put on what might be included in the curriculum at this age.

In Orthodox communities girls do still, remarkably, learn the details of housewifery, particularly insofar as it is affected by Jewish dietary laws of what is permitted (*kasher* or *kosher*), the special recipes for the festivals and so on. In contrast, boys spend a significant amount of time on the ritual dimension of learning to chant the Torah according to the traditional tunes.

This is changing as it becomes recognized that it is nowadays easily as important for boys to have a working knowledge of kashrut, for example, but the curricula are still much restricted by the traditional experiences of the teachers who design the courses. Much of the pressure for change comes from the children themselves whose experience in their secular schooling leads them to demand some shifts in emphasis.

Of course, a century ago it would have seemed strange to start a chapter on Jewish systems of nurture with a description of formal education structures. The starting point for Jewish education was always the home. So indeed it still is in a minority of homes – or perhaps it is in a majority of homes but not to the extent that will ensure a new Jewishly committed generation.

There is still a remarkably high level of residual Jewish practice and identification amongst those whom many Jews would brand as fairly irreligious. They may circumcise their sons, mount mezuzoth (small scrolls containing verses from the Torah) on their doors, light candles on Friday night, fast all day on Yom Kippur (Day of Atonement), hold a Pesakh Seder (Passover meal) of sorts and eat matza (unleavened bread), take time off work on Rosh Hashana (New Year) and Yom Kippur, identify strongly with the plight of Israel and Israelis, socialize mainly with Jews and, yes, send their children to Hebrew classes!

These traditional forms of nurture (for example, the Pesakh Seder is self-consciously an educational event) embed in the processes of Jewish life at least minimal practical experiences of Jewish identity that must prompt even a rudimentary explanation as to what is going on. With the rooting of Jewish practice in the home so firmly, it is almost impossible for the Jewish young person to be entirely unaware of the fact of his or her Jewish identity and some of the key implications that flow from it. (Sadly, of course, some parents are now relatively ill-equipped to answer those questions and might indeed discontinue a practice simply to avoid being asked embarrassing questions about it rather than because they intrinsically wish to reject the practice concerned.)

While this may be the pattern for probably the majority of Jews in nurturing their own sense of identity and thus that of their young, there has, in common with most other religious communities, been a revival of commitment and with it the rising status of education as a key communal concern.

One of the significant results of this shift is the rise in Jewish day schools. Today, over a third of Jewish youngsters attend Jewish day schools. In 1965, it was about a fifth. About half of the schools are state-aided and by far the majority are primary, again replicating the pre-Barmitzvah pattern. The state-aided schools offer a curriculum which fulfils the demands of a secular system, together with between 15 and 25 per cent of time devoted to Jewish studies of one sort or another. This will include the study of Hebrew as well as more systematic approaches to the items on the part-time educational curriculum identified above.

The private schools are frequently private not least because they do not meet the demands of the state in respect of the secular (now National) curriculum. Typically, these schools might devote half or more of each school day to their Jewish curriculum and they produce students highly skilled in Jewish learning of the classical sort with its text-based, rote-learned, dialectically argued approach to the teasing out of truth and understanding.

On any objective scale, the intellectual training offered to quite young children in these schools is unparalleled in any state school. Their sponsors argue that Jewish learning encompasses much that is demanded by the National Curriculum and thus the division is spurious, but they have yet to produce a systematic structure for demonstrating that this is indeed so.

As a pointer though towards the truth of this claim, in the mid-1980s HMI strongly criticized a private Jewish school for failing to pursue a broad enough curriculum. The governors of the school took HMI to court and gained a retraction on the basis that HMI could not understand Yiddish and therefore could not know that much of what was going on under the guise of apparently religious education was in fact natural sciences, history and geography. (Yiddish, the homely vernacular spoken by many Ashkenazis, developed in the Rhineland in the Middle Ages, a Germanic language to which many Hebrew and Aramaic words and phrases were added.)

As remarkable testimony to the growth of the Jewish day school movement stands the Akiva School in north London, the first and, to date, only Reform Jewish day school in Britain. Twenty years ago it would have been unthinkable that Reform Jews would have established, much less sent their children to, a Jewish school. The whole ideological thrust of Progressive Judaism is integrationalist and the fear that Jewish schools might be ghettos would have scotched any such proposal. However, in the 1980s the Akiva School was established, partly in recognition that Reform Jews were sending their children to Orthodox Jewish schools (since there were no others) and partly because of the growing realization that a positive ideology needed a positive environment in which to grow.

Finally, on the formal side are the yeshivot and seminaries. These are centres of higher Jewish learning for boys and girls. They vary in their curricular emphasis but they are in the main patterned on traditional forms of study emanating from Eastern Europe. It is becoming increasingly common for young people to take some time off between school and higher or further education or employment to spend some time at such an institution.

The timetable will be full and demanding. The majority of the programme will centre on gaining a greater proficiency in the study and understanding of traditional religious texts. These will be in both Hebrew and Aramaic, in two different kinds of script and spanning two millennia of literary scholarship.

There is still some debate about the level to which girls should study but there are an increasing number of strictly Orthodox establishments whose programmes for girls are as rigorous and demanding as those for boys.

Amongst Progressive Jews, these distinctions do not exist. However it must be said that the tradition of higher-level Jewish study is not as widely cultivated and the number of outlets for high-level study within the Progressive Jewish tradition is quite small. Certainly, it would be surprising if Progressive Jews laid quite so much stress on textual study, bearing in mind their more flexible placing of text in the hierarchy of authority for the modern Jew.

Over and above these formal structures, which are successful to varying degrees in their stated aims (the Board of Deputies' Redbridge survey in the 1980s disturbingly suggested that the highest level of disaffiliation from the community was amongst those who had had a Jewish school education to secondary level), there is the very vigorous informal education provision which spans the full range of Jewish identity and produces a youth service which is a model for any community.

Besides the traditional-style youth clubs, which used to be attached to many synagogues but are now mainly housed in purpose-built centres, the main form of youth provision, which reaches an estimated 30 per cent of Jewish teenagers, comprises the youth movements. Typically these are organized around a particular ideology, e.g. socialist, Zionist, cultural and charitable activities, help to the disadvantaged or whatever. Interestingly, and as an accolade to this style of youth provision, the youth clubs attached to the Reform synagogues around the country have undergone a transformation and become a youth movement very explicitly propagating and standing for Reform Judaism.

To try and divide Jewish and Zionist activity at youth level is almost impossible and so it is not surprising that one of the high spots of participation in any of these movements is to spend some time collectively in Israel on a tour, some work experience or a study programme. Of course, the more explicitly Zionist youth movements see the highest form of graduation from the movement as emigrating to spend the rest of one's life as an active part of that great Jewish experiment.

It is within these movements in particular, for the most part peer led, that moral and social issues will be most vigorously encountered. All of them have an explicitly educational aim and all participants know that involvement will expose them to teaching and exploration of important issues for young Jews today.

Even the 'table tennis' youth clubs strive to provide explicit educational programmes to enhance or explore their members' Jewish identity. Since these clubs have a less defined ideology, their curriculum is content-free (more or less) and therefore they are frequently more open to encounter with others outside the community. A youth club might, for example, organize a cultural exchange with the predominantly black club down the road or sporting functions with other youth clubs in the area. The movements will make their links nationally with other members of the same movement.

Having said that, all youth movements participate in 'Operation Goodwill', the annual exercise at Christmas in which Jewish people volunteer to work in hospitals and other social provisions to release non-Jews who might want to spend the time with their families. To this extent, Jews are constantly aware of how others might see them and so there is a desire to make good relationships. What is less frequently on the Jewish agenda is how Jews see others.

In conclusion, I should point out that in this chapter I have dealt almost exclusively with the mainstream of British Jewry, the centre 75 per cent. At either end of the spectrum are Jews who do not reflect these patterns.

There are some who feel that continued involvement in the Jewish community and cultivation of a deep Jewish identity is to set their children up for much of the pain and rejection that they themselves might have suffered. Thus these youngsters might see being Jewish as a purely defensive identity and ironically might more learn to see the non-Jew as a threat than those who have been given a more positive perspective.

At the other end of the spectrum are those who are normally called 'ultra-Orthodox'. This is not in fact because they appear more 'orthodox' than many another Jew, but because they appear more 'Jewish' because of distinctive dress, a wider use of Yiddish as a vernacular and a more or less complete lack of interest in relationships with the wider community – which includes other Jews!

These Jews in their various sects have a thriving network of educational provision and the standards of intellectual rigour and levels of retention of young people might be the envy of many another community striving to keep its youth.

There are thus extensive systems established by the Jewish community for enhancing the nurture of young Jews. Increasingly, the provision and funding of such structures are being seen to be *the* priority for the Jewish community of today to ensure that there is a Jewish community tomorrow.

Through these structures, opportunities are provided for young people to gain an affection for Jewish traditions, a familiarity with Jewish practice and a safe environment in which they can experiment with their rebellions.

Since there are many more primary school places than secondary school places in Jewish day schools and since the part-time system still mostly ceases at Bat/Barmitzvah age, the relatively more flexible structures of youth club and movement are the leading strategies by which the Jewish community tries to keep its young people on a loose rein. Within the clubs, and to a lesser extent within the movements, teenage Jews can challenge the adult Jewish community and despair of its timeserving compromises with reality.

Meanwhile, the very engaging in the debate is participation in a time-honoured Jewish tradition – debate and argument have long been the best systems of Jewish education – and so the very resentment or rebellion become their own educational medium for resolution and retention. That's the theory – now we struggle with the practice!

FURTHER READING

Alderman, Geoffrey (1992) *Modern British Jewry*. Oxford: Clarendon Press.
Barnett, Vida (1983) *A Jewish Family in Britain*. Exeter: Religious and Moral Education Press.
Bermant, Chaim (1969) *Troubled Eden*. London: Vallentine Mitchell.
Holm, Jean (1990) *Growing up in Judaism*. Harlow: Longman.
Kosmin, B. and Levy, C. (1983) *Jewish Identity in an Anglo-Jewish Community*. London: Research Unit, Board of Deputies of British Jews.
Lawton, Clive (1984) *I Am a Jew*. London: Franklin Watts.
Waterman, Stanley and Kosmin, Barry (1986) *British Jewry in the Eighties: A Statistical and Geographical Guide*. London: Research Unit, Board of Deputies of British Jews.

Chapter 15

Orthodoxy and Openness: the Experiences of Muslim Children

Peter Woodward

THE NATURE OF THE TENSIONS FACED BY YOUNG MUSLIMS

Language

Inshallah: in translation, if God wills. This says it all. The principal tension that Muslim children face in non-Muslim countries is one of language. They live in a dual culture with twin languages. Every deep, devout thought they have – and often every trite, superficial one as well – needs to be expressed first in Arabic or Urdu or Punjabi or Bengali and then in English as well – or in Welsh or Gaelic or broad Yorkshire or German or Manhattan as the case may be, according to where they live!

For some children, especially those recently arrived in their new country, such dualism is a problem. Their control of English may be limited or their confidence in using it may have sunk to a low level. They may have a knowledge of vocabulary in their second language but lack the skills necessary to hold a conversation in any but the most stilted terms.

But there are others who can turn their tongues to the daily use of two (or more) languages with ease and a facility that comes from regular practice. They seem to be at home with idioms and adjectives. They chatter easily and fluently in either language in the playground as well as in the classroom. And they borrow as many words from their second language to use in their first as they do the other way round. They even seem able to think and to dream in two different languages – a mark of considerable maturity.

These, of course, are the two extremes. There are many, many shades in between, as is equally the case with Hindu and Sikh children living outside India. What is distinctive of the majority of Muslim children in Britain is that in addition to the language of the home (which is often Urdu or Punjabi, or a dialect such as Miapuri; or Bengali or its Sylheti dialect) and the school-based study of English, most Muslim children also study Arabic at the Qur'anic classes they attend when day school is over. They thus develop control of three rather than two languages, and even if their skills in Arabic are limited in some cases to being able to read a text they cannot translate or understand, the extra practice they gain in language work can only be beneficial to their linguistic skills and dexterity.

Twin cultures

This linguistic pluralism is echoed in the cultural dualism which affects most Muslim children in non-Muslim countries. A recent research project on 'Muslim Pupils in British Schools' emphasized in its report to the Economic and Social Research Council how complex are the stringent demands made on Muslim pupils in Britain by the dual culture syndrome in which their lives are set.[1] Within the home they live in an Asian cultural setting where standards of respect, obedience and morality follow the norms of their parents and ancestors, which have often shown little change for many generations. When they leave home for school, recreation or employment they enter a Western society where standards are based on very different premises, and which their parents interpret to be a direct result of the secularization process they fear so greatly.

The dilemma that Muslim children face as a result of this dichotomy emerges in a number of facets, three of which are acute enough to merit listing here.

The first stems from the nature of Islam as a way of life with practical implications for daily living. The children interviewed in the Cambridge-based project mentioned above displayed for the most part a marked loyalty to their faith. On questions of nationality they were often divided, part British and part Pakistani or Punjabi or Indian or Bengali. But on questions of a religious nature they were emphatically Muslim.

Being Muslim in a non-Islamic society is, of course, a sure recipe for encountering problems, especially at times of racial or political unrest. The polarization of views over, for instance, such individuals as Salman Rushdie and Saddam Hussein poses severe problems for Muslim pupils, who feel that their religion-based loyalties are being pulled in tug-of-war fashion in opposing directions. Fellow pupils and school staff expect them to hold strong views and to be willing to express them, but then oppose these views with vehemence whenever they are propounded. Such conflict and tension is not easy to face with equanimity.

A second field of conflicting loyalties emerges in respect of the discipline imposed on Muslim pupils – or not imposed, as the case may be. The discipline of the homes visited in the project to which reference was made above was generally accepted as the norm and rarely questioned. It was seen by both parents and children as caring and fair. School discipline was felt to be more arbitrary, less consistent and often far too lax. In the case of unpopular teachers, discipline was said to involve shouting, a practice the children appeared to detest. The better teachers, as the pupils saw them, were not easy-going but laid down firm and clear guidelines as to acceptable behaviour, and kept to these at all times.

Most Muslim pupils appeared to find little difficulty in moving from school into the discipline structure of the home. Operating in the other direction was less straightforward, especially in such aspects as punctuality, regular attendance and respect for females, and the school's discipline was often seen as touched with uncertainty and was accordingly often viewed with some derision.

A third area of concern, and one which again constituted an important feature of the pupil-based interviews of the ESRC Cambridge-based research project, was the children's expressed concern over the lack of protective support available to them in their schools. In an outer-ring school where Muslim pupils were few in number, this was a view shared with other Asian minority groups. In an inner-ring girls' school it was expressed by the Bangladeshi pupils in particular, who felt picked on by the Pakistani/Punjabi majority, who spoke Urdu and Punjabi and poked fun at members of the Bengali- and Sylheti-speaking community. In both cases pupils wanted the school staff to intervene to protect or rescue them much more frequently and effectively than they did, and felt it was a form of discrimination that they were in effect 'neglected' to such an extent.

Family loyalties

A further conflict related to the loyalty Muslim pupils clearly felt to their parents, and frequently also to other members of their extended family. This often took the form of seeking to shelter their parents from any knowledge of the conflicts they had encountered, usually by omitting to mention at home the difficulties they had faced during the day. In extreme cases they had even been known to suppress information about parents' evenings at which their relatives might learn of these problems, and, in the cases where they are asked to translate for their parents, to gloss over the real nature of these issues.

Such 'protectionism' was, for the most part, intended to shelter parents from the rigours of the two-culture syndrome mentioned earlier, which, with their limited understanding of English language and British customs, many parents appeared to find threatening and frightening – much more so than their children did. This concern speaks highly of the allegiance found within the family unit, which nearly always transcended pupils' loyalty to the school or to other institutions.

Religious allegiances

In religious matters Muslim pupils appeared to follow very closely the examples and attitudes of their homes. Where these attitudes were supportive of mosque worship or loyalty to particular individual leaders, the children nearly always seemed to follow the parental line. In those cases where parents had given up the routine of prayer, pupils often attended the mosque school for some years of Qur'anic study, but rarely continued to attend once that was over. They still regarded themselves as Muslims and generally echoed Islamic views and moral practices, but mosque allegiance appeared to correlate closely with parental example.

In the case of girls this was in any event a situation where non-attendance at the mosque for prayers was the norm. The offering of *namaz* (prayers) at home, the daily reading of the Qur'an, and the observance of the halal food laws usually replaced visits to the mosque as an expression of Islamic loyalty. For the boys the examples of the father, of elder siblings and of uncles all had a profound influence, though in some cases young teenagers spent many hours at the mosque beyond anything that was expected of them. Fasting during Ramadan and most aspects of eating only halal foods received a fairly high profile, whereas other aspects of Muslim behaviour such as the observance of *zakat* (almsgiving) and making plans for *hajj* were often given only limited attention. Private prayer at home was often, apparently, seen as an adequate replacement for the ritual of regular prayer at the mosque.

The conflict of tensions that this range of observance presented to Muslim pupils was further exacerbated when they found themselves in a school and a society where Christian or secular standards seemed to be paramount. For the majority there was security in ritual observance and in following established, family-based patterns. For others the questioning process that schools applaud and introduce in the education they give raised questions about matters of faith that led easily to doubts and uncertainties. To be a Muslim is then not an easy option.

The nature of tensions such as those faced by young Muslims may be illustrated through the situation faced by a fifth-year school leaver who was anxious to go on to further education and was supported in this by her teachers. Her parents were initially opposed to the idea but they were willing to discuss it with her in some detail. Eventually a family conference was held at which a range of possibilities were discussed. These included a speedy marriage and a return to Pakistan, either of which would have decided the issue outright.

Eventually it was the voice of her mother which cracked the traditional stereotype and won the day. She argued that her daughter's character up to that time was the factor that should carry most weight, that the family had nothing to fear since she was such a reliable girl, that the opportunity for her to have a better education than her parents had received was too good to be shunned, and that her career and marriage prospects would be greatly improved by two or three years of study.

In the event the girl continued to live at home, but travelled daily by bus to a sixth-form college not too far away, where she made excellent progress. A similar dilemma will, however, face the family in a short time when career decisions and higher education options have to be clarified.

THE NATURE OF NURTURE WITHIN THE MUSLIM COMMUNITY

The influence of the home

The predominant factor in any study of nurture is the impact made by home and family. This is one of the early findings of a recent ESRC project based at the University of Warwick Arts Education Department, where the Religious Education and Community Project (RECP) has explored, under the overall direction of Robert Jackson, the nature of nurture within four religious traditions.[2] In the case of Hindus and Jews, for example, it is evident that the home exerts an influence greater than any other force not only upon the direction of a child's commitment but also upon its nature and depth.

In the case of Islam the early tribal origins of the faith and the loyalties that accompanied them find an echo today in the ready acceptance of parental jurisdiction. At any time the voice of the head of the family can be questioned, but in the last resort it must always be obeyed. Islamic morality appears to be based upon this concept of tribal fealty and loyalty. Where in other faiths there is a world leader or a national figurehead or a neighbourhood priest, in Islam there is no such figure, even in the local mosque. On very many important issues the head of the family has absolute sway.

Mosque schools and their alternatives

One of the duties carried out by the head of the family is to ensure that his children are trained in the basic tenets and practices of Islam and in the language of the Holy Qur'an. Sometimes this is achieved by sending them for several years to a part-time mosque school. In other cases a tutor may be retained to give part-time lessons, either to one family or to the children from several families. Some particularly observant parents send their children away for full-time Islamic education at a madrassah, often of a residential nature, where religion, discipline, education and morality are all closely interwoven. Whichever path is chosen, the effect is to train the pupils in those elements of Islam that are necessary to be an observant Muslim. If the emphasis is on the recitation of the Arabic of the Qur'an, this is because it is the aspect least likely to be encountered elsewhere, unless specific attention is paid to it.

Most children discover much at home about basic beliefs, postures and practices, at least as far as the adults themselves follow them. The morality of Islam they pick up as they go along. It is the Arabic language, the daily prayers and the text of the Qur'an that are the focal point of much of their teaching, simply because they will learn what they need to know of these in no other way. Then, when they have made adequate progress along these lines, it is no great loss if they go no further with such studies. The seeds of the important aspects of their education are already sown and germinating.

The mosque, prayer and the Qur'an

This early contact with the mosque is, as one would expect, of value in familiarizing children, both boys and girls, with the mosque and in creating a pattern of visiting the masjid that will be useful when the question of attending it for prayers or for festivals comes round. There is in fact a great deal of nurture that takes place incidentally through being in the presence of other people who are worshipping or celebrating. The cumulative effect of witnessing repeatedly the prayers of the devout can be formative on both the accuracy and the orthodoxy of the child's prayer routines and also on the depth of devotion involved in the ritual.

The mosque is, of course, more than a place of prayer. It is a centre for the community to gather, study, talk and plan a whole range of activities, partly religious and partly secular. Here there may be weddings and funerals, political or social gatherings, community activities, and, of course, study sessions.

The Qur'an is studied not just by children, but also by the adults in the community. In particular, many members of the Muslim faith in Britain lack employment and spend a good proportion of their free time in reading, studying and debating the words and message handed down through the Messenger of Allah.

Such study is the life blood of Islam, for the Qur'an is the yardstick of orthodoxy, the incentive to all religious observance and the guardian of the very spirit of the faith. Children who find when visiting the mosque that their elders are content to spend so many hours in Qur'anic study there are inevitably prompted to see such activity as the natural process which is theirs to inherit.

The day school and religious education

Many Muslim parents also expect and hope that the schools their children attend will provide an element of nurture in the Islamic faith, since this is the custom in the villages and towns of the Indian subcontinent where they and their families have mostly grown up. In particular, they are often informed by the school that the RE lessons will include a course on Islam, and many of them assume this will be similar in nature to the lessons provided by the mosque school.

Indeed, in schools where the large majority of pupils are Muslims, parents often feel the school is not fulfilling its natural role if it fails to provide proper courses of Islamic instruction. The twin merits of such courses as these are that they eliminate the need for parents to pay for extra lessons at mosque schools at the end of each day, and they reduce the grumbles of school staff about the heavy demands made on Muslim pupils when they go on to such lessons at the end of the school day, in addition to the home-work the school sets for the evening or the weekend.

The reality of the situation is that schools provide educational teaching and learning situations rather than nurture experiences. Some such courses are sensitive, accurate and acceptable to local Muslim communities. On the other hand, certain mosques encourage parents to object to any teaching about Islam by non-Muslim teachers, and a few actively instruct parents to withdraw their pupils from religious education lessons and school assemblies.

Even in those rare situations where an RE teacher in a secondary school is a Muslim, the courses provided are usually of an educational nature and the nurture content is severely limited. This of course is one of the factors underlying recent Muslim attempts to remedy the situation by developing Voluntary Aided schools for their children, though it is probably a secondary factor, lagging some way behind the desire for single-sex education for secondary-aged Muslim pupils.

In multicultural schools with a high Muslim pupil content the courses in religious education that are provided, along with an element of appropriate assembly material, often fulfil a valuable role in informing all members of the school community about Muslim belief and practice and in providing information about current fasts and festi-vals and major events in the world of Islam. Information is of course a major ingredient in the constitution of any educational course. But whether information alone is sufficient to meet the nurture-orientated requirements of the Muslim communities in the non-Islamic world is a much larger question.

As a final word on the issue of nurture, it would seem relevant to emphasize that similar background and upbringing does not necessarily produce identical results. The personalities of individual children are so diverse that the end product may differ greatly even within families. Two Muslim students I interviewed jointly in a Midlands sixth-form college may bear this out. They were similar in age, background, family, schooling and many other respects. In temperament and attitude to the Salman Rushdie affair they were however as different as chalk from cheese.

The result was a blazing argument. One vowed that he would choke the traitorous author with his own bare hands if ever he knew where he was – and all other Muslims ought to do the same. The other argued just as persuasively, if with more finesse and less vehemence, that while Rushdie's work should be opposed, it was no part of Islam to hound an individual because of the nature of his religious or literary viewpoints. It became clear that similarity of nurture does not of itself lead to uniformity.

Interestingly, the college declined to stage a formal discussion on this issue because the staff were aware how controversial the matter had become and how divided the student community was upon the rights and wrongs of the debate. Any officially sponsored consideration of the issue might be interpreted as taking sides, one way or the other.

GROWING AWAY AND MARRYING OUT

Fears parents have for their children

It would be rash to oversimplify, but among the welter of anxieties that Muslim parents have over their children, two appear to stand out vividly. These are the fear that the children may give up their loyalty to the Muslim faith, and the fear that they may marry a non-Muslim. Both of these dangers occur often enough for parental unease to be justified. Neither happens so frequently that the future of the community is threatened. The two often appear to be closely related, but by no means inescapably so.

The idea that children may grow away from family and faith is partly based on what Muslim parents see of Western society and partly on recent experience within the Muslim community. In a small number of cases children appear to have stopped attending the mosque and have filled the void this leaves by frequenting discos, pubs, clubs, and other 'unsavoury' locations. Major consumption of drink and drugs is probably rare in the British Muslim world, but a habit such as this is usually seen as a rejection of the faith and a turning away from family tradition.

Marrying out of the faith brings a sharper focus. Again it is feared and disliked by Sikh and Jewish parents as much as by Muslims. It is viewed with slightly less disfavour in cases where a Muslim male marries a non-Muslim female, since it is likely that she will convert to Islam. When a Muslim female marries a non-Muslim male, however, the implication is that she will embrace her husband's religion, and that is seen as highly undesirable. One of the functions of the arranged marriage is to prevent such an occurrence.

Nervousness of family response and community reaction

There is inevitably an element of fear, however small, in the response of Muslim children to their parents' views on these issues. While most children do not wish either to move away or to marry out, and have a great deal of respect for family traditions and loyalties, they know of cases where children have been ostracized or expelled from the family home or have suffered violence and even, in a very few cases, death for doing so. Admittedly these are rare and extreme. But it follows that children think very carefully before taking any action that will bring dishonour on the family in the eyes of the larger Muslim community.

Dishonour is a great stigma among Muslims, and any suggestion that the head of the family is unable to exercise full control over the actions of other members of the family group, especially the younger ones, is a source of great concern to the adult leaders of the local community. To be on the receiving end of the scorn and sarcasm that may follow such an episode can be a major disaster that is hard to outlive and that will not be forgotten for a very long time.

Response from the community outside the family can also be a cause of great concern and can lead to much loss of face, even to a level where an element of ostracism may take place towards the whole family who have 'let the side down', for this is how it will often be seen. It is partly to prevent the development of situations that could produce such a reaction that many Muslim girls are sent back to the family home in India, Pakistan or Bangladesh, where they will be surrounded by Muslim influences, friends and relatives, and where the chances of 'moving away' or 'marrying out' are very much reduced. Even should an arranged marriage be rejected there by the 'ungrateful' young-ster, any alternative arrangement is still likely to take place within the Muslim community.

Anxiety over the future of the Muslim community

The basic reasons for such careful provision for the young are mostly personal and family based. There is, however, also an element of concern for the overall Muslim community, the 'house of Islam', and for the standards it seeks to uphold. Many Muslims fear that once the door is opened to what they see as Western standards of morality, there will be a rapid decline in practical loyalty to Islam and in observance of the Muslim way of life. In particular, their fear is that the number of Muslims praying at the mosque and observing Ramadan, Eid and almsgiving will decline rapidly and the future of the faith will be at risk.

For this fear there is clearly some justification. Numbers attending for prayer vary greatly, but there is evidence of a substantial element of the Islamic population who rarely pray at home or at the mosque, especially among the older teenage community. Whether they return once past their youth or come to attend spasmodically is unclear. Naturally, the older generations are very concerned and try to deflect this trend by rein-forcing the role of the mosque school, a strategy that meets with only partial success.

There is, of course, a link here with the question of discipline to which reference was made earlier. The firm but quiet security that the home often affords would appear to have a calming and restraining influence during primary and lower secondary years. For the older teenager whether at school or elsewhere there is more temptation and more peer group attraction for a different way of life, and there appears to be no obvious or universally effective answer to what is basically the age-old question of bridging the generation gap.

Children's attitudes to growing away

Many Muslim children are adamant that they have no intention of growing away from their background. They enjoy the cameraderie of the mosque school and the sense of achievement that comes from proficiency in reciting the Arabic of the Qur'an. They find security in the discipline of the prayer routine and a sense of community in gathering with other Muslims for functions and festivals where they can be proud of being Islamic. They claim that their loyalty to Islam eases tensions between home and school, especially where there are high percentages of Muslim pupils in the schools they attend. They are committed to the principle of obedience to their parents which Islam engenders and for the most part have grown up expecting to have a marriage arranged for them by their parents when they reach an appropriate age.

At the same time there are other children who are much less sure of their faith, often growing up in homes where there is no parental example of regular prayer or mosque attendance. These are much more susceptible to non-Islamic influences and will be likely to move with their parents out of inner-city areas into the more affluent outskirts where Muslims constitute a small minority. In such cases there will probably be fewer restrictions placed on Muslim girls that might hinder their continuing with further or higher education or seeking types of employment that would be unacceptable to their more orthodox and observant counterparts.

Between these two extremes of the ultra-strict and the non-observant there are many shades and gradations. Generalization is clearly unwise and unreliable. It is sufficient to note that many pupils are aware of their parents' concern over such issues and often refrain from any actions that would cause them grave concern. At the same time pupil behaviour and belief today springs less from conviction than was the case in previous generations. Indeed, it is clear that a general decline in Islamic observance is a real possibility when the children currently at school become the next generation of parents.

ILLUSTRATION AND CONCLUSION

In conclusion it may prove useful to close with an illustration that encapsulates where Islam stands on the twin issues of openness and orthodoxy, these loosely linked but seminal semi-alternatives. Several years ago when travelling in Tunisia during the closing days of Ramadan and the festival of Eid ul Fitr that followed, I noticed the erection of a series of small screens in the main street of Tunis. These were made of prayer mats or wall-hangings, woven in bright colours and depicting the holy Ka'ba at Makkah and the green-domed Prophet's Mosque at Madinah.

At first I supposed these were to form a part of some devout religious ritual. I soon discovered, however, that they were erected by local photographers and were designed to be used as a backcloth against which children and families might have their holiday snapshots taken, with instant results available for a reasonable price – reasonable, that is, to those whose bargaining powers were well developed.

Some of the adult community, especially the women, refused to have their photos taken, partly as a result of Islamic orthodoxy as they understood it and partly through fear of the evil eye – the taking of a picture could seize some part of their inner being and they might never be whole again. Their children, on the other hand, both sons and daughters, were more than happy to pose in front of the colourful screens and appeared to have few anxieties when the camera's shutter clicked in their direction.

In much the same way, it has become increasingly clear in recent years that the orthodoxy of the adults in the Muslim community frequently finds itself in conflict with the eagerness of the young. The perennial search for freedom of expression is constantly making itself felt among young people, and is evident today in various forms and to differing degrees among Muslim children in Britain. The type of authority that these parents exercise is, of course, still the unchallenged word of power. At the same time, it appears likely that the future harmony of the Muslim community will necessitate allowing to the young that liberty of expression and the openness to change that only they can fully understand and freely exemplify.

NOTES

1. 'Muslim Pupils in British Schools', a two-year project (1988–90) funded by the Economic and Social Research Council and jointly sponsored by the Department of Education in the University of Cambridge and the Cambridge-based Islamic Academy. Department of Education, 17 Trumpington Street, Cambridge, Cambridge CB2 1QA, or Professor Syed Ali Ashraf at the Islamic Academy, 23 Metcalfe Road, Cambridge CB4 2DB.
2. The four traditions covered are Christianity, Islam, Judaism and Sikhism. In the case of Islam, 40 children aged 7–14, living in the Midlands, were interviewed in their day schools and ten families were then selected for more detailed research in their homes, religion schools and synagogues. A similar number of Christian, Jewish and Sikh children were interviewed, many coming from minority communities of a British Asian background. Further information about the Warwick Religions and Education Research Unit may be obtained from its Director, Professor Robert Jackson, Institute of Education, University of Warwick, Coventry CV4 7AL, UK.

BIBLIOGRAPHY

Al-Naquib al-Attas, Syed Muhammed (1979) *Aims and Objectives of Islamic Education*. London: Hodder and Stoughton.

Anwar, Muhammad (1986) *Young Muslims in a Multi-Cultural Society: Their Educational Needs and Policy Implications: The British Case*. Leicester: The Islamic Foundation.

Ashraf, Syed Ali (1985) *New Horizons in Muslim Education*. London: Hodder and Stoughton.

Ashraf, Syed Ali (1989) *Islam – Teacher's Manual – The Westhill Project*. Leckhampton: Stanley Thomas. Also *Pupils' Books 1–4* and *Photopack*.

Ashraf, Syed Ali and Hirst, Paul H. (eds) (1994) *Religion and Education: Islamic and Christian Approaches*. Cambridge: Islamic Academy.

Bilgrami, H. H. 'Educational needs of Muslim minorities: nature and extent of the problem'. In *Muslim Communities in Non-Muslim States*. London: Islamic Council of Europe.

Halstead, J. K. (1986) *The Case for Muslim Voluntary Aided Schools: Some Philosophical Reflections*. Cambridge: The Islamic Academy.

Husain, Syed Sajjad and Ashraf, Syed Ali (1979) *Crisis in Muslim Education*. London: Hodder and Stoughton.

Joly, Daniele (1983) *The Opinions of Mirpuri Parents in Saltley, Birmingham, about their Children's Schooling*. Research Papers in Ethnic Relations, no. 23. Coventry: Centre for Research in Ethnic Relations, University of Warwick.

Joly, Daniele (1987) *Making a Place for Islam in British Society: Muslims in Birmingham*. Research Papers in Ethnic Relations, no. 4. Coventry: Centre for Research in Ethnic Relations, University of Warwick.

Nielsen, Jorgen (1992) *Muslims in Western Europe*. Islamic Surveys Series. Edinburgh: Edinburgh University Press.

Robinson, Francis (1988) *Varieties of South Asian Islam*. Research Papers in Ethnic Relations, no. 8. Coventry: Centre for Research in Ethnic Relations, University of Warwick.

Rushdie, Salman (1988) *The Satanic Verses*. London: Viking Books.

Sawib, Mohammad Abdul Karim (1983) *A Guide to Prayer in Islam*. London: Ta-Ha Publishers.

Chapter 16

Orthodoxy and Openness: the Experience of Sikh Children

Kanwaljit Kaur-Singh

I would go home and plead with my mother to have my hair cut, so there would be one less level of teasing and bullying. She would always say no, that my hair was my identity, that hundreds and thousands of Sikhs had died fighting for the right to practise their religion. She would tell me that it was a crown and I should cherish it. But I saw it as another layer of skin that prevented me from looking normal. How I cried in the mad playground panic of a fourth-form fight; somebody knocked my turban and it fell on the ground, crumpled underfoot. There lay my crown, my identity, on the hard and dusty school yard. I felt powerless. I still shrink if someone goes to touch my head.

Why did I go to sleep crying, wishing that I would wake up white, so that I fitted in with what was taught in History or English? Only the oppressed in History and the outsiders in Literature meant anything to me.[1]

This heart-rending account from Ravinder Bansal tells of an experience that forced him to deny his faith by cutting his hair, thus removing the symbols of his religion. According to him, it was the only way to survive in the world.

One of the major facts of life in the UK, as elsewhere in the world, in the latter half of the twentieth century has been the throwing together of different religions, different cultures and different races. One can argue at length as to whether Britain's immigration policies have been, according to one view, over-liberal, or according to another, dominated by racist considerations, or somewhat in between. The facts, however, are uncontroversial. Today in Britain, people with different colours of skin (or rather shades of skin), different faiths and different cultures are found together in the same work place, the same school, the same shopping centres. Hindu, Muslim, Sikh and other faiths and cultures, that once were viewed by at least some British people, in a tolerant condescending way, as quaint and exotic, are suddenly present in many local classrooms. In some locations children from such diverse backgrounds are there in substantial numbers, with clearly different attitudes to diet, dress and faith.

Today we cannot keep ourselves remote from different faiths, even if we might wish to do so. Knowledge of other cultures and other faiths is no longer an interesting academic option, but a necessity in the pursuit of communal harmony. Many in this country, from other than white and predominantly Anglo-Saxon backgrounds, even today express bitterness over their acceptance or rather lack of it in British society, as if racial

discrimination found in every country in the world were a peculiarly British institution. Yet the background is worth remembering. Right up to World War II, Britain had one of the largest empires the world has ever known, an empire in which 'Christian' was, however falsely, considered synonymous with white, and whites alone had the right to rule and spread their Christian influence over others.

My husband was in school in Birmingham at the time of Indian independence in 1947. He remembers the debate in which the surrender to a 'half-naked fakir' like Gandhi was being discussed. The word 'heathen' was frequently used. And being brought up in the English environment, even he at the time saw nothing wrong in its use! It is only when we look back at the Britain of the 1940s that we can really appreciate the subsequent degree of change and enlightenment in its attitudes to others that have come about. It is a tribute to the common sense of the British people that changes have been accomplished without major confrontation.

Having said that, tremendous injustices still remain. There is widespread racism, sometimes deliberate, but more often rooted in unthinking ignorance and prejudice. This is all too often found in our schools and other educational institutions, which by the sheer nature of 'education' should be above prejudice and ignorance. Sikh children have been suffering and, still to this day, are meeting unfair, unjust and unequal treatment at the hands of their educators and peers alike. Before we look at the difficulties faced by Sikh youngsters, let us look at how children learn and how schools are failing to provide them with equal opportunities.

Children learn when their experiences of family and community life are valued and the validity of those experiences is recognized; when there is continuous praise for their efforts and they experience success; when their language, their faith and their culture are shared, respected and appreciated; and when their individuality is recognized and valued.

Let us see what happens to a Sikh child when he goes to school. My aim here is not to build a negative picture, but simply to outline the reaction of all too many teachers to Sikh children entering the school for the first time. The reaction to the arrival of a Sikh child can so easily be: 'another problem entering the classroom'. First, his name is Kanwaljit; the reaction is 'Oh, another of those funny names, I can never pronounce them. What, the child cannot speak any English? Why don't the parents teach him English at home?' The audible groans and the body language of the teacher reduce the child's self-esteem; and the child has already been made uncertain by being in a strange new environment.

A further blow to his self-esteem is that Kanwaljit is a boy, and the teacher looking at his long, plaited hair is already calling him a girl. A year or two passes, he discovers that he is coloured and, added to this, he finds that his parents' country of origin, India or East Africa, is never mentioned; the stories about his culture and his religion are non-existent in the school. As he grows up, he enters a world of English history and literature, and English religion, once described by Cole in the *Sikh Messenger* as 'a kind of altruistic morality sanctioned by occasional references to someone called Jesus'.[2] What it actually feels like is again conveyed by Ravinder Bansal:

> My first contact with difference came, at the age of five. It was lunchtime and I was playing a chasing game around a climbing frame in the playground. One of the boys was 'it' and he was trying to catch the others. I cannot remember exactly what was said, but it left an uneasy question in my head. The boy was being called something – something to do

with what he looked like and where he came from. I had not thought about it; I had not even noticed he was black (Afro-Caribbean). I began to realise that there was something odd about me: I did not fit in with the other children. They spoke the same language at home as they did at school (I spoke Punjabi at home), they did not eat chapaties and they believed in Jesus. Whenever anything was mentioned about my home I clothed it in lies, talking about how we ate fish and chips – sowing the seeds of self-hatred.

By the time I started grammar school I had perfected my double life: at home playing the obedient, hardworking, intelligent eldest son of the family, and at school attempting to deny my Sikhism, my colour, my language, my food. My efforts to become truly angli-cized were fiercely accelerated within the 'assimilationist' ethos of the traditional grammar.[3]

In similar ways, throughout the school life, Sikh children may find their language, culture, faith and dress habits devalued and inferior in the eyes of both their educators and peers. An example is the welcome a Sikh boy received when he reached his primary school wearing a turban, a symbol of his faith. The scene is a grey February day in the Birmingham High Court. The occasion is a libel action brought by the head teacher of a Wolverhampton LEA primary school against an allegation of racism arising from his refusal to allow a turbaned boy into his school.

The central fact that the boy was refused admission because he was wearing a turban was not contested. The head said it was not only against the school rules to wear a turban, but also that the turban was 'grotesque' – like something out of a pantomime. A local school teacher of Sikh origins accused the head of deliberate racism, but such are the complexities of libel law that the head won his action and was awarded damages of several thousands of pounds.

'Children are children, whatever their race or origin' and 'we treat all children as equal and don't notice the colour of a child's skin' (although a turban was evidently noticed) are typical of the many hours of well-meaning platitudes trotted out on the head's behalf by the county education authority, teachers and parents. It is interesting to note that in a school where nearly three-quarters of pupils were of Asian origin, not one person, out of a near score giving evidence on the head's behalf, was of non-Christian background, making a statistical nonsense at least of the impartiality of parental support.

Returning to the main theme of professed equality of treatment, when the Sikh boy arrived at school in his turban, the other early arrivals were in the school hall practising the hymn for the day's school assembly. In other words, around a quarter of the chil-dren were being given a basic grounding in their own faith; three-quarters were denied this opportunity, but were obliged instead to share in the grounding in the faith of others. Whilst this cannot by any stretch of the imagination be called equality, it can be argued that it is only right and proper that children from the majority Christian commu-nity should be given basic instruction in their faith. Religion and culture are closely entwined and combine to give stability to society. As has been long acknowledged by Indarjit Singh in the *Sikh Courier*,[4] without such background, children can all too easily grow up rootless and alienated.

Surely, however, what applies to children of one background also applies to those of another. Children from non-Christian backgrounds start with an inherent disadvantage in a predominantly Christian society. This is not said in any way complainingly, but as a simple statement of fact that must be recognized by all involved in education. Some rudimentary knowledge of one's own faith is often picked up in one's home, but it is usually inadequate compared to more systematic school teaching. Most non-Christian pupils have a slight and tenuous background knowledge of their religion when they first go to school, yet it is in this that their self-confidence and their view of themselves and others are rooted.

The role of the educators should be first to learn something of the background of those in their charge, and then to ensure that all children are acquainted with at least a basic outline of these different religions and cultures. It is highly important that this is done as early as possible before the children inherit the sillier prejudices of their elders. It was all too clear from the court hearing that nothing whatsoever in this direction had been done in the school of that particular head teacher. Apparently, the pursuit in this school was not of equality, but of a dull, unthinking and uncaring uniformity.

The turban could not be worn because 'if one child was allowed to wear a turban, another might want to wear earrings, etc'. If the avowed aim of the head and his staff had been deliberately to destroy the self-esteem and self-confidence of pupils from other than a Christian background, they could not have gone about it any more directly.

I would not describe those who gave evidence on the head's behalf as racially insincere. Rather, the difficulty is that it is all too easy to become jingoistic, so immersed in our culture and so convinced by the educational environment of its natural superiority as to be quite blind to the culture and aspirations of others. Many times I have heard from the educators' lips the phrase 'problem child' (who speaks more than one language) and 'if only parents would speak English with the child at home', without the least understanding that it could be possible that the parents might not be English-speakers. At the same time, why should any child be deprived the opportunity of learning his or her 'mother tongue?' Again, the phrase that 'we treat all children the same' is repeated out of ignorance, without realizing that treating all children alike means treating them as if they were all equally of Anglo-Saxon cultural origins, which is not even true for Scots and Welsh. At least until recently, much of the school culture has been geared to an unconscious immersion in the culture of the Bible.

The Mandla and Lee case, which was finally settled in the House of Lords, is well known. Mr Audley Dowell-Lee, headteacher of Park Grove Private School, refused to allow Gurinder Singh Mandla to be a pupil, because he insisted on wearing a turban. Gurinder Singh Mandla was given admission to the school, but was expected to remove his turban and attend as clean-shaven. In other words, he was asked to reject his faith. The court case brought by the Commission for Racial Equality against the head teacher for racial discrimination was lost in the Crown and Appeals Courts, on the basis that Sikhs were not a racial minority, but a religious minority. Since there was no protection in law for a religious minority, it seemed that exploitation could occur unchecked. The head was legally within his right to be anti-Sikh and encourage anti-Sikh practices.

As if this was not enough discrimination, the judges' remarks were like rubbing salt in Sikhs' wounds. Lord Denning remarked that you can discriminate against the Moonies, or skinheads, or any other person to whom you take objection, no matter whether your objection is reasonable or not. Lord Justice Oliver remarked that tribute should be paid to the headmaster's skill and patience in presenting and preparing his own defence before them, 'during a case which must have caused him immense personal distress and anxiety'. This showed sympathy and concern for the very person who later on was proved to be a 'racist'.

It is difficult to understand how Jews throughout the world, with nothing in common except religion, can be considered to be a distinct ethnic group, whilst Sikhs with a common country of origin, history, language, culture and customs, as well as religion, are denied such recognition. Eventually, the sense of justice prevailed and the House of Lords gave the verdict that Sikhs are a minority protected by the Race Relations Act.[5]

Let us see the full implications of such cases. How many parents have the energy, the resources, the know-how, the moral courage and the commitment to go through such lengthy and discouraging procedures to safeguard their freedom of religious beliefs? Very few. The majority succumbs to all the pressures and gives in. It can be no surprise if subsequently they find their children growing up rootless.

I have interviewed many Sikh boys and girls. The girls talked about their experience of the racism encountered by all non-white people, whereas boys found additional difficulties because of their distinctive appearance, with long hair tied in handkerchiefs, patkas and turbans. I was saddened to learn that not even one of them had escaped unpleasant experiences, both from peers and teachers. The following interview with Jasbir Singh was typical.

Jasbir told me that, when he went to his secondary school, he found that many of the Sikh boys (who previously wore turbans) had shaved their hair. In a general conversation, a primary teacher expressed surprise that while many children keep their long hair up to the junior school, fewer seem to retain their symbols when they move to the senior school. Jasbir explained that this was because they could not handle the bullying, the physical violence and the cutting remarks from the teachers.

> I used to feel hopeless when a whole group of boys would chant football songs, with my name filtered into the changed phrases. It was frightening at the age of eleven to be pushed around by 18-year-old boys. The spitting, the pushing and shoving was intolerable. A long running nightmare. The complaint to the teachers resulted only in a mild ticking-off for the ring leader. Many times I had to physically defend myself from the 18-year-old white boys. For a long time I was almost under the impression that the only aim of the sixth former for coming to school was to knock off my turban. Wherever I went, I would hear the words 'nappy head', 'bag head' etc. I had to become thick-skinned to tolerate all this. A few friends (white boys) I had, never stood up to help me. They would disappear at the sight of a mischief monger.

He further explained that

> I learnt to handle the bullying from the boys, but the intimidation from the teachers had the worst psychological effects. The teachers made passing subtle comments about my appearance. These comments were always made discreetly, nothing overt for me to complain about to anyone. One teacher called me 'tea-towel head'. I dealt with this incident in my 'own way'.

Although he never disclosed what this was, on my asking if he ever complained to the head teacher, his reply was that there were so many incidents that he could have been constantly in and out of the head's room. 'But sometimes the boys were caught, beating me, then they were suspended. This happened quite a few times', he added.

> It was the support and knowledge about Sikhism given by my parents that sustained me throughout my schooling and is still the sustenance. If my parents could not give me the knowledge and understanding about Sikhism, perhaps I might have lost my faith in ignorance.

Many incidents of harassment during lessons were reported. To have the ruler being pushed from behind to knock off the turban, while trying to pay attention to the lessons, and then being told off by the teacher for turning round to stop the molester, emerged as a common experience. 'It was common for boys to go around school with swastikas on their bags and written on their heads. Nothing was ever said by the teachers. But I was told off for wearing an anti-Indira Gandhi badge', adds Harjit Singh.

'A teacher knocked the turban off the head of a Sikh student.'[6]

It is a matter of concern for us all that even today, in some schools, where Sikh children are in a majority, the teachers and head teachers make little effort to give encouragement and praise by valuing their pupils' traditions. Just imagine a school where 80 per cent of pupils are Sikh, it is the Baisakhi day and the headteacher comes to the assembly with an invited Sikh guest speaker and does not even take the trouble of greeting the children with 'Sat Sri Akal' (a Sikh greeting). It would have been a small gesture on the part of the head to show that he values his pupils' faith. There are many examples where the pupils' faith, culture and language are ignored and many times purposely denied.

Support for Sikh children in understanding their religion is almost non-existent within the educational system. Today it is not enough to have a faith; it is necessary to understand the religion in order to cope successfully with the pressures which challenge belief of any kind. This is especially pertinent to Sikhs, who have recently become established in Britain. The responsibility for imparting very basic knowledge about Sikhism lies entirely with the 'ill-equipped' Sikh community and the family. The reasons for the ill-equipment are manifold. The older generation, which migrated from India and East Africa, never had to face the challenge of explaining their faith to others. They were and are happy and contented with their religion, however little their understanding of the principles. They had the security of larger numbers and did not feel threatened by society at large. They did not have to face racism such as their youngsters are now confronted with in Britain.

In India and East Africa, the Sikh community was seen as a powerful and flourishing community. Sikhs have been well respected for their honesty, hard work and ingenuity in all professions and businesses. Every turbaned Sikh carried that marked distinction of success. As we have already remarked, in the West it is a different story. Every Sikh, educated or otherwise, is put on the spot to explain her or his religion. It so often seems that media reporters or members of the general public will invite a clergyman and a rabbi to explain about Christianity or Judaism, whereas every Sikh, young or old, is expected to explain the philosophy of his or her faith. However well intentioned, this demand acts as a heavy blow to the self-esteem of those who cannot explain their beliefs and values, and find it easier to hide and disown their religion.

Unfortunately, even when one has the understanding of the religion, the language may act as a barrier for conveying that knowledge to the younger generation. Young Sikhs find it very hard to understand in Punjabi the proceedings and the teachings about Sikhism in the gurdwaras. Their own first language is English. Young people are often rebellious of old ways in every society. But when there is an added language barrier, it becomes quite hard for the community to impart its values and faith even to its own youngsters.

Young Sikhs find themselves in a minority in society, a very visible minority due to the distinct appearance of Sikh boys wearing turbans and, for the older ones, keeping beards. As a minority whose religion is not valued and which faces prejudices at every step in schools, colleges, universities and jobs, there is great need for support from the family and community. In numerous interviews with Sikh mothers and fathers, I have heard of their countless sleepless nights, spent thinking of strategies for giving their children self-confidence and self-esteem to cope with the bullying and prejudices from peers, teachers and employers alike.

My aim here is not to build a negative picture, but to highlight the confined parameters within which the Sikh community is operating. Many Sikh organizations are trying their best to educate their youngsters in Sikhism by holding conferences, symposiums, seminars, lectures and the like on Sikh religion and history. Some organizations hold short or weekend camps where lessons on the Sikh way of life are taught. Most Sikh gurdwaras hold Punjabi and Indian music classes, where reading and singing of shabads (hymns from the Guru Granth Sahib) are taught, so that children may at least acquire competency in reading the scriptures.

Once Sikh children understand their religion, they realize that their sense of personal faith helps them to develop both an understanding of their own tradition and a respect for other religions. Sikhism teaches the one-ness of God and one-ness of humanity. It teaches against false distinctions regarding race, colour, creed or sex. Every human being is equal in the eyes of Sikhs. Sikhism teaches tolerance of other pupils' views even at the risk of one's own life. It encourages full involvement in society. Guru Nanak in his very first sermon bravely declared 'Na koi Hindu na koi Musselman'. In God's eyes, there is neither Hindu or Muslim, only equal human beings. He taught that God is not concerned with labels and artificial, socially created, distinctions between people, but with our behaviour and conduct. Different religions are seen as different paths to the same goal and Sikhs are taught that no one religion has a monopoly of truth. Sikhism's strong belief in one God is shared by many other religions.

Sikhism stresses the one-ness of God's creation. The idea of caste or race, in other words the superiority of one over the other by sheer birth, is quite abhorrent to Sikhs. Guru Gobind Singh, the tenth Guru, writes 'there is only one race and that is that of all human beings'.[7] And again the Guru writes:

> From the divine light, the whole creation sprang,
> Why then should we divide human creatures into high and low.
> Lord the maker hath moulded one mass of clay, into vessels of diverse shape.[8]

Hence all the Sikh institutions are based on this idea of equality. The Sikh sangat (congregation) is composed of any individuals who believe in the one-ness of God. Everyone, regardless of caste, race, creed or sex, can join. The gurdwara, the Sikh place of worship, is open to all worshippers; anyone and everyone can join in the prayers to one God. Regardless of social status, everyone sits on the floor. Men and women are given equal positions.

Each gurdwara contains a langar (open kitchen). It should be remembered that this was begun in a caste-ridden Indian society, where one group would not even associate with another, let alone eat the same food. It served as a social levelling device emphasizing the equality of all humankind. Here men and women of all classes and castes are jointly engaged in preparing and serving for those of equally mixed background, eating in common assembly. Guru Granth Sahib contains the writings not only of Sikh Gurus, but also of men of different religions and of different backgrounds. There are the writings of a king and of poor artisans.

The Sikh Gurus, when they talked about equality of all human beings, included and emphasized equality between men and women. Sikh women enjoy complete equality with men in all walks of life. Since the times of Guru Nanak, Sikh women have taken equal part in all religious affairs. They attend and lead religious services. Guru Amar Das, the third Guru, reminded Indian society, which appeared to regard women as machines to give birth, that 'Blessed is the woman who creates life'.[9] To emphasize the elevated status, Sikh women were given the title Kaur, literally princess, by Guru Gobind Singh.

If there is only one God, and we believe in the one-ness of humanity, then it clearly follows that we should have respect for other people's views. Sikhs are taught to practise and preach tolerance between different faiths. Guru Tegh Bahadur, the ninth Guru, believed so strongly in this that he was publicly beheaded for upholding, in the face of Moghul persecution, the right of Hindus (though he did not believe in Hindu philosophy) to worship in the manner of their choice. Total commitment to freedom of belief and worship is one of the most fundamental beliefs of Sikhs.

Sikhs are enjoined to involve themselves fully in the uplifting of the society. The Gurus criticized those who left their social responsibilities in the pursuit of spiritual improvement. They taught instead that we should live in society, work constantly for its improvement and yet always be above its meanness and pettiness. The Gurus stressed the need for a balanced life. Sikhs are required to pray and meditate, earn by their own efforts and share their earnings with the less fortunate. These are, in brief the principles that guide Sikh boys and girls to understand the difference between right and wrong, as they grow to become responsible members of society.

NOTES

1. Ravinder Bansal (1990) A Sikh by night. *Times Educational Supplement*, 20 July.
2. W. Owen Cole (1985) Sikh children and schooling. *Sikh Messenger*, Autumn, pp. 22–4. London: Sikh Messenger Publications.
3. Bansal, *op. cit.*
4. Indarjit Singh (1982) Editorial: Multicultural education. *Sikh Courier*, Spring–Summer, pp. 1–3. London: Sikh Cultural Society.
5. 'Mandla v. Dowell Lee'. *Education Law*, issue 23, case 30.
6. Burnage Report (1988), p. 140.
7. Guru Gobind Singh, Akal Ustat, 85,15, Dasam Granth. Amritsar: Shromani Gurdwara Prabandhik Committee.
8. Guru Granth Sahib. Amritsar: Shromani Gurdwara Prabandhik Committee, p. 1349.
9. Guru Granth Sahib, *op. cit.*, p. 32.

FURTHER READING

Ballard, R. and Ballard, C. (1977) 'The Sikhs: the development of South Asian settlements in Britain'. In J. L. Watson (ed.) *Between Two Cultures: Migrants and Minorities in Britain*. Oxford: Blackwell, pp. 21–56.

Bennett, Olivia (1990) *Listening to Sikhs*. London: Unwin Hayman.

Burnage Report (1988) *Murder in the Playground*. London: Longsight Press.

Clutterbuck, A. (1990) *Growing up in Sikhism*. Harlow: Longman.

Helweg, A. W. (1979) *Sikhs in England: The Development of a Migrant Community*. Delhi: Oxford University Press.

James, A. G. (1974) *Sikh Children in Britain*. London: Oxford University Press.

Knott, Kim (1987) Calculating Sikh population statistics. *Sikh Bulletin* 4. Chichester: West Sussex Institute, pp. 13–22.

Nesbitt, Eleanor (1987) 'Britain's Sikhs'. In M. Hayward (ed.) *Sikhism: The Report of the Fifth 'York Shap' Conference*. York: RE Centre, pp. 50–7.

Nesbitt, Eleanor (1988) Sikhs in children's literature. *Sikh Bulletin* 5. Chichester: British Association for the History of Religion, pp. 27–34.

Singh, Kanwaljit K. and Singh, Indarjit (1974) *Rehat Maryada: A Guide to the Sikh Way of Life*. London: Sikh Cultural Society.

Singh, Kanwaljit K. *et. al.* (1990) *Learning the Sikh Way*. London: British Sikh Education Council.

International Perspectives

Chapter 17

The Teaching of World Religions in Continental Europe

Herbert Schultze, Hans-Mikael Holt and Wim Westerman

INTRODUCTION: CHANGES SINCE THE 1960S

If we looked at a map of school-based education in continental Europe, drawn when Shap was founded in 1969, we would see, amongst other features, the plain fact that world religions appear only to a very limited extent and that for those leaving school at the age of 18 or 19 years. Only in Sweden was it different. There, the gale force of new, nationwide, comprehensive schools blew away traditional Lutheran instruction and brought in the knowledge of Christianity instead (this was in 1962). Then in 1969 the latter was replaced by an objective and brand-new subject called Religious Knowledge.

Let us now compare the map today. There are many similarities, but also differences. In most countries world religions are to be taught during every phase of schooling, including primary years. The aims of fairness and dialogue are now often part of the syllabuses. We would see on the present map, of course, many differences in detail, but it is the change overall in less than three decades that is striking.

By using a few examples we can illustrate the possible emergence of a new European perspective.

What follows is a survey of the Danish situation by Hans-Mikael Holt and of that in the Netherlands by Wim Westerman. In conclusion, further challenges and approaches from elsewhere in mainland Europe are identifed.

WORLD RELIGIONS IN RE IN DENMARK
Hans-Mikael Holt

RE IN THE DANISH EDUCATIONAL SYSTEM: FRAMEWORK, OFFICIAL GUIDELINES, WORKING CONDITIONS IN GENERAL

Statistically, Denmark is a rather homogeneous society, in terms of religious sociology, of around 5 million people. It is predominantly Protestant (Lutheran), with minorities such as Roman Catholics (about 30,000), Jews (about 7000), Muslims from a variety of backgrounds (35,000), and other numerically smaller groups.

Traditionally, religious education (RE) has the status of a compulsory subject in primary and secondary schools. There is no tradition of RE in subsequent vocational training. In primary and lower secondary schools RE is taught as Christian education. In higher secondary education ('Gymnasium' and 'Højere Forberedelseseksamen') the subject is RE or religious studies.

General guidelines for RE are set up by the Ministry of Education, usually in close co-operation with representatives of the various RE teachers' organizations. Syllabuses may vary from region to region, being subject to decisions of the local education authorities and the boards of parent governors at the individual schools. The only precondition is that all local arrangements should be in accordance – in spirit at least – with the general ministerial guidelines.

Textbooks are provided by the public. The board of parent governors has the right to authorize and refuse to authorize the use of certain textbooks in the primary and lower secondary schools. In practice, this kind of parental censorship is not commonly used.

In primary and secondary schools Christian education is usually a one-lesson-a-week subject; it also belongs to the group of subjects that has no form of assessment/examination. Christian education is therefore heavily dependent on teachers who are dedicated to the subject. Although every teacher has had a basic course in RE at teacher training college, many consider themselves incapable of teaching the subject on both conscientious and professional grounds. Because of that, Christian education in many primary and secondary schools is given rather low status by comparison with what are viewed as more deserving subjects. In spite of these difficult conditions, many dedicated teachers do an excellent job, offering not only Christianity-focused RE, but also frequent sessions studying other world religions. To avoid the pedagogical problems of the one-lesson-a-week situation, teachers often concentrate the lessons of one term in one or two weeks, studying one or two topics, often in co-operation with the teacher in Danish and/or social studies (geography, history and social studies).

In higher secondary schools (16–19 years) the subject is called RE or RS and commonly it includes both Christianity and world religions. According to the 1988 Reform Act of Higher Secondary Schools, RE is to be taught as a compulsory subject in the last year with three lessons a week. RE has full equality of conditions to such other humanities subjects as Danish and history. The final examination in RE is an oral examination.

In both primary and secondary schools, pupils and students may obtain a personal exemption from RE, if they belong to a church or faith not belonging to the Lutheran Church of Denmark. This provision dates back to the last century and is not invoked very often.

WORLD RELIGIONS IN RE

In primary and lower secondary schools, world religions can be included as a special topic. This may very often be done because teachers find it a little easier to approach religion via the 'more exotic' cultures, thereby avoiding indifference or even open hostility shown by many pupils towards Christian education. After the seventh form, world religions can be taken up in their own right as a proper part of the curriculum.

As the pupils have the opportunity to join the teacher in doing the actual planning, one religion and/or culture may well be chosen for study in more detail, often in co-operation with the teachers in history and geography. World religions can also be taught as a part of a social studies programme, thereby including pupils who might have obtained dispensation from the RE lesson!

Amongst RE teachers there is general consensus that RE in primary and lower secondary schools should be planned and implemented in accordance with Denmark being a pluralistic and – especially in such larger communities as Copenhagen and Aarhus – a multifaith society. However, various politically influential groups continue to be a considerable obstacle to these ideas. This situation may well be known to RE teachers in most countries in Northern Europe.

The agreed syllabus in higher secondary education comprises the following areas:

1. Religion and culture of primitive peoples (15–20 per cent).
2. One or two of the following religions: Judaism, Islam, Hinduism, Buddhism, Chinese and Japanese religions (20–25 per cent).
3. Christianity (30–35 per cent).
4. Ethical and philosophical topics (15–20 per cent).

The educational material should comprise texts that are considered to be normative and representative for each of the religions and philosophies of life concerned. Other texts and materials such as pictures, films and tapes may be used to illustrate the life of religions past and present. Textbooks are designed to provide the students with the basic knowledge necessary to develop analytical skills in the interpretation of the material studied.

The final examination for the advanced level is oral but based on the material studied. The student is given some time – about 20 minutes – for preparation. After this, the student makes a presentation, usually in the form of an analysis of a text, which will be similar to ones seen during the lessons devoted to the topic in question. Students are examined in how they treat the text. They are asked to demonstrate their skills in interpreting the understanding of religion and/or philosophy of life expressed in the text. On this basis, the student shows how well he or she is able to take part in an unbiased discussion of major problems related to the specific topic.

From this point of view, RE in higher secondary schools is, both in theory and in practice, an academic subject. In general, and in spite of the various obstacles that face RE and especially Christian education in schools, the present status of RE is fairly high. The conditions for teaching world religions are good, it being a compulsory topic in higher secondary schools. World religions receive a high rating because they are voluntarily given much attention by the students.

A MULTIFAITH APPROACH TO RE?

One of the most popular books used in RE to teach about Judaism is written by the rabbi of the Jewish community in Copenhagen. Other textbooks on Buddhism and Islam are produced either by members of the respective communities or in close co-operation with representatives of the religions. This is also the case when dealing with the Roman Catholic Church.

Recently I reviewed a book on Islam written by a Danish woman converted to Islam. Her reason for writing a Muslim textbook on her new religion was explicit dissatisfaction with the existing books on the Muslim world being currently in use in Danish schools. This point of view, of course, is not a new one. But it shows us a new and promising tendency in Denmark.

Although RE is seldom a matter of great debate in the media and amongst the general public, a growing awareness of the indispensability of an open approach to 'foreign' cultures and their religious beliefs is evident among teachers, educationalists and politicians. This is a good sign that RE in the Danish educational system has both a secure present and an even more promising future.

'*GEESTELIJKE STROMINGEN*': A DISTINCTIVE FEATURE OF RELIGIOUS EDUCATION IN THE NETHERLANDS
Wim Westerman

A new Education Act came into force in 1985 in the Netherlands. This Act regulates the *basisschool* (primary education for the age group 4–12 years). New compulsory subjects were introduced: English and health education. Another newly introduced subject was *Geestelijke Stromingen*, which literally translated means 'Spiritual Streams'.

The introduction of *Geestelijke Stromingen* is connected with one of the recent principles of Dutch primary and secondary education, that schools have to take into account in their entire programme that the Dutch population forms a multicultural society. Schools have to arrange their instruction in an 'intercultural way'.

The children have to be prepared to live in a society with a wealth of (sub)cultures, values and norms, for the Netherlands is a society of approximately 13 million, which includes migrants who originally came as 'guest workers' from Mediterranean states, people from former Dutch colonies (Indonesia, Surinam and the Dutch West Indies), refugees from South America, South East Asia, Africa and the Middle East, gipsies, Chinese from Hong Kong, the People's Republic of China, Taiwan, etc. They have all brought their traditions, cultures and world-views.

History shows that the arrival of migrants is not a new phenomenon for the Low Countries. Over many centuries people arrived in the flat country that is now named the Netherlands. In succession, Romans, Jewish refugees from Spain, Portugal and Eastern Europe, French Huguenots, Flemish and Armenian merchants, German farm-hands, and others since, all travelled to Holland and the other provinces. They arrived in a country which, by contrast with several other European countries, enjoyed a relatively greater freedom of thought, religion and personal expression.

In the seventeenth century, the percentage of 'foreigners' in a city such as Amsterdam was even higher than it is now. But new for our era is the greater variety of cultures (in 1991 more than 130 nationalities in Amsterdam). In turn, Christianity has lost some of its cultural dominance, whereas other religions and world-views have a much higher profile. For instance, Islam and Hinduism have become as visible in the Dutch cities as Christianity and Judaism already were.

So primary and secondary schools have to teach in an 'intercultural way'. 'Intercultural education' is not a subject, but a principle that has to permeate the entire curriculum and the daily school routine and organization.

Since beliefs, norms and values are the roots of the cultures, it is essential that children in the context of intercultural education learn to deal with these roots. This must be done in a way that is in accord with their mental development. Consequently, the priority for the primary school is not with the theories or philosophies of 'faiths and world-views', but with their simply perceptible expressions, such as their books, buildings, festivals, calendars, symbols, art, music, persons and stories. It is important that children learn to communicate with others about *Geestelijke Stromingen*, as expressions of central ideas in human life. That may sound like a platitude, but it is not, for it is not common any more in the Western world to speak in public about your own faith. Sociologists of religion call this development the 'privatization of religion'.

A necessary condition for this communication to be effective is that the students acquire non-biased information, an adequate vocabulary and the skills to explore in a respectful way different faiths and world-views, so they can learn to recognize and to cope with the similarities and the differences between the various *Geestelijke Stromingen*. Coping with similarities and differences of cultures, beliefs, norms and values can be learned in different ways.

For instance, the hopscotch game does not come from any one country. It is played almost everywhere. Even young children immediately recognize hopscotch designs drawn, scratched or chalked on the ground, so they recognize the worldwide similarities in this game. But they are also realistic enough to recognize the many different hopscotch designs and the variations in the rules of the game. From their own experiences they often know that even within one suburb or village hopscotch is played in different variations. Speaking about the similarities and differences in the hopscotch game, after having been playing it, can be a preparation for a more explicit approach of *Geestelijke Stromingen*, for religions and non-religious world-views also have their similarities and differences, for example, all of them have rules, commands and prohibitions that try to regulate the essential things in life. But the rules vary.

So, while playing, the pupils can be prepared for contacts with the unity and the varieties in cultures and religions. The same effect can be obtained by telling stories (every belief system has at least one story that tells how the 'ideal situation' has to be seen), visiting buildings of worship (in most churches you can find a font, but not in a synagogue or in a mosque), etc.

Non-biased and respectful information in the content of *Geestelijke Stromingen* deserves special priority. The Education Act specifies that this subject matter has to be taught in an objective way. It must be 'objective', as distinct from RE, which has, according to the act, a subjective character.

The debatable contrast 'objective–subjective' is used to make possible the introduction of *Geestelijke Stromingen* as a compulsory subject in all schools. This is because of the Dutch educational system, which is divided between *openbare* schools (founded and administered by the government or by local public authorities) and *bijzondere* schools (founded and administered by private bodies, often groups of parents or churches, and mostly with a religious starting point). In most of the *bijzondere* schools, RE is compulsory for the students. That is not the case in *openbare* schools, where religious instruction can be taught by representatives of religious bodies (e.g. churches or mosques) to students whose parents agree with these lessons.

So instruction in *Geestelijke Stromingen* is not the same as 'religious education'. The first is information about various religions and world-views, while the latter is instruction in the particular religion to which the students belong or to which their parents wish them to belong.

While RE is seen as subjective, *Geestelijke Stromingen* had to be categorized as objective to make it an obligatory subject.

Broadly outlined, it can be said that till now most of the *openbare* schools (public schools, about a third of all Dutch schools) have no tradition at all in instructing about faiths and world-views. Most of their teachers are afraid to be subjective while openly teaching about religions and other world-views. Most of the teachers of the *bijzondere* schools (private schools, two-thirds of all schools) do not have this fear. They teach as they like about religions. But their own views are often so one-sided that they give caricatures of other religions.

For both groups of teachers the official introduction of *Geestelijke Stromingen* as a subject is a real challenge. The main challenge for the first group is to learn to begin teaching this subject, while the others have to learn to teach it in a more genuine way. A central problem for both groups is that most of the teachers themselves did not learn very much about any stream other than the one to which they themselves belonged.

In the Dutch educational tradition, the government cannot officially prescribe the contents of the curriculum. Only the subjects are named in the Education Acts. However, this does not mean that there is not a certain national tradition regarding the content of the lessons. Especially for the 3 Rs, the tradition is rather strong. Parents know what to expect, since they themselves were trained within that tradition, schoolbooks reflect it, and secondary schools expect that primary schools will teach certain amounts of knowledge, etc. If a primary school has too deviant a curriculum, it will indirectly be corrected by outsiders.

But with respect to *Geestelijke Stromingen* there has been no real tradition. So it is officially and in practice still the individual school that decides which *Geestelijke Stromingen* will be taught (only world religions or also non-religious world-views?), where it will be taught (in which age groups?) and how it will be taught.

It is predictable that in the next ten years the foundations for a new educational tradition will be laid and that the textbook authors will be very influential in this process. The last prediction is based on the experience that textbooks normally determine to a large extent the contents of what is taught. This is already the situation, even when there is not yet a tradition of *Geestelijke Stromingen*.

Until now, most of the information about religions has been found in history and geography textbooks. Most of the history books give only some information about Islam and Judaism, and that only in the context of the Crusades. This gives implicitly the impression that those religions are only historical phenomena and that the only characteristics of world religions is that they fight each other.

As history textbooks normally place world religions far away in time, most geography textbooks place them far away from home. One of the most popular geography series does not give real information about *Geestelijke Stromingen* in Europe. It only says that in the Balkans you can find Eastern Orthodox people 'who have icons instead of statues'. The texts describing North and South America, Africa and Australia give the impression that on those continents religions are completely absent. But in the setting of lessons about the Middle East, India and the Far East religions appear. The hidden message is that religions are only an Asian affair.

Most of the geography and history textbooks give the impression that faiths and other world-views belong to 'there and then' and not to 'here and now'.

Moreover most of the information is presented in caricatures: 'the cows of Hindu India are sacred, they eat what they like, while millions of Indians starve of hunger'. The reverse is now shown: European supermarkets with their rows of tins of food for cats and dogs show that these animals are very important to consumers, even though we too in the West know about the starvation throughout the Third World.

Connected with the caricatures is a lot of exaggeration. One of the geography books says, for example, that you can find in 'the holy city of Kyoto 1600 Shinto temples and 600 holy places'. But the tourist organization of the same city proudly announces about 40 temples! This exaggeration looks like the stories of the sixteenth-century explorers. After their voyages they told that they had seen 200-metre-long sea monsters, mermaids, etc. Too few people could check their stories to contradict their messages!

The same mechanism can be seen in the area of *Geestelijke Stromingen*. The exotic prevails and the plural situation round the street corner is ignored. It seems much easier to write texts about religions far away than about religions near by. Maybe this is one of the reasons why Christianity and Humanism are nearly absent in all textbooks, except – of course – the textbooks for RE.

It is essential that information about *Geestelijke Stromingen* is not restricted to RE textbooks, while schools are free to decide if *Geestelijke Stromingen* will be a separate subject on the school timetable or if it will be integrated into other subjects like geography. This last option conforms to the idea of intercultural education, not as a subject but as a principle that influences the entire curriculum and the daily school routine.

During the last decade, primary schools in the Netherlands have become more and more accustomed to an integrated approach to the curriculum. While traditionally the subjects were separated, we now find combinations such as geography and history together, or social studies. In such combinations *Geestelijke Stromingen* can easily find a place. It is even one of the principles of the new Primary Education Act that the subjects, where possible, have to be presented coherently with each other. This principle gives *bijzondere* schools the opportunity to combine *Geestelijke Stromingen* and RE. This possibility is one reason to put a question mark against the statement in the Education Act that says that *Geestelijke Stromingen* have to be 'objective'. In educational practice the concept 'objective' could better be replaced by 'in an open way' or 'non-biased'.

Since the 1960s, attention to all kinds of prejudices (racism, sexism, ageism, handicapism, etc.) in children's literature and textbooks has gradually grown. Yet, until now the prejudice towards faiths and world-views has not attracted much attention. However, recently, several studies of anti-Jewish prejudice and articles describing inaccurate information on Islam have been published. In the next few years one of the challenges for the Dutch textbook authors will be to give appropriate and reliable information about *Geestelijke Stromingen*.

CORRESPONDING DEVELOPMENTS ACROSS EUROPE

Herbert Schultze

Who in the continental European countries is responsible for the teaching of world religions? In all Western European countries it is the education authorities. They are in some cases nationally organized as, for example, in Sweden with its central board of education. Sometimes they are regionally structured, as in Switzerland, with its 25 or 26 cantons, each with its own educational sovereignty.

But who decides on matters of content, topics to be taught, etc.? This differs tremendously. In *Switzerland* the conference of cantonal directors of education employs an expert for immigration issues. In that country, world religions appear under the label of 'immigration'. In *France* there exists no place at all for religion in state schools. An exception is the regulations for the eastern *départements*, which are similar to those long established in the *Länder* of western Germany. But teachers in these *départements* are themselves more caught in a tension than privileged, for the aim of the school is to educate French citizens; churches, synagogues and other religious communities are just registered organizations. In *Sweden* the curriculum is worked out for all school subjects by an integrated system. Educationalists, experts and administrators work deliberately to adapt to the classroom the ethos of a democratic and plural society with equal rights for adherents of every religious group or even non-religious stances.

In some countries, according to national legislation, the 'religious communities' decide on the content. This has sometimes led to a sort of 'equal rights' solution. In *Austria*, for example, twelve officially recognized religious communities have the right to issue syllabuses and to train to appoint teachers for 'their' RE in state schools. The condition is that they must find five, or exceptionally only three, pupils at one school to form a class for RE; then all expenses will be paid by the state. A different but comparable regulation exists in *Belgium*, where seven types of RE, including a humanist one, are known. Most of the RE classes in these two countries are Christian, i.e. Roman Catholic, Protestant, Old Catholic, etc. This means in fact that the Churches decide mostly on the content. Because of this fixed diversification, the space for teaching world religions is often very small, sometimes non-existent. In *West Germany* prior to reunification, the influence of the Churches was laid down in the constitution both of the Federal Republic and the federal states (*Bundesländer*), and this principle is now extended to the grades. School classes used to be divided into two parts: a Roman Catholic and a Protestant one. Nevertheless, the major world religions can now be found in every syllabus. Judaism is officially recognized in Austria, Belgium, and Germany; Islam is recognized in Austria and Belgium, but not in Germany.

Some people in the countries mentioned dreaming of the Jefferson amendment to the constitution of the USA, with its separation of Church and state. But the iron is so hot that politicians dare not touch it. This can be illustrated by a look at *Italy*. There, RE is traditionally Roman Catholic, and the relation to the Church was confirmed by the Concordat. Simultaneously, and for the first time, a treaty was entered into between the state and the Protestant church federation. Consequently, the state also offered Protestant religious education in schools. But Protestants declined. They prefer separation of school and Church, whilst the Roman Catholics prefer the opposite. Thus things remain as they are.

In Eastern European countries, the situation is just as mixed as in Western Europe. *Poland* remained, during decades of communist regime, a Roman Catholic country with a small Protestant minority. Any teaching of religious issues was taken over by the Churches. There was not very much space reserved for world religions.

In the pre-union *German Democratic Republic*, the traditional missionary societies survived as Church institutions. They contributed information on world religions to the training of teachers in Church education and, in particular, the teaching of Judaism and Islam benefited. This corresponded to initiatives from the World Council of Churches for dialogue which were quite favourably received in the GDR.

Any attention to world religions was excluded altogether from the schools of the *Soviet Union*, although the topic was treated in some studies from the Soviet Academy of Sciences. Now, however, in the face of rediscovery of the Christian past and the evidence of other strong religious allegiance in the form of Islam and Buddhism, much rethinking of the nature of RE is currently underway throughout the former Soviet Republics.

The six dimensions of religion identified by Ninian Smart, and promoted as a basis for a broader approach to RS and RE, in England in the 1970s are well known to almost all authors of syllabuses and learning material in Western European countries. In a Dutch national curriculum project they became explicitly standard. In other national contexts they were adapted or modified. But the teaching schemes depend also on many other factors.

TRAUMA, HISTORICAL FATE AND CURRENT EVENTS, AS FACTORS OF INFLUENCE

Some traumas determine the image of adherents of another world religion than one's own. Muslims, for example, are for many Western Europeans still the people of the oil crisis. The consciousness of exercising colonial power against Muslims is not as vivid as the memory that these people turned off the tap of oil. In Austria and Germany, Muslims are also seen as those who besieged Vienna. This fits in with the image of strong or even brutal warriors, and fanatic and fatalistic people.

The problem with trauma is greater in history lessons and history textbooks than in RE. A major difficulty is the reduction of history to wars, victories and lost battles. In the time between those events, Jews or Muslims, for example, seem to disappear from history. And, in addition, a failure to distinguish between such processes of conflict and the religion of Judaism or Islam must be recognized. On the other hand, in some syllabuses and books for RE, historical development plays only a minor role. This also leads to a one-sided picture.

Photo-agencies make their money not only with the press, film, television, etc., but also with publishers of textbooks. Attractive or sensational photographs are more and more popular. Some schoolbooks in various European countries present, for example, among five or ten other pictures on Islam, one of Ayatollah Khomenei. After he died, this information, or better indoctrination, by a photograph will influence the pupils for another ten years. And whatever they hear will be combined with this as regards the religion of Islam.

Furthermore, the fate of adherents of a world religion in certain countries has provided opportunities for them to be observed. The Jews in *Finland*, for example, are now established as good patriots. As such, Jewish men have served loyally in the Finnish army. This was also the case during World War II, when the Finnish army and the army of Nazi Germany were allied. There is also a Muslim community in Finland, no less patriotic. Finland, a country on the border, received its neighbours from other religions with the same hospitality as it had the Russian Orthodox. Consequently, Judaism and Islam are well represented in Finnish RE as well as in history lessons.

In *Italy* the capital, Rome, has functioned for years as a gateway for immigrants from Africa, Asia and Latin America. Their cultural and religious heritage should, according to official statements, be respected. However, administration and social services seem to find this rather difficult. Happily, where they fail, impressive voluntary activities do the appropriate work. In some of these activities, young people are involved. But in school, children and young people learn more about classical deities like Jupiter and Venus than about Allah and Muhammad or Buddha. The national heritage of modern Italy is seen in the Roman Empire, even though the state was born out of the movements of enlightenment and liberalism.

Sometimes, sad events make world religion a matter of interest. The television programme on Indira Gandhi's funeral provoked in many European classrooms questions from children and young people which only could be answered by information on Hinduism. Similarly, in West Berlin when the popular quiz master Hans Rosenthal died, the programme on his funeral led subsequently to a great number of lessons on Judaism.

Trauma, fate and quite ordinary events can influence the agenda of teaching world religions. There are, of course, also the pupils' interests. But their interest, for example in liberation theology, is directed more to liberation than to theology. And their questions about Buddhism concern methods of meditation rather than the message and the way of Buddha. Personal situations and questions of pupils are acknowledged not only by almost all syllabuses but also by national and regional school laws on the continent.

From these regulations we can conclude as follows. RE of one type or another is generally compulsory for the pupils. They can withdraw for reasons of conscience. From 14 years on they themselves can invoke this; younger children need a declaration by their parents. Teachers are generally free to teach RE or to refuse this. They need in most of the countries a professional qualification, which is variously defined. Only a few of the continental school systems still use the instrument of a permission (*missio* or *vocatio*) authorized by the Roman Catholic or Protestant Churches. The use of schoolbooks depends on the law of a free market in most countries. Exceptions are *Austria* and *West Germany* and, in some respect, *France* (because of the 'programme', the national curriculum), where central controls are exercised.

To these remarks it must be added that there is a wide variety of what is followed in practice; the picture often varies from one school to another. There are parents who move from one nation to another. Their children sometimes have fascinating experiences but sometimes they face depressing situations. This is particularly true of the studies of world religions.

EUROPE AS A COMMON HOME FOR PEOPLE OF DIFFERENT RELIGIONS AND PHILOSOPHIES OF LIFE?

Are there some lighthouses pointing a direction for the teaching of world religions in the present situation? There are the poets; but the more inspired are often non-religious people. The German poet Peter Hacks, for example, proclaimed the following message:

> Love and brutality
> two ships sailing on the ocean of time;
> brutality goes by after years
> love remains for eternity.

And then there are new theories for the teaching of world religions. In Sweden some scholars and educators have explored the theoretical basis or principle for a balanced and fair presentation of different world-views in schools. Some of them prefer a thematic approach, and others a historical or systemic one.

In the Netherlands the General Synod of the Dutch Reformed Church declared in 1981 that openness and dialogue are the conditions of both a good school education in general and a trustworthy religious education in particular.

Hans Küng travels from one country to another to proclaim his message that there will be no peace in the world without peace between religions and a global ethic. Some scholars in Germany have developed theories and teachers' guides which adapt such visions to the nationally administered structures.

These and other valuable efforts are surrounded by clouds of prejudice in all the countries. Moreover, the claims of industry and business organizations are taken much more seriously by politicians, and it is they who issue the guidelines for education authorities in most of the countries.

Nevertheless, the facts are that Buddhists from Vietnam became citizens of many European countries, and that city areas like Rotterdam Cosswijk and Berlin Kreuzberg have developed into big Muslim cities ranking after Istanbul and Ankara. Despite the controversial discussion on multicultural societies, the number of school classes with children from diverse religious and cultural backgrounds is increasing all over Europe.

The day after the visit of President Gorbachev to the Council of Europe, the Parliamentary Assembly discussed the vision of Europe as a common home. For the first time delegates from the then Soviet Union, Hungary, Poland and other Eastern European countries offered their assistance in building this common home. It was a kind of religious atmosphere. But no delegate either from the West or from the East used the word 'religion'. The secular world with secularly thinking people is reality. It is time to announce the good news for which religions are known. This begins in school education. A continental European Shap has now been founded. Before the regulations come which mean that all sausages are the same, all rolls the same, and all cheeses the same, a place should be guaranteed for the appreciation of religions in all their rich diversity.

BIBLIOGRAPHY

Brokerhof, D., Schultze, H. and Ytsma, W. (eds) (1985) *Religious Education and Schoolbooks.* Enschede: Stichting voor de Leerplanontwikkeling.

Schultze, H. and Selander, S. A. (eds) (1983) Religion and schoolbooks in Europe. *Didakometry,* **68**, 1–65. Malmö School of Education.

Spinder, Hans (ed.) (1993) *Religious Education in Europe.* InterEuropean Commission on Church and School (c/o National Society RE Centre, London).

Chapter 18

Freedom, Authority and the Study of Religion in the United States

Ninian Smart

Attitudes to religion and education are remarkably different in the USA than in Europe. They are determined by several forces. First, there is the United States Constitution, which lays down, through the First Amendment, a separation between Church and state. Second, there is the actual history of religions in the USA. A predominantly Protestant atmosphere gave way in the late nineteenth century to a phase when both Roman Catholics and Jews came to be vital ingredients in the melting pot. And later, non-Western faiths and other new creations have emerged as a vigorous new motif, particularly during the decades from the 1960s until the early 1990s. Third, US experience contains a high degree of individualism, in part because of the mobility of the US people, first during the push westward as the frontier met up with ocean-borne immigration in California. Partly, too, individualism arises from the continuing mobility which is a consequence of a vital industrial capitalism. Another factor is the relative fragility of the US family, mostly nuclear in scope anyway. A third factor in US experience is the large number of private schools, particularly at college level, which has meant a fairly heavy investment in classes on religion, often the major source of knowledge among those who have left high school. Fourth, even more strikingly than in Europe, the USA is a plural society ethnically. The institution of slavery brought many uprooted Africans into the country, so that Black religiosity is itself an important part of total US religion. Contiguity with Mexico has multiplied Hispanic presence in the USA. In California, labour recruitment among Chinese and Japanese in the late nineteenth and early twentieth centuries has given Far Eastern populations a solid presence, as have more recent migrations of refugees and others from Vietnam, Indo-China more generally, and Korea. But even rather small groups, such as Indians from South Asia, are making themselves felt. Malibu Canyon, the back from Los Angeles offshoot where many stars reside, now boasts a great replica of a South Indian temple. In Los Angeles everyone, even Anglos, is in the minority.

These phenomena affect rhetoric and language, and this is vital to grasp, since the rather divergent US vocabulary can cause confusion. Generally speaking, the USA has experienced aggressive secular ideologies. Though the Enlightenment was vastly important in the foundations of the country, its suspicions of religious establishment and emotionalism were clothed in the polite dress of deism, not of atheism. There was never a really strong socialist or Marxist movement, sometimes deeply hostile to all forms of faith, in the USA. Generally, therefore, public opinion looks on religion as a good thing. This has been taken up in the social civil religion (Bellah and Hammond, 1982). It is common for presidents to invoke the name of God in exhorting the nation; there is typically an invocation at presidential inaugurations; and the White House has, since Eisenhower's time, been the scene of prayer breakfasts (Cruise O'Brien, 1988). There is usually among practitioners of civil religion an awareness of the old trinity of Protestantism, Catholicism and Judaism. In short, there is a general ethos in the USA in favour of religion, while in Britain and Australia, and in a different way in France or Italy, there is a strong strand of anti-religiousness and anti-clericalism. In brief, public rhetoric in the USA is favourable to religion. On the other hand, the strong sense of the importance of dividing Church from state leads often to vigorous opposition to public or official manifestations of religion: thus city halls may be criticized for putting up Christmas decorations and public schools for incorporating anything faintly suggesting religious commitment in the curricula. Sometimes there is a collision between public piety and devotion to liberalism as according to the Constitution. Ronald Reagan could call for prayer in public schools (but even he had to allow that all it could be would be a period of silence, when faced with the question of the formulation of prayer).

One result of the differing configuration of religiosity in the USA is that the expression 'religious education', which is so common in Britain and elsewhere, has a narrower sense. For British theorists, the incorporation of the term 'education' in the phrase is to be favoured: it shows that we are involved in genuine education, with all that that implies, and not just 'instruction'. Now, of course, in British usage religious education covers both what goes on in what may be loosely called state schools and what occurs in faith contexts. In the USA, the expression 'religious education' covers only the latter. Consequently, practitioners of what in Britain would be called religious education refer to the subject in public schools as 'Public Education Religion Studies', a somewhat awkward locution (Will, 1981). The general clearance by the Supreme Court for work of this kind occurred through the decision known as Schempp (1963). This had a wider consequence than some changes in high school and primary education: it also helped to release energies for the setting up of programmes and departments in public universities.

Here it is worth reflecting on another difference in styles of English usage. Because so many colleges in the USA are privately founded and funded, from Harvard to Grinnell and from Rice University in Houston to Mills College in Oakland, it has long been common for them to have departments of religion (sometimes merged with philosophy). Such were typically centred upon the main faith of the founder or founding group – so they could be Catholic or drawn from a variety of Protestant groups, or Jewish. So it is that a programme on religion has a more tradition-bound shape than one of the new departments of religious studies formed in the State universities since the second half of the 1960s. Consequently, too, the majority of members of the main professional body, the American Academy of Religion, are from denominational institutions and many look on themselves as theologians rather than pluralistic students of religion as according to the religious studies model. Moreover, many private institutions have seminary-type activities and so have divinity schools. It is not normal in the USA to talk about theological faculties, and not normal at all to have theology departments, as occurs frequently enough in Britain. (The term 'faculty' in the USA typically refers to professors, i.e. the teaching staff of a college, and also to high school and other teachers – and, by the way, 'staff' usually refers, not to faculty, but to what are often called 'assistant staff' in the British university scene.) And so there are divinity schools and seminaries in addition to undergraduate religion programmes. Mostly they offer professional and graduate training. Famous seminaries are Union Theological Seminary in New York and Hebrew Union in Cincinnati. These represent important centres of learning, but are denominational in essence, and hence unsuitable as parts of public universities.

Despite the difference indicated above, religion programmes have increasingly converged with the religious studies model. This was partly due to the revolution in student opinion and tastes during the 1960s and early 1970s. This put pressure on many institutions to widen their curriculum. Courses in Buddhism, Native American religions, Chinese religion, African religions and so on became common, as well as more traditional offerings in forms of Christianity and Judaism. Religion programmes thus became plural. On the other hand, the religious studies model evolved something more – an integrated approach which was both plural and multidisciplinary, drawing, that is, on the methods of history, sociology, anthropology, phenomenology, philosophy and so on to illuminate the various dimensions of religion. Consequently there are vigorous religious studies departments and programmes at various of the large State universities, such as Virginia, Iowa, Arizona State, Colorado, Kansas, California (at Santa Barbara) and elsewhere. However, it must be noted that the chief beneficiary of the 1960s revolution was maybe the University of Chicago, whose history of religions, dominated by the guru-like figure of Mircea Eliade, supplied many of the doctorally trained professors in the new programmes. Chicago is a private university, and the history of religions was a segment of the divinity school offerings. Also influential was Harvard's Center for the Study of World Religions, also part of the divinity school, under the leadership primarily of Wilfred Cantwell Smith. It may be noted that an aspect of the ideology of the centre was pluralism in the sense of acceptance of the claims and equality of the great religions, and not just the promotion of the plural or cross-cultural study of religion. In principle, on the other hand, the State institutions espoused a more neutralist position, since it was their job to study religion and the religious, and not to promote any particular doctrinal position, even the position that all ways lead to the same Truth.

The Church–state separation in the USA has sometimes led to a fearful negativity because up to Schempp and beyond the prevalent interpretation was negative about both teaching about religion and teaching of religion. This has raised a question among conservative Christians, particularly in the 1980s, when they were influential during the Reagan era, as to whether humanist values were not dominant among high school teachers and administrators. Was not humanism itself an ideology which was being imposed on the curriculum? There was some logic in such critiques of educational practice, though it was often expressed arrogantly – for instance, through a campaign to have Creationism taught in schools as a contrast to Evolutionism (conservatives tended to think that the biblical doctrine of Creation denied the theory of evolution). The fault of this logic lay in supposing there were only two alternatives, namely biblical fundamentalism (of a sort) and the scientific view that human beings arose by evolutionary processes. Their critique may have had merit, in so far as there was in most schools no attempt to show how one could be both an evolutionist and a Christian, or a Buddhist, or a Muslim, and so on. A thousand flowers should actually bloom, not just two, both rather sickly ones, in that they did not display the blooms of deep philosophical thought.

The fact is, of course, that in the USA the conservative wing of Christianity has a much greater influence than it does in Europe. This leads to some polarization between the liberal cast of the Constitution and much public opinion on the one hand and conservative piety on the other. This affects school districts, since conservative factions can exert some degree of censorship, through parents' associations and the like. The reasons for conservative influence are threefold. First, there is the traditional weight and extent of highly Protestant viewpoints, such as those of the Southern Baptists. Second, there is the problem of education: so many high schools and colleges teach technical and business education without giving students much sense of a liberal perspective in religion. Third, there is the clever use of the media by conservatives, who until the late 1980s (when a series of scandals undermined their influence) were much better at using modern media, notably television. Basically, in my view, the problem is an educational one, though one should also note that liberals may succumb to different temptations than those of anger and angst, and adopt a politer form of cultural arrogance.

The special configurations of US religiosity which I have lightly sketched above account for some of the major differences from the European scene. They deeply affect the way in which the study of religion can be promoted in the USA. They also deeply affect aspects of the problem of freedom and authority. Basically, I would argue that authority as a whole, considered as an offshoot of tradition or located in tradition, has faded away greatly in the USA (and in California in particular: I am writing this in California which, because it is the end of the US frontier and has a freshness in conceiving of new lifestyles and ideas, is often regarded as the Future). There are many indications, especially in the Northern world, of the crumbling of traditional authority. It is evident, for instance, in Catholicism, where the papal teachings on birth control are obviously widely disregarded, even in Italy (northern Italy has the lowest birthrate in the world).

Traditionally there are various sources of authority in religion, and they are everywhere in some trouble, but most of all in the USA. Thus, for instance, Catholicism depends on a monarchical and bureaucratic hierarchy in Rome, and a subsidiary hierarchy in the USA. The advent of J. F. Kennedy as a presidential candidate marked a significant turning point. In order to become President he had to pledge his adherence to the Constitution, which was at variance with certain aspects of Catholic thought. These elements of the old traditionalism were challenged at the same time during the Council of Vatican II (1962–65). Indeed, the long campaign against Catholic Modernism carried on by the Papacy collapsed at that time: in other words Catholicism embraced a liberal perspective. It is interesting that in more recent times liberal Protestantism has undergone statistical decline: the mellownesses of liberalism are perhaps a way in which Protestants get to be effete. Yet at the same time liberalism has never had it so good, since it has largely conquered the Catholic Church. But there remains the important tension between the Papacy and the new liberalism. This liberalism in effect is the embracing by Catholics of an individualist perspective. They adhere to the Catholic tradition because they choose to. Indeed, Catholic loyalty is impressive: but

the logic has changed. There is no need to stay Catholic. Who is afraid of excommunication except, of course, for a few priests?

In Protestantism things are different, for the only Pope left is that famous old paper one:
the Bible. The way that book is interpreted is, of course, multi-form. In fact, on the far
right, where fundamentalism reigns, the situation is ironic: it is the charisma of the
preacher that counts. The results are similar to those in Catholicism. As the loyalty of
Catholics to the Pope governs his acceptance, so the decisions of individuals shape Protestant groups. In short, individualism prevails even among those who choose community.
But an even wider critique of tradition is taking hold. Why choose the Bible rather than the
Bhagavad Gita? Why the Buddhist canon rather than the Hebrew scriptures? The Zen
Centre in Los Angeles is full of Jews; Hare Krishnas recruit among Roman Catholics;
Islam has strong appeal among African American Christians. Others simply choose their
mixture of values. In short, the wider question of authority is obviously important among
individualists, and individualism is probably the main US ideology.

Now, of course, individualism as an ideology relates to the study of religion in high
schools only on one flank. That is to say, one aspect of the educational process is to
prepare young people for sensitive decisions about important matters. From this flank,
the study of religion is in a way a form of philosophy. It is a way of introducing young
people to alternatives in their lives. The information that may be given about religion
and religions has relevance to the choices in life that they can make. The general ethos
is that people should make up their own minds. This is one problem for parents, who
sometimes have a different slant. They do not want their own children to opt for
anything but their tradition. Individualism is thus itself a threat to their position (at
which they themselves may have arrived from an individualistic direction).

But on the other flank the educational process has nothing much to do with choices. It
concerns knowledge of history and of cultures. From this flank the study of religions
has to do with understanding the world. It was this aspect of education that the Supreme
Court in 1963 chiefly drew attention to. There are aspects of human history which
require for our understanding an insight into religion and religions. Therefore the study
of religions needs to be woven well into general history, whether of the USA or of the
wider world. Recent events, since the Khomeini revolution in 1979 in Iran particularly,
have given Americans at large a sense of the vitality of the study of religion as a key to
the understanding of world history.

It is largely for this reason that in many public high schools the study of religions has
been included in the curriculum. Still, there has been little systematic preparation of
curricular materials. But there have been programmes, for instance in California and
Illinois, which have combined the descriptive approach, rather than the existential one,
with local studies. It so happens that in many, indeed all, regions of the USA (except
for highly localized areas) there is a large or significant presence of migrants from
various parts of the world. This gives the opportunity for students to have first-hand
knowledge of alternative traditions. It also gives the local traditions the opportunity to
express themselves. For instance, at the University of California Santa Barbara we have
been pursuing (since 1987) a programme called Religious Contours of California
(similar programmes have been launched in Illinois and elsewhere), which aims to
introduce students to world religions, from Catholicism to Buddhism, through their
manifestations in California itself, for instance the Catholicism of Chicanos (people of
Mexican descent) and the religion of Chinese Americans.

It is hard to separate out such education in religions from programmes designed to promote ethnic understanding. One of the major concerns of US high school instruction is the necessity of combining both something of the melting pot idea and at the same time the appreciation, in a positive way, of differences. The result perhaps will be the emergence of a two-tier set of values, one expressing the US ideal, of a freedom-loving, egalitarian, opportunistic mode of living, and the other expressing different ethnic and religious values, dwelling together, however, in harmony. This will help to reinforce a certain privatization of religion. This is already apparent in some communities, even outside of the three main strands of Judaism, Catholicism and Protestantism.

Another major effect of the diminution of external authority has been the emergence of syncretisms – blended kinds of religion. At one level such blending occurs individually. This is summed up in the figure of Sheila in Bellah and others' *Habits of the Heart* (Bellah *et al.*, 1985). She represents the religious individual who has made up her own mélange of spiritual values. At a more communal level there are movements which merge differing strands from world religions and elsewhere – such as Unificationism, which has elements of Confucianism and Christianity, Transcendental Meditation, which blends South Asian techniques and Western individualism, and various forms of new age ideology.

So far our exploration of freedom and authority in the US scene suggests that the question of freedom of belief is no longer a serious one. It is true that school boards of a conservative cast may wish to censor materials in schools. But generally a kind of libertarian individualism is dominant. There remain, however, problems of promoting curricula in the field. To these I shall come back. Meanwhile, one aspect of the conservative critique of humanistic values is worth dwelling on. As I have noted above, though often conservatives draw the wrong conclusion from noting that certain values are being promoted in school textbooks (for instance, there may be an absence of reference to religious factors in history), there is a vital issue underlying such a line of criticism. It is the question of the proper definition of religion.

It is a somewhat ironic thing that many professionals in the field think that religion cannot be easily or at all defined. Wilfred C. Smith's *The Meaning and End of Religion* (Smith, 1963) projected a strong critique of the Western notion of religion, especially when applied to non-Western phenomena. However, it would seem that the right conclusion from such a critique is that there is no clear demarcation between religion and so-called secular world-views and systems of practice. If so, then secular ideologies should equally be taken into account in dealing with the question of whether education involves an even-handed and plural approach. This seems to me something which the conservative critique has raised, even if it tries to resolve the issue in a narrowing rather than a broadening direction. But the step of treating all world-views similarly has not been taken in the US educational world, as yet. There would of course have to be the recognition that the doctrine that all world-views are to be treated impartially is not itself a world-view in the relevant sense – or it too would have to be taken equally with the view that educational impartiality should be disregarded, and this would be a contradiction. The point is that liberal neutralism would give each position maximum fairness, but lack of such neutralism would involve unfairness.

Of course, it can be argued that liberal neutralism is already protected by the US Constitution. There is no doubt that on the whole Americans, because of loyalty to the Constitution, do take freedom of religion seriously: on the other hand, during the

McCarthy era, a secular ideology was identified as un-American. Interestingly, his witchhunts would never have worked had they been directed against Jews or even Moonies: his perception of communism as a common enemy paved the way for the full acceptance of Catholicism in the political process, as witness the election of John F. Kennedy as President. When Protestantism fully dominated the US public scene, there was often much overt anti-Catholic rhetoric. But the US is still some way from world-view neutrality (Smart, 1982). The conservative critique brings out the point that a certain set of values is often promoted in public education which in a broad sense comprise a form of scientific humanism, without paying attention to those philosophical issues which indicate ways in which science and religion, whether Christian, Islamic, Buddhist or Jewish (say), are compatible. Often therefore, the only viewpoint contrary to scientific humanism which high school students hear about is a highly conservative one, and this may reinforce the scientific humanist ethos. Another factor is that in many college and university philosophy departments world-view neutralism does not at all prevail, nor even a lesser degree of pluralism: this typically gives scientific humanism a privileged position. It is interesting to note that secular, that is to say pluralistic, universities have never addressed the question of world-view homogeneous departments (such as many economics, sociology and political science departments, as well as philosophy departments).

The Schempp decision rested on the perception that religion is an important factor in many phases of history, social development and so on. It is therefore primarily the descriptive and historical treatment of religion that has entered into public school curricula. Hence treatment of religions appears within the broader embrace of such subjects as social studies, economics, world history and so on. Also in the USA there is quite a lot of interest in courses on the Bible as literature, and by implication other scriptures as literature. The fact that so much education simply ignored religion, in order not to cause turbulence and possible illegality in the face of the Constitution, led to a felt need to treat the Bible as literature in view of its important place in the English literary heritage. It is quite common for such courses to be given in colleges and universities in departments of English.

The result of the integration of religious material into 'other' subjects such as social studies is that most teachers who handle the field are not especially trained in it. This is creating a growing concern in public universities and especially in State colleges to help to educate teachers in this area. (By 'State colleges' I mean that second tier of universities in many States below the so-called State university – thus as well as the campuses of the State University, for instance the University of California, there are various State universities such as California State University Northridge, Cal State San Francisco and so on: the whole nomenclature is confusing for outsiders. The State colleges tend to be more closely tied in with the validation of school teachers in the various subjects.)

In brief, the major form in which the study of religion appears in high school and other curricula is as the descriptive or historical exploration of the role of religion in human affairs. Nevertheless, because young people are at a formative stage, and because ethical issues are frequently tied to religious ones, the existential and philosophical concern with issues of truth and falsity can hardly be avoided, and here considerable sensitivity, in view of the Constitution, and of the more vital role played by local school boards, is necessary.

In this connection it is vital that the distinction, alluded to by the Supreme Court in the Schempp decision, between teaching religion and teaching about religion be kept to the forefront of attention. Or to put matters a different way, pupils need to be clear about the classroom situation and that of the religious community. Here different forms of authority are evident. The teacher's authority springs from his or her standing as representative of a wider society concerned with passing on knowledge and the means to form sensitive and sound opinions. The teacher, from this base, should be seen as a kind of chairperson in conducting debates, if the kind of material under discussion turns to existential and ethical issues. The role of the pastor or priest or rabbi, by contrast, springs from her or his role in a committed community, concerned to pass on a certain framework or style of commitment. It is often difficult for the distinction of roles to be kept in mind, and this can lead a faith community into trying to pressurize the wider community to accept its particularistic standpoint by censoring literary texts, insisting on Christian-oriented textbooks and so on. This remains a clash of authority not without significance on the US scene. Nevertheless, one should not overlook the role which liberal Church organizations, for instance the Council of Churches in Minnesota, have played in promoting religion studies in the school system.

In more recent years the pattern created in California, known as the Religious Contours paradigm, has been influential. This was to explore world religions through the presence of religions in the State. For instance, there is a strong Chinese community, especially in the Bay Area, which can be used as a bridge to the history of religions in China. Similarly, there are many Hispanics in the State whose religion is predominantly (though not only) Catholic. There are many new religions and old religions in new places, like Zen Buddhism (many of whose members are Anglos and Jews), which has a flourishing centre in Los Angeles. A series of studies of California's religions has been launched through the University of California Press (edited by Phillip Hammond and Ninian Smart). Similar experiments have occurred in Illinois. The fact that such a paradigm works by looking at local communities helps to reinforce the distinction between teaching a religion and teaching about one.

So far I have mainly sketched the situation in relation to public schools. What of private ones? The pressures appear to be towards the convergence between the two segments of education. In colleges and universities there is increased pluralism, which is fuelled by student demand. While an interest in Eastern religions is not as intense in the early 1990s as it was at the beginning of the 1970s, it is still highly significant. Moreover, the new ethnic self-consciousness drives demand for courses in Native American and African religions. Moreover, events since 1979 have brought the question of Islam to the fore of many American minds. Individualism reigns as much among private school students as among their public school peers. All this of course raises deep questions of authority among religious educators within the various communities. Apart from those groups which try to deal with the problem by isolating their members from within the midst of an open society, it appears to me that they need to rely increasingly upon intrinsic rather than extrinsic authority. It is not possible to have one area of human life sheltered from the rest where appeal is made to obedience. In an educational system which is greatly problem-oriented, it is not easy to lay down the religious law.

By 'intrinsic authority' I mean that authority has to spring from the intrinsic qualities of what is appealed to. It is the holiness and perceived judgement of the guru, not his gurudom, which counts. It is the plausibility of arguments for revelation which counts rather than a bare book. It is the poetry and depth of a scripture that counts rather than sacral status. It is the strength of argumentation which counts in a theological book rather than its being commended by some bishop or community. It is the fruitfulness of religious life that counts rather than tradition. It is the experience of faith rather than its orthodoxy which should weigh. It is the power of ritual rather than its provenance which counts. Such intrinsic authority poses challenges to all communities and traditions. It is true that there are severe backlashes as the disturbing implications of such a concept become manifest. But beyond every backlash lies another generation, where the hardnesses of fierce commitment are mellowed. The USA has probably sailed further along this individualist voyage than any other society.

REFERENCES

Bellah, R. N. and Hammond, P. E. (1982) *Varieties of Civil Religion*. San Francisco: Harper & Row.

Bellah, R. N. *et al.* (1985) *Habits of the Heart*. Berkeley and Los Angeles: University of California Press.

Cruise O'Brien, Conor (1988) *God Land*. Cambridge, MA: Harvard University Press.

Schempp: 374 US 300, 1963.

Smart, Ninian (1982) *Worldviews*. New York: Macmillan, Scribner.

Smith, Wilfred Cantwell (1967) *The Meaning and End of Religion*. New York: Harper & Row.

Will, Paul J. (ed.) (1981) *Publication Education Religion Studies*. Chico, CA: American Academy of Religion.

Conclusion

Since its formation in 1969, the Shap Working Party has striven to broaden the basis of education of children and adults in England and Wales through a greater appreciation of the world's religions. It has done this through publications, conferences and an annual calendar of religious festivals, all designed to contribute to richer teacher education and warmer community relations. Its impact has extended to a Scottish Shap, continental European conferences, and, particularly through Ninian Smart, one of its founders, to North America.

In 1988, the Education Reform Act gave out mixed signals for England and Wales as to how inclusive RE should be. There was talk of the special place of Christianity, but there was also for the first time in British history the declaration that no locally agreed syllabus for use in schools would be legal unless it attended to the principal religions found in contemporary Britain. Since then, government circulars have given guidance about the interpretation of the law which have seemed to want to narrow the focus again. But these are not statutory.

In 1994 National Model Syllabuses for RE were prepared and published at government expense. They were the fruit of extensive consultations between teachers and leading representatives of six faith communities: Buddhists, Christians, Hindus, Jews, Muslims and Sikhs. Although they do not remove the discretion of Local Education Authorities to develop their own alternative schemes, within the terms of the 1988 Act, they make it plain that the commended religious ingredients of education in England and Wales are diverse and demanding.

After a quarter of a century of lobbying, the curriculum in Britain's schools is almost Shap-shaped, at least in theory. Many obstacles remain, however. First, much has to be done to equip teachers in primary and secondary schools to be able to take on the challenge of effective delivery. It would not be easy even were they all to be specialists, which they are not. Second, the persistent suspicion between the faiths, but most especially between some self-appointed defenders of Christianity and those then provoked to respond as minorities, needs to be gently anaesthetized. This at least should facilitate better opportunities for mutual inspection, prior to normal life being resumed with heightened readiness for understanding. Third, the pariah of secular humanism, excluded from all the official syllabus-making, deserves to be acknowledged as a living presence in society. Unless that happens, it can the more easily appear to undermine any of the religious traditions, as so commonly it does within established media influences, without itself being put under the same critical scrutiny as the religions themselves.

Shap will continue to make its contributions to this entire educational process. The subject matter of this book is a reminder of the tensions which exist between freedom and authority, both within and between different religions. They cannot always be resolved. For the greater benefit of our collective condition, they certainly deserve to be understood.

Author Index

Subject Index

'Abide with Me' 128
Abraham 51, 117
Adam 51
'Adrienne' 132
aesthetics 38
Agni 28, 30
ahimsa 120
Akbar 31, 32, 40n16
Akiva School 152
alcohol 66, 67
Ali, Caliph 48
alienation 97
Amar Das, Guru 172
Amaravati 115, 118, 119, 124
American Academy of Religion 189
American Constitution 188
Amos 52
amrit 62, 68
Amritsar 62, 63, 64
Ananda 10, 12, 14, 17
anarchy 23
Anglicans 20, 69, 129
Anglo-Irish Agreement 81
animals 120
anti-semitism 24
apostasy 42
apostolic authority 20
ʿAqida 42
Arabic 155, 159, 162
Arabs 87, 91, 92
Aramaic texts 152
archaeology 87
Arjan, Guru 59, 60, 61
Armada, Spanish 78
artha 29
Arya Samaj 33, 64, 71, 144, 145
Ashkenazi Jews 89, 90, 149
Asoka 11–12, 14, 31–2, 115
Assembly of God 130

Atman 28, 38
Aurangzeb 31
Aurobindo 33
Austria 183, 185
authoritarian vii, 11, 23, 89, 145
authority viii, 4–7, 10, 11, 12–16, 31–7, 44, 51–2,
    68, 70, 80, 87, 97, 142, 146, 164, 195
    crisis of vii
authority reasoning 101–6
autonomy 23, 101
avatara 32, 59
Ayatollahs viii
Ayodhya viii

Baba Batra 53
Babur, Emperor 60
Bahadur Singh, Banda 63
Baha'is 87
Baisakhi 62, 69, 170
Bal Vikas 139, 144, 145
Balaam 86, 93
Bangladeshi pupils 157
Baptists 20
Bar/Batmitzvah 150
base communities 20, 25
Bat Kol 57
Belgium 183
'belly-button battle' 89–90
Bengali 155
Bernadette 21
Bethlehem 92
Bhagavad Gita 19, 144
Bhai Bij 142
bhakti 32, 37, 40n18
bhikkhunis 115, 118
bhikkhus 115, 118
Bible 19, 23–5, 56, 129, 132, 194
Birmingham High Court 167
birth control 67